Black and White Media

BLACK AND WHITE MEDIA

Black Images in
Popular Film and Television

KAREN ROSS

Polity Press

First published in 1996 by Polity Press in association with Blackwell Publishers Ltd.

2 4 6 8 9 10 7 5 3 1

Editorial office:
Polity Press
65 Bridge Street
Cambridge CB2 1UR, UK

Marketing and production:
Blackwell Publishers Ltd
108 Cowley Road
Oxford 0X4 1JF, UK

Blackwell Publishers Inc.
238 Main Street
Cambridge, MA 02142, USA

ISBN 0-7456-1126-5
ISBN 0-7456-1127-3 (pbk)

A CIP catalogue record for this book is available from the British Library and the Library of Congress.

Typeset in 10.5 on 12 pt Palatino
by Best-set Typesetter Ltd, Hong Kong
Printed in Great Britain by Hartnolls Limited, Bodmin, Cornwall

This book is printed on acid-free paper.

Contents

PART II   TELEVISION

PART III   FILM AND TELEVISION

Acknowledgements

I would like to take this opportunity to thank all my colleagues and friends, both in the academy and outside, with whom I have shared ideas and arguments down the years. Thanks, then, to my colleagues at the Centre for Research in Ethnic Relations (University of Warwick) who helped me on my way when I was but a lowly post-graduate student and, in particular, to Harry Goulbourne who gave me direction, books and a disciplined approach. Grateful thanks are also due to my colleagues at the School of Continuing Studies (University of Birmingham) whose ears I sometimes bent during the writing of this book, especially my colleague, room-mate and friend, Dawn Lyon: also to Jennifer Tann who gave me the time to make the drafting of this book possible. I would also like to thank my colleagues at the Centre for Mass Communication Research (University of Leicester) and, in particular, Annabelle Sreberny-Mohammadi who has gently encouraged. My thinking has greatly benefited from discussions and conversations with numerous colleagues and friends including Colin Prescod and Claudine Boothe and I am grateful to them and all those other scholars whose work I admire and have learnt from. I would also like to thank my editor, John Thompson, for keeping faith and persuading me to do the same. But I am mostly grateful to Chris for his support, his supply of tea and his patient reading of early drafts and tactful suggestions thereto: at times of madness, he kept me sane.

Author's Note

Notwithstanding the continuing debate around the usefulness of the term 'black' and its rejection by some subaltern communities, the term still provokes a powerful political resonance and functions as a crucial symbolic signifier not only of oppression but, more importantly, of resistance. Throughout this text, therefore, the term 'black' is used in its old 'political' sense to describe peoples of diaspora communities who experience oppression and discrimination (used particularly when discussing black images in white media) and as an oppositional descriptor when discussing the work of alternative black media practitioners. In reality, particularly when discussing early media examples, 'black' will mean people of African or Caribbean descent, usually African Americans (US) or African Caribbeans (UK) but will also include peoples of South Asian diasporas when discussing more contemporary films and programmes. The terms 'South Asian', 'African American' and 'African Caribbean' are also used in the text, mainly when discussing particular actors or media professionals.

Black, White, Grey: Some Preliminary Notes on Identity

> One of the greatest disappointments at this end of the 20th century
> has been the regression of the human race into ethnic factions. It is as
> if we have learnt nothing from the vast bloodied landscape of human
> history . . . instead of moving towards a greater global sense of hu-
> manity, we are moving back to our little secure units, our ethnic
> suspicions, our nationalist legends of superiority over others and
> eternal difference from others.
>
> Ben Okri, 'Time to Dream the Best Dream of All'

Individuals living in the economically developed countries of the
world are increasingly reliant on the mass media to provide them
(us) with information, education and entertainment. In particular,
other people in other places are powerfully evoked through
the words and pictures which emerge from TV. As the late twentieth century witnesses momentous changes taking place across the
globe – the dismantling of the Berlin wall, the dissolution of
the Soviet Union and Yugoslavia, the triumph of Nelson Mandela –
the media are on hand to sift, filter and shape the reporting of
those events for our information, education and enjoyment. What
those global moments signal, among many other things, is the fracturing of so-called 'national' identities as individuals and groups
seek to establish their own racial, ethnic and cultural identities for
themselves on their own terms. This book considers the media's
presentation of those shifting identities and explores both traditional and emerging representations of blackness as diaspora communities mobilize resistance against those orthodox images of the
black 'other' which have been perpetuated (and perpetrated) by the
white media industry.

Nations, nationalities and nation-states have never been 'natural'
nor mere political entities – they have always been symbolic for-
mations, systems of representation which produced ideas and

ideals of nationhood. The nation was never real, it was always an 'imagined' community, inflected with meanings which its 'members' were invited to read and thus know themselves by, as subjects and citizens. But these nationals were never homogeneous, they (we) are all ethnic hybrids and the nationalist enterprise has always been to represent the nation as one primordial people. This insistence on 'unity' is expressed as eloquently through 'patriotic' war abroad (World War II, Suez, Vietnam, the Falklands, Haiti) as it is exposed for its emptiness by exactly the same imperative at home (Northern Ireland, Yugoslavia, Soviet Union, Rwanda). 'Identity is always . . . a structured representation which only achieves its positive through the narrow eye of the negative. It has to go through the eye of the needle of the other before it can construct itself' (Hall, 1991a: 21).

Various analyses have been invoked to account for the unexpected revival in nationalism and ethnicity which contemporary society is experiencing and which, as Hall argues, is transforming cultural life itself (1993). It could have been expected that the discourses attending the grand theories would have resulted in a dislocation of nationalism towards a more inclusive global consciousness rather than its opposite: no more attachment to space, place or nation but submersion in a global melting-pot future. However, 'when the era of nation-states in globalization begins to decline, one can see a regression to a very defensive and highly dangerous form of national identity which is driven by a very aggressive form of racism' (Hall, 1991a: 26). In America, Britain and across Europe more generally, Western societies are currently exemplified by the resurgence of fascist organizations and the retreat into a right-wing fundamentalism which is intent on re-erecting and maintaining 'ethnic' boundaries. This particular historical moment is overlaid by the pervasive presence of the mass media, whose global images cross and recross linguistic frontiers with speed and fluency, and satellite television is perhaps the most potent example of the global imperative, unregulated by national conventions and free to roam the universe and drop its load at will.

Nation and identity

The desire to create and maintain discrete ethnic identifications within 'national' boundaries has been prompted by a variety of historical circumstances but is always the expression of subject peoples contesting the dominance of the ruling elite. 'They are movements of popular mobilisation, at least in their rhetoric and slogans, if not always in deed' (Smith, 1991: 140). The struggle is against the status quo, the social, political and economic relations between majority and minority *ethnies* (to use Smith's use of the French equivalent, to mean ethnic communities) and the marginalization which accompanies such majority–minority inter-actions. Although Smith is talking more about the development of ethnic nations within (hitherto) national parameters, as in the former Yugoslavia or Soviet Union, his analysis can be usefully applied to the rise of ethnic affiliations and identities in countries such as Britain and America. Here, ethnic communities are not territorial in that they are not fighting for ethnic enclaves within national borders, but rather have developed as movements for change, mobilizing around specific issues such as the Civil Rights movement in the 1960s and numerous anti-discrimination protests subsequently. Smith suggests that a fundamental part of the forma-tion of emergent new ethnicities (both majority and minority) is the return to an idealized image of 'what we were', which could serve as a guide for ethnies in the making (1991). This impulse can be seen very clearly in both Britain and America, in the search for roots amongst African Caribbean and African American communities who need to recover their histories in order to make sense of their todays and tomorrows, and in the insistence on ethnic purity amongst the various white 'tribes'.

The return to this 'imagined' past, this mythologized history, will expose, it is hoped, the community's authentic essence to itself even when it means inventing large parts of this 'self'. As Oguibe points out, 'Africa is a historical construct rather than a definitive. Many have argued, prominent among them the Afrocentrist school, for the antiquity of a Black or African identity, an argument which falls flat upon examination' (1993: 4). The danger in not acknowledging the essential fictiveness and symbolic recovery of ethnic histories manifests itself in the easy slide to fundamentalism. In Britain, the pull towards engaging with an expansive European identity has been countered by the development of a vigorous 'English' identity which is decidedly exclusive. In Hall's discussion of 'Englishness', he argues that as an ethnic category, Englishness has always been mongrel, a hybrid masquerading as a pure and homogenous cul-ture as it absorbed and obscured all its many different constituent parts (1991a). The historical relationship between national identity and the nation-state is beginning to fracture as a result of many factors including economic decline, loss of status and the migration of labour. This unstable moment is highly charged and highly dangerous. The resurgence of neo-Nazi and fascist parties across Europe signals a significant retreat into nationalist notions of 'pure' ethnicities and a form of cultural racism which has shifted away from crude ideas of biological determinism and has mutated into an altogether more sophisticated framework. This seeks to present an (imaginary) definition of the nation as a unified *cultural* commodity which engages a national culture which is perpetually vulnerable to incursions from enemies within and without (Gilroy, 1987). Our children are taught particular histories from particular perspectives and parents are now rebelling against the celebration of Christmas *and* Diwali, against the teaching of Byron *and* Walcott, against the reading of Kipling *and* Naipaul. The 1990s have already witnessed a significant backlash on both sides of the Atlantic against policies designed to encourage 'multiculturalism', encouraging both Britain and America to retreat into a defensive WASP-ish consciousness.

But what is important in the project of reclaiming the histories of the oppressed is not simply the capture of an absolute truth, which after all could only ever be partial, but to rehabilitate a history which has been denied, to excavate a proud and potent past which could provide lessons for the present. There is a clear requirement for the widespread circulation of such recovered histories to mobilize both affirmation and rebellion. For all those communities who share a history of oppression and colonization, reclaiming the past to make explicit the horrors of imperialism and slavery is as important as excavating an authentic history for the purposes of celebration. The popularity of Alex Haley's *Roots*, on both sides of the Atlantic and among both minority and mainstream audiences attests to the power of popular media to make palatable a hateful history, but also invites a critical enquiry about precisely who this rags-to-riches story is for. Similarly, the BBC radio broadcast of the *Ramayana* was presumably intended to broaden out the range of cultural iconography available to audiences but scarcely hit the mark. The *Ramayana* is an epic Hindu poem which is one of the two most important and sacred Indian texts and has been in existence, in one form or another, for at least four thousand years. It has had an enormous influence on both literary and oral traditions and predates that other great work, the *Mahabharata*. But the narrative treatment of The *Ramayana* had to be so theatricalized to appeal to a white British audience, or so some of the programme-makers believed, that the simplicity and subtleties of the text were entirely destroyed: it became just another fantasy adventure. The dangers of cultural imperialism are ever present and easily invoked.

A third space

The migrated peoples of the new diasporas are not, however, meekly accepting the refusal of dominant white cultures to acknowledge their existence, their contribution, their right to ethnic, cultural and any other type of identity. The peoples of these diasporas have learnt new skills, learnt to adapt, to negotiate and translate across (at least) two cultures. They are struggling, as Hall puts it, at the margins of modernity but they are also at the leading edge of what will become the 'truly representative "late-modern" experience. They are the products of the cultures of hybridity' (1993: 362). For Hall, then, these settled but still foreign communities retain their links with 'home' but will never actually return there and even if they did, it would not be to their remembered homeland but to a place transformed by time to make them as foreign there as they are foreign here. For example, the formation of black diasporas in the post-war migration period transformed British social, economic and political life. Prohibited from taking on a 'British' identity, black migrants began to search for more solid ground in their history. The new identity they took on was 'black', a term which had emerged from the Civil Rights movement and was adopted worldwide thereafter.

> Black was created as a political category in a certain historical moment. It was created as a consequence of certain symbolic and ideological struggles . . . in that very struggle is a change of consciousness, a change of self-recognition, a new process of identification, the emergence into visibility of a new subject. (Hall, 1991b: 54)

Diverse diaspora communities acknowledged that what they had in common was greater than what divided them and they united under this new identity to fight for equality and against racism and discrimination. However, Gilroy argues that the community of blacknesses which had forged a fragile unity because of their shared experience of oppression has now fractured and split off into discrete ethnically 'pure' groupings. 'This retreat from a politically constructed notion of racial solidarity has initiated a compensatory recovery of narrowly ethnic culture and identity. Indeed, the aura of authentic ethnicity supplies a special form of comfort in a situation where the very historicity of black experience is constantly undermined' (1993: 86). The unifying notion of 'black' has thus been replaced by more particular and specific notions of cultural difference. Despite the rejection of this term and the retreat into categorical ethnicities, Hall insists that the impulse for organizing around the constructed identity 'black' remains as strong as ever. But what must be acknowledged is the fact that the black identification tag silenced many who felt they had been reluctantly incorporated under that mantle.

Peoples of the various diasporas not only carry with them the traces of their past, but reproduce and transform themselves, producing new hybrids, new models. It is precisely this process of transformation which informs the work of those black film- and programme-makers whose work is discussed in this book. It is precisely within this hybrid existence, in what Bhabha calls the 'third space' (1989), that new transgressive modes of being are articulated and expressed through popular cultural forms such as film and music. This ability to negotiate across boundaries, to work through differences of class, gender, race, sexuality and ethnicity is precisely what gives contemporary modes of cultural production their vitality and relevance. Within the cultural context, marginality, notwithstanding its peripheral location, has never been as productive as it now is, not simply in its penetration of dominant discursive spaces but also in its celebration of a cultural politics of difference through the 'appearance of new subjects on the political and cultural stage' (Hall, 1992: 24). Music, in particular, has been the experimental site of exciting cultural fusions, by black and white artists and those in between who are making new musics from selected samples of older forms, who set Hindi lyrics to rap rhythms and drink water as they dance to jungle. 'In reinventing their own ethnicity, some of Britain's Asian settlers have also borrowed the sound system culture of the Caribbean . . . as part of their invention of a new mode of cultural production with an identity to match' (Gilroy, 1993: 82). Such cultural hybridity takes its form and develops as a consequence of both acculturation and resistance, where individuals affiliate to multiple groupings, have multiple identities, are both this *and* that, *both* not *one*. However, new musical forms, such as bhangra and jungle, with their fusion of traditional rhythms and modern rap argot have provoked significant debates relating to their authenticity. But as Gilroy points out, the globalization of vernacular forms means that the 'original' sound is becoming harder to locate (1993) and the rhythms are no longer suffused with secret and ethnically specific codes which confuse the uninitiated. We are all world musicians now.

The interconnectivity and flow of cultural capital across the Atlantic is an important aspect of cultural hybridity and the influence of America on Britain is extremely powerful: 'Black America is reiterated and relived through the lives of Black Britons' (Small,

1993: 38). Within mainstream America itself, popular culture has always incorporated African American vernacular traditions, whether it wants to acknowledge such a fact or not (Hall, 1992). The everyday is precisely the site of ongoing negotiation over cultural production. This notion of hybridity is explored in films such as Ngozi Onwurah's *Coffee Coloured Children* (1988) and Gurinder Chadha's *I'm British But . . .* (1989), where the ambiguities and ambivalences of living through difference and making multiple identifications are played out through the narratives. The tensions associated with living in two cultures have been a constant site for exploration and negotiation within film narratives, with a desire to articulate cinematically precisely those equivocal themes (Malik, 1994). The ties of loyalty and belonging both bind and bisect other ties of identification, encouraging the possession of multiple identities across a range of characteristics – ethnicity, gender, sexual orientation, nation, community, region – and provide a dialectical response to the push towards compartmentalism. This is not to argue that such identifications are entirely situational, to be paraded at will depending on the circumstance, nor to suggest that one or other affiliation will be in the ascendancy at any given moment. But the holding of multiple identities does seem to be more expressive of the way in which life is actually lived in contexts which include other people with whom we share some characteristics some of the time.

An Afrocentric identity and its critics

The discourse attending and through which the politics of identity is now being expressed has been the site of considerable struggle and, in particular, over the articulation and specificity of 'blackness'. Against the rhetoric of diversity and hybridity has emerged an equally assertive but essentialist position which seeks to circumscribe the construction of black images. As white America attempts to unify itself against all the 'others', so 'Afrocentric perspectives and nationalist constructions of identity are increasingly attractive to various sectors of the black community' (Gray, 1993b: 365). While acknowledging the seductions of essentialism, Hall insists that the question is no longer (if it ever was) about the struggle between either/or, total victory or total incorporation, but is actually the struggle over cultural hegemony. The site of contestation is the shifting balance of power in the relations of culture, 'It is always about changing the dispositions and the configurations of cultural power, not getting out of it' (1992: 24). Hall suggests that identity is formed 'at the unstable point where the "unspeakable" stories of subjectivity meet the narratives of history, of a culture' (1987: 135) and it is crucial to recognize that all identities are constructed across and through difference, forged through the experience of living within a politics of difference. For peoples of the various diasporas, the colonized subject is always located somewhere else, displaced and disenfranchised from a sense of belonging to *here*. The taking on of a 'black' identity has always been subjective and situational: 'black' has never been a stable category but rather a construction, like all the other takes on identity.

The push towards an essentializing notion of blackness and/or the adoption of a specifically Afrocentric perspective can be viewed as a logical and reflexive response to the old (and now rehabilitated) discourses of exclusionary nationalism. Conspicuous forms of boundary maintenance, I and not-I, become more pressing when those boundaries are under pressure. 'Ethnic identities which embody a perceived continuity with the past may in this way function in a psychologically reassuring way for the individual in times of upheaval' (Eriksen, 1993: 68). Ethnic identities thus become sources of personal authenticity in a world otherwise in a state of constant flux. The adherence to a discrete ethnic identity can be used as a symbolic tool in political struggle, as the differentiating feature between them and us. Even as Hall indicates the overlapping terrains of those old nationalist identities and the emerging new ethnic ones, he insists that the two are not the same. Ethnicity *can* be found as an element in the more regressive types of nationalism or national identity, but it can also begin to connote alternative meanings and to open a new space for the development of affirmative identities (Hall, 1987). If nothing else, its insistence on locating every voice as a separate voice, spoken from a specific location at a specific time at a specific historical moment gives the speaker a concrete identity, a real place from which to speak. The essentializing moment is weak, for Hall, because it naturalizes and dehistoricizes difference. This is not to say that there is no such thing as black history(ies) and specific black experiences, but rather to emphasize their diversity instead of their sameness, not 'mistaking what is historical and cultural for what is natural, biological and genetic. The moment the signifier "black" is torn from its historical, cultural and political embedding and lodged in a biologically constituted racial category, we valorize, by inversion, the very ground of the racism we are trying to deconstruct' (Hall, 1992: 29–30).

But if these pulls and pushes towards ethnic nationalism are simply replacing one set of rigidities with another – Afrocentrism vs. Eurocentrism – the material circumstances which produce the privileged discourses through which they are articulated must be fully acknowledged and understood. Cultural expression and the representational image are both sites through which the politics of identity are played out but also constitute precisely the terrain over which the struggles occur. The work of African American male filmmakers such as Spike Lee speaks fluently of an authentic black experience which is unapologetically nationalist and Afrocentric but which at the same time operates within implicitly homophobic and misogynistic codes. A proud nationalism is paraded unself-consciously, but simultaneously silences those other black voices, of women, of gay men and lesbians. A rejection of these totalizing conceptions of blackness which normalize certain characteristics such as gender and sexuality has grown up in parallel and a significant critical literature now exists which takes black self-representation in popular culture as its subject. The essentializing project privileges a robust masculine heterosexuality as the 'real' black signifier and organizing motif.

'Black romanticism is high on the political agenda of people like Louis Farrakhan and the Nation of Islam and various rap groups prioritizing their very narrow versions of black masculinity It mythologizes the past as it erases memory' (Julien, 1992: 257). The immense popularity of rap as the epitome of blackness, both as a musical style in its own right and as the aggressive rhythm of black 'gangsta' films such as *New Jack City* and *Boyz N the Hood*, has made it more difficult for alternative black cinematic representations to achieve a similar potency. As Julien incisively comments, 'Afrocentrism's privileging of a new black aesthetic is not dialogic enough to think through the "hybridity of ethnicity", let alone liberated enough to include "queerness" in its "blackness"' (1992: 258).

Popular culture does not provide a nourishing framework through which we can all find our true selves but is instead an entirely mythical arena. It is a place in which we can try on different identifications for size, play around with our imaginary selves. Gilroy also wants to repudiate the dangerous obsession with racial purity and ethnic absolutism which inflects both black and white political discourse (1993). There should be no more finite cultural categories, no more fixed identities but rather an expansive, multi-layered, multi-ethnic culture, a 'black Atlantic' culture which em-braces Africa, America, the Caribbean and Britain all at once, whose themes transcend ethnicity and nationality, synthesizing into a new and vibrant cross-culture. Eschewing both Africentric (*sic*) notions of ethnic essentialism *and* anti-essentialist positions, Gilroy suggests that the grey area between these two positions could provide a more fruitful ground for analysis. Rather than viewing cultural tradition as a pristine set of practices, ongoing cultural production could be interrogated for evidence of its disruptions, its fractures, its inventions. Black identity is thus better understood not as essential or non-essential, but as a 'coherent (if not always stable) experiential sense of self' (1993: 102). The history of the 'black Atlantic' expresses the continuous nature of fluid and dynamic identities, always un-finished, always being made over and over. In particular, Gilroy argues that the appropriation and transformation of externally-derived musical forms by migrant communities on both sides of the Atlantic has been the most popular route into the establishment of a potent new sense of self-expression and self-knowledge, enabling the progression from arrivé to settled blackness. But as Gray points out, much of this critical anti-essentialist thinking has remained in the privileged corridors of the academy where the possibilities of a more flexible and comfortable location within the social hierarchy are realizable, rather than taking place on the street, where indi-viduals have fewer choices. The appeal of nationalist ideas and rhetoric to less advantaged communities is not difficult to under-stand. Gray insists that an acknowledgement of personal location and life chances needs to be foregrounded and worked through before offering simple rejections of the essentialist position. 'Totalizing conceptions and condemnations rather than critical and strategic interventions and deployment simply up the ante without actively moving the debates into those zones where they enlist and mobilize complexly positioned African-American subjects and subjectivities' (1993b: 371).

Media myths

It is inescapably true that the position of black people in the image hierarchy has been framed, historically, by the ideological contours of race and representation. For Taylor, the arguments about 'positive' or 'accurate' portrayals are entirely spurious unless one understands the structures of dominance within which black communities are and have been situated. 'Dialogue about which film is better or more authentic than which may already be hope-lessly entrenched within the favoured discourse of cultural imperi-alism' (1989: 90–1). The problem with focusing on 'race' and 'race relations' is not just that it gives the *idea* of race a veracity which the term does not merit, but that it continues to focus on black communities, whereas in fact the requirement is for an examination of racism with the spotlight on white people. The subject for investigation should be the way in which certain relations have been 'racialized', presuming that black populations are the cause of racialized hostility instead of being simply the target of particular (racist) white attitudes and actions (Small, 1993). The seduction of retreating into black ethnic absolutism in the face of white chauvinist exclusion is not difficult to see as the colour line forecast by W. E. B. DuBois continues to constitute deep and deepening social, economic and political cleavages. Guerrero argues that the biological determinist traps that a filmmaker like Spike Lee may sometimes fall into must be understood in the context of a rampant and homogenizing white essentialism which seeks to proscribe black discourse (1993).

Given the primacy of media products in the everyday lives of most people this book seeks to analyse how white media depict differentness, otherness, blackness, 'us' and 'not us', and looks at the claims made to verify these portraits. It asks questions about precisely whose history, whose culture, whose identity is being paraded as the incontrovertible truth and considers how the media is implicated in this interpretative exercise. Popular mass media play a significant role in the transmission and maintenance of cultural identity, through a repetitive display of cultural norms and values which eventually become seen as simple 'truths'. What is now at stake, in the context of global media, is not simply the representational image itself, but what it connotes in the social world, its meaning and value in both the public imagination and, more crucially, in the social order. The way images of black communities have been historically constructed from a white perspective and, moreover, from a position of considerable domination, has had clear consequences for the perception and portrayal of those black communities in Western societies. How do contemporary 'plural' democracies such as Britain or America now come to terms and cope with a history which is bloodied by slavery and imperialism?

Studies of the media rest inevitably on the tension between who or what has ownership and control over the words and pictures. Despite suggestions to the contrary, forms of cultural expression do not reproduce a pristine and incontrovertible 'reality' but rather offer something which stands in for an aspect of reality (Gidley, 1992). The fundamental argument is that if mainstream media do not tell us what to think, media discourse certainly tells us what to think *about*. If most media products are inscribed with the same cultural assumptions because their producers share the same cultural experiences, then their underlying norms and values are transmitted as an unselfconscious truth. But when we see a portrait of blackness, it does not describe the actuality of being black but rather references a particular way of thinking about blackness: it is not about *being* black but being *thought of* as black. Although it is clear that different types of images produce greater or lesser degrees of truthfulness and are differentially close in appearance to optical impressions, no image is other than a social construction viewed from a particular perspective and situated in a particular historical moment. 'The politics of representation considers the changing institutions which govern the encounters between constructed images and constructing eyes' (King, 1992: 132). Notwithstanding the ability of individual viewers to negotiate or challenge the implicit messages of the text, the amount of work required to decode against the grain, so to speak, militates against such negotiation becoming a routine practice. Is *The Cosby Show* a straightforward sitcom about an affluent black middle-class household going about its business or is it *really* a cynical attempt by corporate America to pretend that hard work can overcome every obstacle, including racism?

Semiological and cultural studies approaches to the media have correctly insisted that the text is capable of diverse readings because the viewing public is comprised of discrete individuals rather than a lumpen mass. But such approaches perhaps obscure the limited number of significantly 'alternative' readings which are possible, over-estimate the motivation of the viewer to challenge the text and under-estimate the ideological power of the media to persuade by the reiteration of the cosily familiar. The value of negotiation as an analytical concept is that it allows space to the subjectivities, identities and pleasures of audiences (Gledhill, 1992), but negotiation has to be understood as a finite activity. At some point, all possible readings are exhausted and the viewer makes a judgement based on a nexus of factors, both internally and externally driven. If black communities are constantly framed by media texts within a narrow repertoire of meaning, then viewers who do not have first-hand experiences of those communities will have no reason to challenge them, since their frame of reference would not include opposing conceptions of blackness. The notion of representation then is highly complex, particularly in its relationship to the real world. The greater the experiential distance between the viewer and the subject (for example, the white audience and the black image) and the more complex and sophisticated the image, the closer the perceived fit of screen image to actual reality. But what the image offers is the illusion of reality if for no other reason than that images can only ever be constructions of *a* reality, not *the* reality, and this is true as much for fictional as factual portraits. As Mitchell reminds us, the representation of fictional people or events can never be entirely separated from political and ideological questions and it is never clear, in any case, the extent to which art imitates life or the other way round (1990). The very term 'representation' refers to the presentation of an image which stands in for a symbolic something in the first instance and then beyond that superficiality, to signal the social, political and historical circumstances which are implicated in the image (Attile and Blackwood, 1986). What is clear is that film- and programme-makers who produce art works which purport to represent the 'other' will inevitably do little more than reflect their own assumptions and experiences. As Said's groundbreaking work has shown us, the 'other' is usually understood in terms of how 'they' are different from 'us' (1978, 1994). There is thus a tendency to dichotomize into we/they contrasts in order to make sense of the other and thus the more appropriate question to ask about the representation of blackness by white practitioners might be, what aspect of *themselves* is represented in their work?

> Can one culture use its own terms to say something about another culture without engaging in a hostile act of appropriation or without simply reflecting itself and not engaging the otherness of the Other? . . . can we ever escape our provincial islands and navigate between two worlds? (Armstrong, 1991: 157)

Toni Morrison, the 1993 Nobel Laureate for literature and the first black woman to achieve the award, argues in similar vein when she seeks to understand white literature's use of African and African American characters. Reading white American fiction, she initially believed that black people signified little or nothing in these texts, other than functioning as the objects of 'jungle fever', to provide local colour, to provide homilies, humour or pathos. However, when she starts to read as a writer, she discovers that far from signifying nothing, black characterizations reflect a complex of personal fears and desires which reside in the bosom of the writer: 'I came to realise the obvious: the subject of the dream is the dreamer. The fabrication of an Africanist persona is reflexive, an extraordinary meditation on the self' (1993: 10). Hall argues incisively that the way in which the discourse of race is articulated by and through the (white) media must be understood not simply as the outcome of individual pathologies but in the context of specific structures and practices which inform and inscribe media formats and which function as a result of social, political and economic agendas rather than personal ones (1981). For Hall, the media as an inclusive industry constitutes a largely political institution primarily concerned with the production and transformation of ideologies. An intervention in the media's construction of race becomes an interruption in the terrain of ideology itself.

Black media images: modern and trad

The representation of black people in popular media has traditionally utilized an extremely narrow repertoire of images which have their provenance in early travellers' tales, bogus biological determinism (racism) and the vast colonial project. Traditional and enduring motifs such as the happy slave, the noble savage and the entertainer are now rehabilitated for a contemporary audience as the argumentative house-keeper, the starving Ethiopian, the high-profile pop star. In the relative absence of black images, those which are available take on iconic dimensions, signifying in one constructed image, the complex of diverse and heterogeneous communities, reducing individual uniqueness to a false and essentialized black 'other'. As part of the enterprise of reinventing nation-states, the mass media have a primary role in standardizing representation and language, in normalizing the circulation and promotion of dominant values. They play an important part in reproducing and strengthening nationalist sentiments.

Representational orthodoxy dictates that if the black 'other' is allowed to make films, then those films must be authentic portraits of that other's own community, whereas white filmmakers have the whole world as their backdrop. ' "Correct" cultural filmmaking usually implies that Africans show Africa; Asians, Asia; and Euro-Americans . . . the World' (Minh-ha, 1989: 136). But black filmmakers are not limiting themselves to pseudo-anthropological texts which satisfy the white audiences' interest in the exotic, but rather are constructing all manner of diverse and exciting narratives for themselves. While popular oppositional practices in America are led largely by African American filmmakers, in Britain there is an emerging body of work by both African Caribbean and South Asian writers and filmmakers. Films such as Gurinder Chadha's *Bhaji on the Beach* (1993), Ngozi Onwurah's *Welcome II the Terrordome* (1994) and Hanif Kureishi's work represents an exploration of and engagement with the dynamics and complexities of diaspora experiences in Western locations (Ghani, 1994). The success of a number of black filmmakers has meant that mainstream black and white audiences can now enjoy a greater range of black-originated work showing a greater diversity of black images than has been possible hitherto. It is no longer adequate to read black media subjects as simply the passive result of white imaginings. We also need to consider the contribution black media professionals have made and continue to make to the development of a dynamic black media culture.

Form and function

While this text concerns itself with the representation of the black 'other' in popular film and television in Britain and North America, it cannot be exhaustive, nor does it claim to provide definitive words on the subject. However, it does signal key ideas and texts which have influenced and extended the debate around black representation and popular media. Where many previous works have tended to focus only on black people in white media, this book considers but then goes beyond this preoccupation and examines the way in which black media workers are reclaiming the right to compose their own words, to define their different identities and to (re)present themselves in their own image. Not one song, but many. 'Perhaps, instead of thinking of identity as an already accomplished historical fact, which the new cinematic discourses then represent, we should think, instead, of identity as a "production" which is never complete, always in process and always constituted within, not outside, representation' (Hall, 1989: 68).

This, then, is a book which acknowledges the complexity of representational issues and the differently nuanced texts which are produced by media practitioners whose works reflect their own unique experiences of blackness and whiteness. It aims to map the history of black images from the earliest days of cinema to contemporary film and television and to identify the provenance of particular 'types' of characterization which have been traditionally allocated to black actors and the way in which those types are being subverted by the work of contemporary black media practitioners. It is precisely this alternative black media practice which contests traditionally racist iconography in popular media which is forcing a reassessment of what identity and nation can mean and extending the possibilities.

The book is split into two broad sections – film and television – with two further chapters which explore black media criticism (chapter 6) and the future for film and television (chapter 7). The text is primarily concerned with popular media and although it discusses black filmmaking practice, it only focuses on widely exhibited films such as *Boyz N the Hood* and *Bhaji on the Beach*, rather than short films and videos which have had limited release, important though these are. What it also does not do is discuss other media, such as radio or the press, nor does it consider media at the institutional level. The text looks both backward, in order to understand the present, and forward to speculate on the future for film and broadcasting practice. Although the great majority of texts on race and the media originate in North America and focus on American products, it will happen that some of the references to British films and programmes in this book may be unfamiliar to a non-British audience. But the global media marketplace means that most popular media texts find their way across the world sooner or later and in any case, most of the programmes and films mentioned illustrate general points of principle which have universal applicability.

In the first section, chapter 1 looks at black images in white film, moving from *The Birth of a Nation* to *Demolition Man* and considers much in between: for example, the so-called 'blaxploitation' movies and Spielberg's much criticized treatment of Alice Walker's novel, *The Color Purple*. The provenance of contemporary black characterizations is also examined: *The Birth of a Nation* was seminal not just for its articulation of a determinedly racist text but because it defined, for the first time, the way in which Hollywood would choose to represent black people in the future (Diawara, 1993) and as such, constitutes an exemplary master narrative. Chapters 2 and 3 explore the way in which black filmmakers have sought and continue to subvert the traditional iconography of black communities as imagined by white media folk through the development of a separate black filmmaking practice, looking at the histories of Britain and North America. Black filmmaking did not begin with the work of popular contemporary practitioners such as Julie Dash, Spike Lee, Gurinder Chadha and Isaac Julien, but with the pioneering work of Oscar Micheaux and his co-independents in the early years of the twentieth century. The related development of black filmmaking in both Britain and North America is mapped out in these two chapters, exploring the independent workshop movement in the former and more commercial work in the latter.

The second section looks at television, with chapter 4 tracing the development of early television characters in series such as *Amos 'n' Andy*, *The Black and White Minstrel Show* and the first black British soap, *Empire Road*. It then moves on to consider contemporary television programmes and maps black characterization through three specific genres: comedy, drama and soap opera. Chapter 5 explores the way in which Britain has responded to the 'problem' of black people, by setting up specific 'multicultural' programme departments within mainstream television companies (BBC and Channel 4). It looks at the context in which these units have developed and questions the route that such strands have taken in their effort to respond to market forces and the eternal quest for the audience. The last section contains the final two chapters. Chapter 6 considers the discourses which have arisen around the need to develop a different framework through which to make critical responses to black-originated media. Specifically, black media cannot be read and interpreted within the traditional framework of mainstream film criticism because this is inflected by a set of Eurocentric assumptions and encoded with the grammar of race. Chapter 7 considers the future for black images and black media praxis in an environment of continuing deregulation and globalization.

PART I

———————

Film

Down and Out in Beverley Hills: Black Film Portraits and the White Imagination

It's not just what we inherit from our mothers and fathers that haunts us. It's all kinds of old defunct theories, all sorts of old defunct beliefs, and things like that. It's not that they actually *live* on in us; they are simply lodged there, and we cannot get rid of them. I've only to pick up a newspaper and I seem to see ghosts gliding between the lines.

Henrik Ibsen, *Ghosts*

Since the very beginning of the film industry, race and racist imagery has been a constant theme pervading and persuading the film narrative. The type of imagery used in the cinema has been borrowed directly from the narrow and derogatory repertoire of images that has inflected the white imagination for hundreds of years and can most easily be understood by attending to the notion of 'the stereotype'. The relationship between black communities and popular culture has often been discussed in terms of stereotype and misrepresentation, where commentators take up various positions along the positive–realistic continuum. But, as Mercer points out, the debate on ethnic stereotyping has become 'a collective ritual of rhetorical complaint' (1989: 3), so that the constant reiteration of the evils of negative images and misrepresentation becomes circular and unhelpful. Whilst the stereotype offers an analysis based on repetition, it tends to ignore difference or else reduce it to simple variations on a theme but without working through what those differences might connote (Neale, 1993). Not only is a truly exact repetition not possible – every instance of the happy slave or the bumbling buffoon is similar but different – but each character gains her sense of self by comparing herself with others for evidence of difference. The description of a text as racist results not from the observation of racism as it actually exists in the text but rather

through the reading of that text within a framework which acknowledges racism. 'A text can only be read as racist if the discourse
through which it is read contains that term and, hence, an explicit or
implicit definition of it' (Neale, 1993: 46). But of course the use of
stereotype is immensely seductive since it provides a lazy short-
hand way of quickly invoking a 'type' whose characteristics are in
some way 'known' to the audience through their experience of a
shared cultural code. So, for example, it is possible to tell 'mother-
in-law' jokes which work precisely because the audience already
has a shared understanding of what mother-in-lawness connotes:
the very term conjures up particular images and sets of behaviours.
But while stereotypes may have no basis in reality, they are nonetheless real in their social consequences and are used as a basis on
which social roles can be allocated (Pieterse, 1992).

Ethnic and racial stereotypes function in precisely the same way,
provoking a shared assumption amongst the audience about the
'essence' of African Caribbean people, Indian people, Irish people
and so on. Knowledge about those who are different from 'us' is
often gained vicariously through various media forms. The repetitive framing of particular images in certain ways eventually leads
to those images being seen as the definitive statement on 'those'
people and the groups to which 'they' belong. Images thus become
transformed over time, from being merely symbolic to connoting
reality. The media's tendency, in any case, towards simplification,
means that sophisticated discussions which contextualize complicated ideas, histories and events are routinely ignored in favour of
reductionist explanations which the imagined mass audience will
more easily understand. Contained within the stereotyping process
is the structuring of implicit power relations where the gaze is of the
dominant, looking at the subordinate: how *they* are different from
us rather than how *we* are different from them. The gaze has traditionally been white, where whiteness is taken as the profoundly
unproblematic norm against which all 'others' are measured. As
Dyer points out, whiteness as a discrete ethnic category has never
been the subject of serious scrutiny (1993), since the powerful have
no need to explain or justify themselves to the powerless.

Have racisms, will travel

The provenance of such stereotypes, then, can be mapped against
the history of writings about 'race', much of which emerged from
travellers' tales and documented accounts of explorations, and later

exploitations, conducted by voyagers travelling to the African coast (see Fryer, 1984; Walvin, 1973). But notions of 'otherness' existed prior even to these early expeditions, since Europe had for several centuries been colonized by the superior powers of the Islamic world (Miles, 1989). Although many of the reports brought home by travellers were factual and alluded to the high living standards and riches of some of the African merchants, such facts were often interspersed with fantastic fictions.

the Ethiopians had no noses . . . the Arimapsi had a single eye in the forehead . . . the Anthropophagi [lived] on human flesh . . . the Gamphasantes went all naked . . . the Blemmyes had no heads at all but eyes and mouths in their breasts. (Hacket (1566) cited in Fryer, 1984: 6–7)

The rapacious exploits of European adventurers such as Christopher Columbus and his so-called 'discovery' of America, together with the development of slavery as a lucrative trade, has meant that for at least five hundred years, the vast colonial project has kept black communities in chains, both literally and metaphorically. This rich seam of denigration has been vigorously mined over hundreds of years and if slavery as an explicit practice was formally abolished in the late nineteenth century, the rationale invented for its justification – the inherent inferiority of non-white peoples – retains a signal potency in the contemporary world. The nineteenth-century theorist, Arthur de Gobineau, occupies a pivotal place in the development of racist ideologies about blackness and whiteness with the construction of a racial typology which placed white, yellow and black people in a descending hierarchical order of superiority. These three 'races', according to Gobineau, had readily identifiable characteristics which were true for each member of that 'race'. Thus, black people were inherently lacking in intellectual ability: 'his intellect will always move within a narrow circle' and yellow people had 'a general proneness to obesity [and] little physical energy and inclined to apathy'. White people on the other hand were 'gifted with reflective energy [and] an extreme love of liberty' (Gobineau cited in Biddis, 1970: 135). The strength of this ethnocentric perspective can still be seen in the work of some contemporary commentators. Halstead, for example, writing in 1989, questions the basis for rejecting theories of race as explanations for physical and intellectual difference. His sentiments would not be out of place in the biological determinist theories of the seventeenth and eighteenth centuries.

It needs to be acknowledged that the Asian communities, from India, Pakistan, Bangladesh or from East Africa belong to the Caucasoid race or sub-species. The Afro-Caribbeans are Negroid and the immigrants from Hong Kong, China and Japan Mongoloid. (Halstead, 1989: 11)

But as well as the circulation of academic theories around race, the reduction in printing costs and increasingly sophisticated printing processes resulted in the mass production of cheap (and racist) literature during the late eighteenth and early nineteenth centuries. An eager readership received a regular diet of tall tales, including stories of African adventures where the barbarians were captured or civilized by the white man, as well as more philanthropic tracts penned by missionaries and abolitionists (Walvin, 1973). Despite their very different perspectives, both types of literature served to reinforce the existing stereotypes of black people as heathens and savages: both looked to the white man to civilize the barbarian, baptize the pagan.

For many writers of the late eighteenth century, the routine subjugation of black African to white British will was so obvious as to scarcely merit comment. It was a popular perception at that time that not only was white superiority natural, it was also of inestimable benefit to the brute African, without whose discipline he would revert to bestiality (Kiernan, 1969). While some writers during this period supported the anti-slavery campaign being waged both in Britain and America, Dabydeen suggests that much of this apparent support was mere opportunism (Dabydeen, 1980). Writers and particularly poets of the eighteenth and nineteenth centuries wrote movingly about the plight of the slave but their support often disguised a less altruistic motive.

From the 1770s onwards England was deluged with anti-slavery verse [but] there is little evidence ... to suggest that any of these poets devoted any personal time or effort, or dug deep into their pocket, to support the abolition cause. (Dabydeen, 1980: 44)

A primary function of literary works during the nineteenth century was to filter encounters with the 'New World' through a European perspective so the contrived reality of such encounters was mediated through the pen and perceptions of the writer (Ridley, 1983). Colonial fiction expended much energy in justifying the imperial mission abroad, where such stories bridged the twin publics of both colony and mother country and represented each in the context of the other, conveying ideas between the two. The adventure story, replete with savages, cannibals, missionaries and brave white hunters, was a highly popular literary genre and its themes made the easy transition across media, to permeate nascent film narratives. Even a text which purported to speak in defence of black communities, such as Harriet Beecher Stowe's *Uncle Tom's Cabin* published in 1852, resounds with familiar stereotypes such as the original Uncle Tom, crafty George and a skirtful of women who alternate between deep (pagan) superstition and even deeper religiosity. The language and imagery of *Uncle Tom's Cabin* appears arcane to the contemporary eye, particularly for a text which was hailed as radical in its day, with the constant juxtaposing of black/white, evil/good, believer/infidel.

> There stood the two children, representatives of the two extremes of society. The fair, high-bred child with her golden head, her deep eyes, her spiritual, noble brow . . . and her black, keen, subtle, cringing, yet acute neighbour. They stood . . . the Saxon, born of ages of cultivation, command, education, physical and moral eminence; the Afric, born of ages of oppression, submission, ignorance, toil and vice! (p. 255)

The novel's publication spawned a variety of new forms, including a variety hall musical genre where four different Uncle Tom musicals played during the Christmas season in 1852 and, by the end of the 1860s, more than fifteen minstrel companies had been formed, establishing the black entertainer stereotype in the public consciousness (Lorimer, 1978). Black performers, but more usually white actors in blackface, toured the country as minstrels, pretending to provide a realistic account of the lives and songs of black slaves in America.

From one medium to another

With the emerging technology of film, these pre-existing images and stereotypes of black communities burst into vibrant life. The development of cinematography was predicated on the assumption that the actors in front of the camera (and of course behind) would be white, and celluloid was originally developed for the white body (Dyer, 1993). Thus the technology itself was culturally normative around whiteness and with the introduction of black characters for contrast and variety in early film enterprises, numerous technical problems were encountered, particularly when lighting black artistes. The limited range of perceptions about black people from

the view of the white film industry meant that difficulties in lighting
were neatly turned to advantage by routinely placing black artistes
in shadow to suggest darkness or evil. Yearwood suggests that an
integral aspect of the system of pleasure in cinema has been the
representation of the black body in traditional ideological terms
(1982a). This pleasure is centred around the appropriation and
domination (both actually and symbolically) of the black body and
requires the collusion of the spectator (audience) to perpetuate established social and economic relations between black and white
through the objectification of the former by the latter. 'Hence, traditional cinema produces a structure of seeing within which the
black body is constituted as the object of the look, thus reproducing
traditional relations in society' (Yearwood, 1982a: 43). When the
film medium was in its infancy, Thomas A. Edison and his associ-
ates were producing films such as *Pickaninnies* (1894), *Negro Dancers*
(1895) and *Dancing Darkies* (1897). The attraction of using black
artistes in these early film efforts lay in the vitality and mystery that
surrounded these 'exotics', characteristics which were missing from
the 'normal' white subject (Pines, 1975). Black communities were
thus given their identity by describing what they were not, that is,
not *white*. The differentness of black people was deliberately exaggerated to demonstrate their essential dissimilarity with white people, their lack of sophistication exemplified by their enjoyment of
singing and dancing which further reinforced assumptions about
their primitive and uncivilized natures. In early-1900s America,
cinema defined black communities in white terms, reinforcing the
totemic structure of America's racial arrangements. White
filmmakers restricted their narratives to safe and non-threatening
images of black communities suspended in a white world which
ignored stable black institutions such as the family and the church.
This type of imagery offered audiences nothing new but merely
reiterated and confirmed the traditional view of black people which
had become embedded in white culture from the earliest travellers'
tales. 'Movies were a tool, free of language barriers, transferring the
social mores and popular culture of the day at the expense of the
cultural realities and social existence of Black Americans' (Bowser,
1982: 43).

Uncle Tom and Aunt Jemima

Typical roles for black artistes in the early years of film included 'the
Uncle Tom derivative, the faithful servant type; the slapstick buffoon type; and the knife-carrying savage type' (Pines, 1975: 30).

Bogle provides a similar typology in his book *Toms, Coons, Mulat-toes, Mammies and Bucks* (Bogle, 1989). Clearly there is little disagreement between Pines, and Bogle's categorizations and the latter has simply added two extra stereotypes which were most commonly accorded black women artistes, namely the tragic mulatto and the pneumatically upholstered mammy. Later on, a third type would be added to this lexicon of denigration: black woman as siren/whore. Whilst black men in early films were usually relegated to the faithful servant/wily villain/lovable fool roles, roles for black women were often more varied inasmuch as they were sometimes 'allowed' to be wise-cracking and smart (Cripps, 1967). Black women were often cast as dominant personalities, particularly in their relationships with their menfolk, which served the purpose of reducing the threat of black male power and sexuality by the cinematic emasculation of black men by their women. Black women were much less threatening in real life than black men, so the industry could afford to be more generous in the characterizations of black women in film because white society knew that in reality, black women were powerless. The mammy stereotype is particularly interesting in the context of black sexuality since she was often drawn as the complete opposite to what a white woman should be, that is, delicate, weak, pale and silent. However, the characteristic which both groups of women shared was their servility, mammy to the white family, and the white mistress to the master. Mammy characters were rarely portrayed as overtly sexual beings and there was certainly never any hint of sexual tension between mammy and master, an instance of art very definitely not following life.

The mammy character has had a long and distinguished career in American films and the endurance of this 'type' has been significantly reinforced by the powerful iconography of her physical characteristics and recognizable traits. She embodies two deeply cherished myths of black womanhood: the faithful servant and the earth-mother. Taking care of white children at the expense of her own family, for whom she was usually sole parent, was part of mammy's personality in numerous films well into the 1950s. But the construction of mammy was not simply an attempt to romanticize a malignant chapter in American history. The location of mammy in the Big House served a dual purpose: to remove power from white women (transferring maternal authority from mothers to mammies) and to fracture black family life (DelGaudio, 1983). The success of Hattie McDaniel as Mammy in *Gone with the Wind*, for which she won an Oscar encouraged Hollywood producers to believe that mammy was a *big* attraction, in every sense of the word.

> Hollywood, prone to replicate successes and now convinced that audiences would 'walk a million miles for one of mammy's smiles', wrapped a bandana around the head of each working black actress faster than you can say 'Ah's a comin.' (Mapp, 1972 reprinted in Patterson, 1975: 197)

Although mammy was often rebellious, she knew her place and could always be relied on in times of need. Her sometimes cheeky manner with her white owners/employers was invariably tempered by her unfailing loyalty and devotion to her 'family'. Another favourite role for black women was/is sex object, forever used and abused by black and white men alike. For those black women who were included in narrative plots for romantic interest, the seductress was a popular role and artistes such as Dorothy Dandridge began their careers playing such characters. The sexual dimension of American racism is strongly reflected in the images of the black woman in film where her portrayal, even more than her male counterpart, has been determined by people other than herself.

The lack of progress of black women behind the camera (and this is still largely true in the 1990s) has resulted in a cinematic history of stereotyping and a steady procession of mammies, sirens and whores. Although the stereotypes discussed above were certainly not invented by the film industry, the exciting visual style of film enabled a much fuller exploitation and exaggeration of these types to be demonstrated. The titles of early silent films such as *The Wooing and Wedding of a Coon* (1905), *How Rastus Got His Turkey* and *Rastus in Zululand* (both 1914) show quite explicitly the perceptions that white filmmakers held about black communities and such films were among the first racist 'comedies' which relied on audiences understanding that black meant buffoon. As filmmakers began to search for more interesting material than the rather studied 'black fool' comedies, films began to appear which rehearsed topical problems and provided moral guidance on issues as varied as miscegenation and insubordination. Many of the plantation films of this period, particularly the numerous versions of *Uncle Tom's Cabin*, both celebrated white supremacy and applauded the faithful black servant. The film of *Uncle Tom's Cabin* was originally released in 1910 but the indictment against slavery contained in Beecher Stowe's work was softened in order to make it more acceptable in Southern film theatres. The overridingly negative characterization of black people in early silent films as variously stupid, frightened, lazy or savage set the popular tone for cinematic portraits in subsequent decades.

The greatest show on earth

In terms of significant moments in film history, it was arguably in 1915 that a crucial turning point was reached with the exhibition of D. W. Griffith's infamous *The Birth of a Nation*. From a purely technical point of view, the film was masterly in terms of conception and structure. It was the longest film that had yet been made, cost $200,000 and was the first film to be accompanied by a specially arranged orchestral score. But it is for its controversial content that the film is best known, constructed around the explicitly racist text of Thomas Dixon's *The Clansmen*. The film was an outstanding success when first shown and was the first film to be 'honoured' by a White House screening. The film demonstrated how the South had been 'right' about black people and how the North was 'right' about preserving the Union. It argued that the reconstruction which freed black people also endangered the most precious asset of the South, that is, its (white) women, who would require the heroic deeds of the Ku Klux Klan to vanquish the rapacious lust of black men for pure white womanhood. In his history of American film, Jacobs discusses the use of stereotype and caricature contained within the film.

> The film was a passionate and persuasive avowal of the inferiority of the Negro . . . the entire portrayal of the Reconstruction showed the Negro, when freed from white domination, as arrogant, lustful, villainous. Negro congressmen were pictured drinking heavily, coarsely reclining in Congress with bare feet upon their desks, lustfully ogling the white women in the balcony. (1939: 177)

The film articulated many of the fears of white society and indicated, yet again, the unwillingness of the industry (and white society generally) to conceive that black communities could use power responsibly. In the world of the silver screen, if black people are given power they are immediately corrupted by it and must come to an untimely end, often at the hands of a white hero. The mulatto-mistress in the film, Lydia Brown (played in blackface by Mary Aldin), is the unhappy would-be white yearning for acceptance. It is she who seduces the white abolitionist, Austin Stoneman, and, as the film's title card proclaims, she is 'his one weakness and the cause of his downfall'. The screen typification of black woman as whore has its roots in slavery and its construction can be seen as one way of absolving the collective guilt of slave masters. The systematic rape of black women slaves was reformulated as black women's insatiable lust for sex and, as Carby points out, the institutionalized rape of black women has never been as powerful a symbol of black oppression as the spectacle of lynching. Rape has always involved patriarchal notions of women as being, at best, not entirely unwilling accomplices, if not outwardly inviting sexual attack. (1987: 39)

The Birth of a Nation used the 'inevitable' corruption of black people by power to justify the consequent rise of the Ku Klux Klan to contain and control them. Taylor suggests that while Dixon's original text was clearly racist, Griffith's own racism was unconscious, in as much as racism as a group psychosis is unconscious (Taylor, 1991), but this is an extremely generous reading of his work: Griffith's later attempts to make amends through less vicious portraits of black communities can be viewed as nugatory and little more than an attempt at retrospective damage-limitation. Although an organized movement against such representations was still in its infancy, many people saw the film for what it was and demonstrations were held in a number of states. The National Association for the Advancement of Colored People (NAACP) tried to have the film banned and issued leaflets against its screening, but Griffith rallied to its defence by publishing his own pamphlet entitled *The Rise and Fall of Free Speech in America* in which he cited numerous good reviews of the film. Working on the principle that no publicity is bad publicity, the furore surrounding the film guaranteed its popularity at the box office and also firmly established the effective power of film. But the glorification of the Ku Klux Klan not only did untold harm to the drive for equality but enabled it to embark on a major recruitment drive and enjoy a certain amount of respectability and legitimacy (Reddick, 1944). Nearly eighty years later, in 1994, the film was released on video so that, notwithstanding the appalling racism explicit in the narrative, viewers could finally have the opportunity to watch a 'masterpiece'. But as Phillips so acutely asks, is the price too high?

I have no passionate feelings about Griffith [and] I certainly don't want his film banned. On the other hand, at a time when ethnic cleansing has become a familiar term for the kind of atrocities practised by the Ku Klux Klan, it may also be time to debate seriously what meaning we should attach to the disinterment of *The Birth of a Nation* as a 'neglected masterpiece'. (M. Phillips, 1994: 69)

Rastus and Sambo: comic genius in the making

Because the majority of important 'black' roles in early films were played by whites in blackface and because films in this fledgling period were written, produced and directed by whites, characterizations were usually stiff, embarrassing and crude. Looking specifically at comedy films, Reid argues that blackface minstrelsy was an early popular form of American race humour where white minstrel 'comics' objectified African American oral traditions, physiognomy, dress, dance and song (Reid, 1993). By masquerading in blackface, white artistes implicitly commodified the authentic black experience, appropriating black traditions and culture as a suitable vehicle for racist humour. As with the immensely popular *The Black and White Minstrel Show* on British television, the mask of blackface effectively neutralized the sexual charge between black men and white women and allowed a white audience to enjoy the pretended romance. When black artistes were engaged to play more substantial roles in film, they were often exoticized and endowed with insatiable sexual appetites. Equally, a number of the industry's revered stars such as Harold Lloyd and Buster Keaton used black characters in their productions to generate 'darkie' jokes or to function as the butt of slapstick misfortune. The lack of realistic narrative in early films was compensated for by an abundance of melodies, spirituals and engaging black faces but sheer volume did nothing to obscure the fact that these films used the same old tired clichés but with a bit more rhythm: black people are happy (and so is white society) when they know their place. Ironically, although these films helped to establish and sustain the careers of black performers such as Stepin Fetchit and Clarence Muse, their continued employment was dependent on repeating the successful formula of all-singing, all-dancing, all-happy-working-for-the-massa routines.

Once black performers had become part of the mainstream film scene and, moreover, had demonstrated their ability to attract an audience, black artistes were regularly seen in films of the late 1920s and through the depression years of the 1930s. Although it is tempting to be dismissive of films of this period, Bogle suggests that artistes such as Stepin Fetchit, Paul Robeson, Hattie McDaniel and Fredi Washington all contributed to the development of the idea in the public's imagination, that black performers could act in their own right and did not always have to function simply as a foil to the white folks. But it is hard to find evidence to support this highly optimistic perspective. 'Their high sense of style elevated them, and through style the black actors turned their cheap, trashy, demeaning stereotyped roles inside out, refining, transforming and transcending them. The great black performers did not simply *play* characters. Rather they played *against* their roles' (1989: 2).

The pre-war years

By the time *Gone with the Wind* (1939) was actually screened, the pre-distribution publicity ensured that its audience would break all previous box-office records. Although the film was technically far superior to *The Birth of a Nation*, there are nonetheless some revealing parallels between the two productions. Both were about the South, the Civil War and black people but where *The Birth of a Nation* was overt in its message, *Gone with the Wind* was more subtle. To a large extent, the later film took up the baton handed over to it by *Nation*, further establishing in the white American mind the 'rightness' of the Southerners' slant on slavery and black people.

> The defeat which it [the South] suffered on the field of battle was more than repaired by its victory over the minds of the American people through history books, novels and now the motion pictures. Some critics felt that the final touch to this victory came with the award to Hattie McDaniel of an Oscar . . . for her role as 'Mammy'. (Reddick, 1944 in Patterson, 1975: 15)

Once again, there were vigorous protests against the film and the NAACP were successful in getting some of the more offensive scenes edited out of the final cut. Commenting on the effects of the persistent stereotypical representation of African Americans, Reddick argues that such portraits established associations and further confirmed pre-existing assumptions about black communities. The medium of film thus operated to confound black ambitions and aspirations and popular films such as *Gone with the Wind* and *Swanee River* (1940) retained the traditional racist motifs of faithful servants and happy black folks. Butterfly McQueen who played Scarlet O'Hara's maid, Prissy, recalls that she soon fell foul of typecasting efforts. 'When I wouldn't do Prissy over and over, they [the studios] wouldn't give me any more work' (McQueen quoted by Sheila Johnston, *Independent*, 25.9.1989). When Lena Horne was put under contract with MGM she was asked to test for the part of a maid in their forthcoming *Cairo* (1942). During the test, Horne was found to be too light-skinned to be realistically cast as a maid, so the make-up department experimented with different shades of blackface until she achieved the 'right' colour (Bourne, 1983).

While black actors were often forced to adopt the standard caricatures accorded them by white writers and directors, several black women performers refused to play by white rules. At a time when the black press was full of advertisements for skin lighteners and hair straighteners, Bessie Smith was only ever interested in pleasing a black audience, insisting that her chorus girls were at least as dark as she was (Melly, 1988). Her disregard for positive images made her the antithesis of what organizations such as the NAACP wanted from their black heroes and the Association tried but failed to ban her only film, *St Louis Blues* (1929). Actors such as Cicely Tyson and Gloria Foster who steadfastly refused to act in films which denigrated black women were destined to be out of work more often than employed. Hattie McDaniel, on the other hand, was usually typecast in mammy roles – her most famous being in *Gone with the Wind* – and she pragmatically argued that it was better to *play* a maid for $700 a week than *be* one for $7 (McDaniel quoted in Patterson, 1975: xiii). This simple economic truth cannot be easily subverted by an appeal to the greater harm being done to the black community as a whole through black artistes perpetuating stereotypical thinking by acting out the fantasy life of white producers. Woody Strode was cast in a number of John Ford's westerns and visibly challenged the view that all cowboys were white. However, he was also willing to play more stereotypical roles and featured in a number of Tarzan movies and was reported to have said: 'I'm tired of this black, black, black business. Me, I don't care. If the money is right, I'll play Mickey Mouse' (Strode cited in Bergan, 1995). Stepin Fetchit who started life as a porter on a film set, cannot be blamed for enjoying the transition from handyman to film star, even if his characters became increasingly ludicrous as the comedic requirement for laughing at rather than with a black fool became ever more desirable.

Commenting on the protests which have ensued over stereotypical black portraits in film, Cripps argues that far from eliminating all such images, specific actions have led to the least objectionable stereotypes being the ones that continue to have currency. Thus villainous black men stayed off the screen at the price of allowing the comically idiotic Stepin Fetchit to typify the entire black community (1978). The apparently sensitive use of 'positive' characterizations resulted in the development of black roles which denied autonomous agency, since black actors were only allowed to be amusing (but stupid) sidekicks to a white male lead. Hollywood's efforts to avoid sexual stereotyping of black women and men meant that black actors were often desexualized, becoming little more than ciphers. Even in all-black films of the 1950s such as *Carmen Jones* (1956), the fear of portraying black sexuality led to the construction of wooden and artificial characters who were entirely unrealistic because the human dimension of sexuality was denied.

James Baldwin criticizes the character of Joe (played by Harry Belafonte) in *Carmen Jones* precisely because he is reduced to cardboard cut-out (Baldwin, 1955).

The slightly more realistic dramas of the immediate post-war years facilitated the emergence of one of the most significant black acting talents in the 1950s and 1960s in the shape of Sidney Poitier. Without having to resort to singing, dancing or fooling, Poitier was able to produce some powerful performances in his numerous roles as the quietly dignified and intelligent urban black man. Early examples of his work such as *Edge of the City* (1957) and *The Defiant Ones* (1958) signalled a radical departure from the more traditional roles assigned black male actors although his characters were unusually prone to sacrificing themselves in order to save a white compatriot: Hollywood demands that if a black man does something heroic, then disaster must necessarily follow. The fear which operated at the root of much racist mythology was defused by the domestication of black customs and culture – a process of deracination and isolation – or else by stories in which minority groups were shown playing by the rules of white society (Diawara, 1988). Later films such as *To Sir with Love* (1966) and *Guess Who's Coming to Dinner* (1967) allowed Poitier to develop different strengths and Leab argues that the very presence of Poitier set a precedent, even if his saintly image was forced upon him by an industry indifferent or hostile to black concerns (Leab, 1975). But Cripps is highly critical of black actors such as Poitier, Harry Belafonte and Sammy Davis, accusing such stars of trading in stereotypes and giving rise to 'conscience liberalism' (Cripps, 1980). For Cripps, then, such stars diminished their own authentic personalities by portraying what were essentially white characters with black skins.

Integrating the black

The 1960s saw a shift in cinema portrayals of race and a number of films of this period treated with the theme of integration and accommodation of African Americans into mainstream society. Hollywood was, however, generally clumsy in its efforts to explore the brutal drama of the Civil Rights movement and most films of the decade were made with the intention of showing the best side of the black (and of course the white) community (Null, 1975). Films such as *All the Young Men* and *Sergeant Rutledge* (both 1960) featuring Sidney Poitier and Woody Strode respectively, were both army

films and demonstrated mainstream cinema's preferred presentation of black individuals as superheroic rather than real people with
real problems. African Americans were welcomed into the bosom of
Hollywood by cautious degrees but certainly not by their economic
and social competitors in the real world (Cripps, 1993). While the
elite could happily pay lip service to the notion of equality, safe in
the knowledge that the black community would never constitute a
genuine threat to their position, less privileged Americans were
rather more ambivalent about the strangers in their midst. These
tensions were reflected in some of the films which emerged during
the 1960s so that as black people began to intrude into the consciousness of the white masses, their place in society provoked
divergent images. While *Pressure Point* (1962) introduced the
American audience to the notion of a black doctor (although this
character was played by the safe Sidney Poitier), John Ford's *The
Man Who Shot Liberty Valance* (1962) cast Woody Strode as an archetypal Uncle Tom who shambles off the picture after being hit by a
bucket of whitewash. Sammy Davis is best remembered as playing
derivative 'Sambo' roles to Frank Sinatra's various characters in a
number of films during the 1960s such as *Ocean's Eleven* (1960),
Sergeants 3 (1962) and *Robin and the 7 Hoods* (1964).

However, Hollywood's collaboration with black writers led to a
number of black-oriented films being produced which described
more genuine experiences of black family life (Reid, 1993). By the
end of the 1950s studios were hiring black writers to develop and
write scenarios for studio-produced films which dealt with black
themes and this led to pressure for more diverse and authentic
filmic representations. Films such as *Native Son* (1951), *A Raisin in
the Sun* (1961) and *The Learning Tree* (1969) were film adaptions of
black literary classics which provided alternative readings of the
diversity of black communities and which, in the original, were
enjoyed by both black and white readers. Whilst the major studios
were cautious about funding works by African Americans, they
were more willing to underwrite film treatments of successful black
literary works, recognizing the potential audience.

In Britain, too, films began to be produced in the 1960s which
looked more realistically at race and racism in contemporary
Britain, largely as a result of the Notting Hill Riots in 1958 after
which 'race relations' became a legitimate topic for discussion in its
own right. This new mood of realism led to the production of two
landmark films, *Sapphire* (1959) and *Flame in the Streets* (1961). Both
these films articulated white society's response to the black presence and the contextualizing framework of race relations allowed

the former to portray the black community as 'victim' while also allowing the latter to identify the same community as 'problem' (Pines, 1991a). These dual strands of victim and problem/perpetrator continue to constitute the dominant motifs in contemporary film and television programmes which delineate aspects of 'race'. The narrow construction of the black subject, as victim and social problem, places a structural limit on the possibility of developing black characters or representing black experiences beyond the boundaries of the race-relations problematic. Not only are mainstream commentaries on race issues prefigured by their development inside the white imagination, but the continued insistence on problematizing black people as victim/villain endlessly corroborates the popular myth of black communities as an underclass perpetually on the edge of criminal breakdown. In addition, as Dyer argues, those studios which chose to focus on groups which were defined as 'oppressed' or otherwise disadvantaged, then became part of the very process of oppression (Dyer, 1988). The act of studying black people in isolation reinforces their differentness from the wider society while at the same time ignoring the role of that wider society in the maintenance of racism. The assumption that minority groups are the exception leads inevitably to the conclusion that the dominant group is the norm.

Blaxploitation as genre

In an ideas-bankrupt Hollywood at the beginning of the 1970s, with white Americans leaving the cities in droves, it was hardly surprising that Hollywood looked at the success of black-produced films such as *Sweet Sweetback's Baadasssss Song* and *Super Fly* and jumped on the black bandwagon with alacrity. The potential of movies to reach a newly urbanized black audience began to look financially viable and the new film formula of aggressive black hero who beats the system and ends up with the money *and* the woman was used in a series of derivative films. Thus a new phase of hard black hero types took hold and a succession of films like *The Legend of Nigger Charley* (1972) and *Hell up in Harlem* (1974) were designed to give a thirsty black audience black heroes of their own. Blaxploitation stars contrasted sharply with the black saint image peddled by Poitier's various incarnations which appealed more to a white and emerging middle-class black audience. The aggressive individualism of the new black heroes represented a significant shift away from the traditional accommodationist constructions which had informed films of previous decades (Pines, 1991b). Whilst these blaxploitation movies were condemned because of their negative portrayal of black urban ghetto life and the glamorization of crime, it was less the fault of black artistes than an avaricious Hollywood keen to turn an easy buck. Black audiences could enjoy the sight of black heroes kicking against the (white) system and winning, even as they condemned the violence and recognized the implausibility. Here were the ultimate escape movies for black audiences, where they could cheer with the black hero on screen and then walk out of the theatre and back into real lives blighted by racism.

In black films of the 1970s (then as now) women tended to be seen as accessories to the black male lead, massaging away their crises of confidence with soft words and sex. Precious few women existed outside the orbit of their men: women were only rendered visible in the context of hard male bodies and strong male fists. Black woman as whore was, as ever, a particularly popular motif, and black prostitutes were much in evidence in many of the black films of the 1970s including *The Hit Man* (1971) and *Sweetback*. Hollywood's answer to criticisms against stereotypical black female roles was to produce films like *Cleopatra Jones* released in 1973 by Warner Brothers, followed by *Cleopatra Jones and the Casino of Gold* (1974) and American International's offerings of *Coffy* (1973), *Foxy Brown* (1974) and *Friday Foster* (1977). All these films showcased emerging black women actors, but the visual imagery employed was clearly meant to appeal to the fantasies of a white male audience. Both Tamara Dobson and Pam Grier who featured in these films had bodies which were both athletic and sexually appealing and although they had to appear as powerful and threatening to accord with the conventions of the genre, they nonetheless remained vulnerable and feminine. Reid suggests that both women were seen by the (white) male viewer as amazons who deserved to be sexually and racially disempowered (1993). In the end, the male gaze is more disempowering than the women's aggression is liberating, and in any case their violence was usually directed against other women (as in *Cleopatra Jones*) so that the possibility of female solidarity was instantly closed off as a potential threat. At the end of their labours, our heroines always returned home to the reassuring arms of their lovers.

Huey Newton, a significant activist in the Black Panther movement condemned most of the 'black' films of the early 1970s as being counter-revolutionary but singled out *Buck and the Preacher* (1972) and *Sweetback* as brave exceptions. For Newton, most of the remainder did not treat with the possibility of revolution or when they did, made such ideas appear stupid and naive (Newton cited in Patterson, 1975). More sensitively drawn alternative black portraits such as *Lady Sings the Blues* and *Sounder* (both 1972) also provided correctives to the cardboard cut-out heroes of the blaxploitation genre and during the 1970s, mainstream cinema began to take seriously the talents of black directors such as Sidney Poitier and Ossie Davies (Bogle, 1989). Criticizing the blaxploitation films from a rather different perspective, Tony Brown, then Dean of Howard University's School of Communications, regarded films such as *Super Fly* as symptomatic of black self-hate and highly dangerous both in their glorification of deviant and criminal activities such as drug-dealing, but also in the encouragement of an uncritical identification with the alleged 'heroes' (Brown cited in Patterson, 1975). Kael, too, was concerned about the after-effects on a black audience, of a steady diet of black-beats-white scenarios.

> How is it going to be possible to reach black audiences after they have been so pummelled with cynical consumerism that any other set of values seems hypocritical and phony ... blackness is a funky new trist – an inexpensive way to satisfy the audience that has taken over the big downtown theatres now deserted by the white middle classes? (Kael, 1972: 264)

But the sudden interest in black themes during the 1970s, including the blaxploitation movies, did at least enable black actors to demand not only more authentic characterizations but a more equitable financial arrangement for actors and cinema-owners alike. Commenting on the film *Melinda* (1972) which he directed, Hugh Robertson recalls the battles he fought in order to develop the character of Melinda into something more than cipher.

> I had to fight and fight for any human elements in the story ... they kept pushing for all sex and violence. I had to insist on the dinner scene between Melinda ... and Frankie ... so we could see some kind of relationship between them, not just bring her into the story and suddenly have her dead the next morning. (Robertson, cited in Patterson, 1975: 245)

It was also during the 1970s that many of the black comedians who had appeared on television variety or comedy shows began to appear in comedy films. The first financially successful black comedy produced by a major studio was *Cotton Comes to Harlem* (1970) which was directed and co-written by Ossie Davies. The film's main narrative concerned the exploits of two detectives who uncover various shady goings-on and although a contemporary audience might flinch at the poor production values, *Cotton*'s box office success helped to demonstrate that a low-budget black film could find a mainstream audience. Sidney Poitier's directorial debut came in 1974, with *Uptown Saturday Night* in which he also co-starred with Bill Cosby. As with *Cotton*, *Uptown* assiduously avoided any comment on the social or economic location of real black communities. Reid argues that the function of what he describes as 'hybrid minstrel comedy' is to satisfy the pleasure requirements of a mainstream audience rather than provide accurate portraits of the black experience (1993). However, it was also the case that the box office success of *Uptown* and Poitier's sequel *Let's Do It Again* (1975) and the fact that these types of films attracted both black and white audiences, encouraged major studios to continue funding black-directed projects, provided, of course, that they were in the same mould. Criticism of these kinds of black film centred on the fact that the humour contained within the narratives could have been oppositional and resistant, subverting the humour which traditionally mocks black people by deriding the humour itself. Instead, their narratives simply reinforced the traditional stereotypes without offering anything new and without engaging in a political discourse which spoke to the lived black experience.

The next generation

A new wave of black independent filmmaking broke during the 1980s, with the commercial debut of Spike Lee and colleagues such as Robert Townsend and Julie Dash. This movement was mirrored by Hollywood's renewed interest in things ethnic. Stephen Spielberg's film adaptation of Alice Walker's novel *The Color Purple* (1985) became an unlikely success story in the mid-1980s and, unusually, put black women centre stage. Although the film was a box-office success, it did not attract critical acclaim largely because it was seen as entertainment rather than an accurate social commentary. Johnson, for example, is caustic in his analysis of the film, positioning it as standard romantic melodrama with too many factual and historical errors to be aimed at anything other than an audience of idiots (1990). The uncompromising depiction of Mister as evil incarnate was one of the main causes of criticism against the film, particularly from black male commentators. It has been argued that the films's simplistic portrayal of Mister (and therefore black men in general) as quintessentially evil prevents the narrative from dealing adequately with other issues such as male–female relations, racism, sex or religion with which the original text was also concerned (Diawara, 1988). Discussing the characterizations of black men in *The Color Purple*, Spike Lee argues that the reason they were so one-dimensional and crude lay in the way in which Alice Walker herself perceives black men. He is highly critical of women like Walker and Ntozake Shange who, he argues, vilify black men and whose works are then embraced by white producers, eager to share in the condemnation of black brothers by black sisters (Lee, 1986). He cites the work of Terry McMillan as not falling into this unfortunate category, commenting that he would be very pleased to turn McMillan's texts into film. McMillan, however, does not share Lee's vision and when asked if she would consider him directing her bestselling novel *Waiting to Exhale*, she said no, because Lee 'knows nothing about women' (McMillan cited in *The Voice*, 19.1.1993). However, the criticism over the film is more properly to do with Spielberg's adaptation of Walker's novel, than the text itself.

> Whatever the factors which personally motivated him to downplay and in some ways almost completely ignore the transformation of Mister, it had the political impact of transforming Walker's text (which was not anti-black male, which did not portray black men as if they are not complex individuals) into a one-dimensional frame where black males were depicted in a conventional stereotypically racist Hollywood manner. (bell hooks, 1991: 69)

Buddies

Whilst black filmmakers such as Spike Lee were endeavouring to retain control over their own art works by producing films independently, the commercial sector was rediscovering the pleasures and profits of a black comedian acting as foil to the white hero. Richard Pryor and Eddie Murphy were catapulted into superstardom during the 1980s with films such as *Stir Crazy* (1980), *48 hrs* (1982) and *Trading Places* (1983), usually as the more zany half of a black–white twosome. Whilst Pryor's work has received considerable acclaim, Murphy's career has been less favourably assessed. Bogle suggests that while Pryor's influence on Murphy's characterizations are clear, what is also obvious is that Murphy has not properly understood Pryor's work (1989). He argues, for example, that whereas Pryor gets inside the characters he creates and explores their pain and their dignity, Murphy regards his own characters as essentially low-life wasters and is too willing to indulge in profanity to score cheap points. On the other hand,

Murphy's characters are always completely self-assured and confident and despite portraying street-wise dudes who find themselves thrust into a strange white milieu, Murphy's characters never back down, are never subordinate.

Murphy's various roles have all tended towards the comedic with some social commentary overlaid on the slapstick humour but in *Beverley Hills Cop II* and *III*, the charm of Murphy's original character, Axel Foley, begins to lose its strength as his antics test the boundaries of viewer belief. In a number of Murphy's films, the action is located within predominantly white environments so that any threat which might be associated with a young black urban male is quickly deterritorialized by virtue of his having to operate on more familiar (to the white audience) turf. In *48 hrs*, Murphy is cast opposite Nick Nolte and plays the loud, inconsistent exhibitionist young blood, Hammond, against Nolte's more dignified, authoritative police officer, Cates. For the black viewing audience, the fact that Hammond remains a villain means that full identification with his character cannot take place, since his misdemeanours are subject to a normative process of discipline and punishment. He is not therefore the hero of the piece, although he may well be the star of the show. Black protagonists such as Apollo Creed (Carl Weathers) in *Rocky II* (1979) receive a similar treatment where their defeat is a requisite to the development of the white hero figure. Diawara argues that not only is the black viewer denied the possibility of identification with black characters – because they are typically represented as losers in various ways – but the pleasure of narrative closure is often an ambiguous experience since questions of blame or guilt are often left unanswered or else resolved against the black characters (1988).

The *Lethal Weapon I, II* and *III* movies (1987, 1989, 1992) were articulations, once again, of buddy themes, this time teaming up Danny Glover with Mel Gibson. In a reversal of the matched pairing in the *Beverley Hills Cop* series, here it is the white partner who takes all the risks while the black colleague can only look on in amazement. The innate humanity of a black–white relationship which transcends race difference is very appealing to all kinds of audiences, suggesting that anything is possible if we could just get to know one another. While this simple message does, of course, have some force, it also serves to focus attention away from the more pressing social and economic iniquities which separate black from white in the real world. Glover is quick to question the usefulness of labelling, of saying this film is comedy, that film is social comment, suggesting that political elements can be found in films which do not describe themselves thus.

I think what we term political is awfully limited and relative. There is something political about *Lethal Weapon*. The fact that we introduce a family and change ideas about black relationships. You can make that argument. The fact that we deal with the issue of apartheid in *Lethal 2*, the issue of gun control. It's accessible rather than a straight political piece. (Glover in interview with Leone Ross, *The Voice*, 27.10.1992)

Making Whoopi

The female equivalent of Eddie Murphy in terms of box office success, must be Whoopi Goldberg who first came to public notice in Spielberg's *The Color Purple*, although her gift for comedy was submerged beneath the sentimental demands of the script (Johnson, 1991). When she received a Hollywood Golden Globe for best actress in a dramatic role for her part in *Purple*, she paid tribute to Hattie McDaniel in her acceptance speech saying: 'Hattie McDaniel – here it is' (Goldberg quoted in Bourne, 1993: 11). Her second feature, *Jumpin' Jack Flash* (1986), directed by Penny Marshall allowed some of her talent to emerge, but nonetheless managed to (mostly) confound a genuine comedic intelligence by insisting on bizarre clothes and a propensity to adopt the wide-eyed manners of the fool in an effort to buy a cheap laugh. Goldberg has not been allowed to develop the sexual/romantic dimension of many of her characters and more usually plays asexual or at least sexually uninterested women. In *Clara's Heart* (1988), Goldberg is governess to a confused white child and in *Homer and Eddie* (1989) she is running away from a mental institution and teams up with a similarly unbalanced adventurer, Jim Belushi.

Several forgettable films later, for example, *Fatal Beauty* (1987) and *The Telephone* (1988) Goldberg starred in the popular and award-winning *Ghost* (1990), providing comic relief in an otherwise lengthy and determinedly tear-jerking story, and achieving an Oscar for her pains. In 1992 she starred in two more films, the movie version of the stage play *Sarafina!* and Disney's *Sister Act* (followed by *Sister Act II* in 1993). Although *Sister Act* was a huge box office success and Goldberg received the NAACP's Image Award for Best Actress as well as a Golden Globe nomination, her role was undemanding and her character, a second-rate lounge singer called Deloris Van Cartier, lacked depth or context. With few exceptions, Goldberg's career has been made on her talent for playing desexualized clowns, non-threatening black fantasy women who can appeal to a mass white audience and her improbable impersonation of a nun. But perhaps part of Goldberg's appeal may be precisely that her characterizations provide a comforting respite from the constant negotiations about race which other films featuring black performers require, since her ethnicity is never a controversial issue. In *Made in America* (1993), in which she starred with Ted Danson, the storyline does turn on racial identity – her daughter thinks that the white Hal Jackson (Danson) is her father – but race is not really prefigured in any meaningful way. The numerous 'ethnic' references – she works in an African bookshop, wears 'African' clothes and wears her hair in locks – only serve to accentuate the difference between her unconventional and whacky lifestyle and that of the strait-laced and macho Danson; they do not have any real narrative importance as signifiers of meaningful cultural difference. As with the relationship between the characters played by Whitney Houston (Rachel) and Kevin Costner (Frank) in *The Bodyguard* (1992), the emerging relationship between Hal and Sarah in *America* is seen as strictly romantic rather than daringly and truthfully trans-cultural.

On the other side of the Atlantic, Britain produced a number of films in the early 1990s which featured black performers. These included *The Crying Game* (Jaye Davidson) and *Peter's Friends* (Alphonsia Emmanuel) (both 1992) and Branagh's *Much Ado About Nothing* (Denzel Washington, interestingly cast as Don Pedro, 1993). Where *Peter's Friends* employed a traditional stereotype – upwardly mobile sexy black woman, played with some pathos by Emmanuel – *Crying Game* was altogether more ambitious, casting Davidson as Dil, a fey young black individual who operates as a woman but is biologically male. Other than a few throw-away remarks by Dil which relate directly to race and racism, the narrative is essentially about the white hero, Fergus (Stephen Rea), and his obsession with Dil which continues despite his discovery of Dil's maleness. It is therefore more like an orthodox love story with the twist of sexual ambivalence than an exploration of black–white relations.

In 1992, Sidney Poitier became the first black performer to be awarded a life achievement award by the American Film Institute. To celebrate his new status, he starred alongside Robert Redford in *Sneakers* (1992), a lightweight thriller in which he played a member of a team of computer experts hired to test the security systems of hackable information networks. When asked why a performer of his considerable talent and experience should engage in such a project he replied that careers should be engineered to take in diversity and *Sneakers* was part of the lighter side (Poitier quoted in *The Sunday Times*, 8.11.1992). Whilst not quite pushing back the frontiers of reactionary typecasting as he did in, for example, *Lilies of the Field*

(1964), for which he received an Oscar, his membership of the
computer group as an ordinary, everyday expert rather than a *black*
expert at the very least provides some evidence of integrated casting. But mainstream films in the 1990s are not blazing new trails in
black representation, they are not privileging black actors in lead
roles but merely expanding slightly the repertoire of possible
characterizations.

Native American chic

The year 1992 marked the quincentenary celebration of Columbus's
so-called 'discovery' of the Americas. In contrast to numerous festivals carried out in the developed world, much of South America
demonstrated its protest against the hijacking of its history by Europe and the subsequent mythology which was invented from the
privileged purview of a European gaze. Five hundred years on,
many parts of South America are still engaged in the same old
fights, repelling the imposition of imperialist rule over indigenous
peoples. Released in October 1992 in good time for the celebrations,
Ridley Scott's *1492: Conquest of Paradise* was a lush historical set-
piece, showcasing the contoversial French actor, Gérard Depardieu
as Columbus, and ostensibly charting the journey that our 'hero'
makes from the coast of Spain to the Caribbean. As an exercise in
showy costume drama, the film was definitely successful but the
numerous historical inaccuracies and the rehabilitation of Chris as
an eco freak without an avaricious bone in his body leads to a
certain disenchantment with the notion of an authentic history.
What the film gives the viewer is yet another adventurer-as-hero
figure with the disagreeable details of precisely how paradise actually was conquered and the ugly fate of the indigenous peoples
thereafter, receiving a Hollywood-style nip and tuck treatment.
    Also released to coincide with the Columbus celebrations,
Michael Mann's *Last of the Mohicans*, adapted from Fenimore
Cooper's original text but also influenced by Phillip Dunne's 1936
screenplay, burst into spectacular life. The story is set in the moun-
tainous frontier wilderness of the colony of New York in 1757 and
charts the adventures of the heroic Hawkeye (adopted as a child by
Mohican Chingachgook when his white settler parents were killed)
against the background of war waged between the English and the
French and relations between the Native Americans and the settlers.
As with Rice Burroughs's Tarzan hero, Hawkeye is imbued with
many 'noble savage' characteristics but he is privileged above the

ordinary natives because of his whiteness and is therefore endowed with a moral superiority which allows him to function outside both his native and his adopted culture. Although it starts promisingly as a (reasonably) accurate historical comment on war, it quickly floats into romance, as the relationship between Hawkeye and the colonel's daughter becomes the central narrative focus. As would be expected from a Hollywood treatment, truth is once again sacrificed for the sake of a good box-office rating. Staying with the Native American theme, yet another film on this topic released in 1992 was Michael Apted's *Thunderheart*, which featured Val Kilmer as a part-Sioux FBI agent who is sent back to 'his people' to investigate a murder on a Navajo reservation. Apted raises what could have been a formula thriller to a more sociological level, using the narrative to rehearse some contemporary questions about race and class. However, the pacing is never completely comfortable and sequences of social commentary rub roughly against the more orthodox thriller sections, so that although the film is inevitably pitched into the genre of the latter, it nonetheless manages to be patronizingly smug about the former.

More black two-steps for the 1990s

A modification of the male-bonding thematic which was played out in police buddy movies such as the *48 hrs* and *Lethal Weapon* series was repackaged for the 1990s in several films including *White Men Can't Jump* (1993) featuring Wesley Snipes and Woody Harrelson as respectively black and white basketball enthusiasts who team up in order to pull off a scam and along the way develop a genuine friendship against the odds. As with earlier efforts to reverse the orthodox white-good/black-bad dichotomy which characterized many of the 'race' movies of the 1970s, the home-spun philosophizing which the no-hoper white character Billy receives at the hands of his family-oriented, sensible black friend Sidney sits a little too neatly. However, the film does manage to capture something of the simmering racism and resentment which lies scarcely submerged beneath the veneer of civilized American society. As Billy and Sidney trade insults in an effort to get on top, their barbs are inflected with the racist taunts which are a commonplace, although their macho discourse slowly gives way to grudging acceptance and partly discarded bigotry.

Wesley Snipes was much in vogue in the early 1990s, starring in Mario Van Peebles's *New Jack City* in 1992, and *White Men Can't Jump*, *Rising Sun*, *Demolition Man* and *Boiling Point*, all in 1993. *Rising*

Sun, directed by Philip Kaufman and also starring Sean Connery, has Snipes playing the student to Connery's sage in this formulaic cops and robbers thriller. Snipes plays a Los Angeles police officer who is responsible for Japanese liaison and his casting in this role (in the original novel his character is white) is bizarre, given the poor status and perception of black people by the Japanese community. The overt xenophobia which riddles Michael Crichton's original book is underplayed in the film, but the Japanese are nonetheless seen in an almost exclusively bad light, pandering to American fears of colonization and the red enemy. Kaufman's efforts to head off complaints of racism produced a rewriting of Connery's character as a Japanophile and his sidekick as black, but these gambits are not enough to camouflage the central racist motif.

As in *White Men Can't Jump*, both *Boiling Point* and *Demolition Man* see Snipes teamed with a white star (Dennis Hopper and Sylvester Stallone respectively). *Demolition Man* has Snipes cast as the blond-haired psychopath, Simon Phoenix, pitted against good guy cop, John Spartan, with the action taking place in the year 2032. It is a frothy number, true to the action-packed, sci-fi convention of guns and violence. Snipes's acclaimed versatility is part of his own master plan to secure a suitable power base from which he can choose and control his own filmmaking future. Although he has made more than a dozen films since 1986 and continues to feature in highly popular white-produced films such as *Demolition Man* and *Passenger 57*, as well as in black-originated work – such as *Sugar Hill* (1994) – he remains unconvinced that black performers will ever be identified as simply American rather than African American stars.

Snipes has been joined in his privileged position as a top box-office black star by the equally talented and flexible Denzel Washington who starred in Spike Lee's much-hyped film biography, *Malcolm X*, in 1992 and then in Branagh's *Much Ado About Nothing*, the award-winning *Philadelphia* and *The Pelican Brief*, all released in 1993. Washington's role in *The Pelican Brief*, as an investigative journalist with the *Washington Herald* who becomes involved in an extremely convoluted conspiracy thriller, is played to his usual high standard – he is already an Oscar winner for his supporting lead role in *Glory* (1990) about one of the first black regiments to fight in the Civil War – but even he is unable to rescue the rather laboured plot. The firm closure at the end of the film, with all the loose ends neatly tied represents Hollywood's deliberate shift in perception about political intrigues. Whereas earlier examples of the genre such as *All the President's Men* (1976) allowed viewers to make up their own minds about guilt or innocence, *The Pelican Brief* brooks no argument about precise culpability.

While Washington turned in a strong and sensitive performance as the black lawyer Joe Miller who Andrew Beckett (Tom Hanks) recruits to represent him in his forthcoming lawsuit against his former employers in *Philadelphia*, it was Hanks that was nominated and subsequently received an Oscar for his part in the film. It remains a mystery why Washington was not even nominated in the support role. While Andrew is certainly the more deliberately sympathetic character, the film really turns on Joe and his rites of passage as he comes to terms with and begins to resolve his own homophobia. The narrative of *Philadelphia* is less to do with being gay and having Aids than with being straight and homophobic and is groundbreaking not just because it deals specifically with Aids but in that it positions a black man as the embodiment of all-American family values (Taubin, 1994). It was clearly a solid commercial decision by director Jonathan Demme to cast Washington in the 'defender-of-the-faith' role since he is currently extremely attractive at the box office and his inclusion guarantees a black audience who might not otherwise have been interested in a story about white privilege gone sour. While part of the reason why Joe takes on Andrew's case is because he recognizes the oppression of discrimination, the crucial revelatory scene in the film, when Andrew's essential humanity is suddenly comprehended by Joe, is compromised by a colonialist subtext. The scene has Andrew asking Joe if he knows Maria Callas's work and when Joe replies that he's not that familiar with opera, Andrew then puts on a recording of Callas singing 'La Mamma Morta', from *André Chénier* and proceeds to interpret the song for him. The entire, lengthy scene is sentimental and overplayed and the dramatic tension requires that Andrew gives Joe a lesson in high culture while at the same time exposing his own vulnerable humanity. Thus Joe's sympathy for Andrew is achieved at the expense of insisting on his ignorance about opera. In his Oscar acceptance speech, Hanks remarked that Washington had made a serious commitment to the film, putting his reputation on the line in playing Joe, but time will tell if Hollywood's nod to political correctness endures beyond the lifetime of this film. If Washington and Snipes are working to push back the boundaries of acceptable black characterizations in mainstream cinema, they are remarkable because they are still so few. But at least in films like *Philadelphia*, black men are allowed to have families, play with their children and be ordinary members of society, not just villains and pimps.

Giving a contemporary spin to both the black as fool and black as athlete stereotypes, Disney's *Cool Runnings* (1993) presented the real-life story of the first Jamaican bob-sled team and its efforts to get to the 1987 Olympics in Calgary. Because it is a Disney creation and considerable licence has been taken to embellish the actual story, the production values are excellent and no expense has been spared in location shooting. Apart from the phoney Jamaican accents/patois – the lead is played by the American actor, Leon – the film is enjoyable and well acted, with the cultural cues managing to avoid ridiculous caricature. The final scene, with the much vaunted but seldom actualized homily about the taking part rather than the winning, is very effective but it has less to do with overcoming racism than providing a 1990s slant on the timeless story of David and Goliath. Throughout the film there are the requisite taunts of the 'go back to where you came from' variety from the German-speaking competitors and a slapstick scene at Calgary airport where the boys are apparently unaware that Canada is cold (they arrive in tropical shirts, shorts and sunglasses), but the real story, as with all Disney films, is that true grit and old-fashioned determination will bring its own reward. The Jamaican and therefore the 'race' angle is incidental to the crucial message of the film, but it is nonetheless a well-crafted work which manages to avoid the more pernicious stereotypes of young black men, although social commentary is not a strong point.

Apart from the films of the ubiquitous Whoopi Goldberg, there have been few interesting and important roles for black women in Hollywood during the early 1990s, although there have been some notable exceptions, particularly using the same-sex black–white buddy convention. The American independent filmmaker John Sayles's *Passion Fish* (1993) featured Mary McDonnell as the recently disabled white soap star Mary-Alice and Alfre Woodward as her reluctant black nurse, Chantelle. Mary-Alice returns home to Cajun country to recover from her accident and come to terms with her disability and her irascibility chases off all but the last nurse who is sent to look after her. Chantelle is a strong and determined woman who is also trying to control her own internal demons. Although Woodward is cast in a servile role, is recovering from a serious drug habit and has a young daughter Denita (Shauntisa Willis) from whom she is estranged, she nonetheless manages to confound the limitations of her character with her sensitivity, pacing and acute presence. The film is more atmospheric than straightforwardly narrative, with languid scenes of steamy Louisiana waterscape and awkward moments of near passion standing in for long passages of dialogue. The fact that it is set in the American South but includes no hint of racial tension leads the viewer to be slightly wary of the film's authenticity, but as with *Cool Runnings*, this is more an emerging buddy movie than strict reportage.

One of the most controversial films of the early 1990s which was very much *not* a buddy movie but rather seen as explicitly 'womanist' by many commentators, was the screen version of Tina Turner's autobiography, *What's Love Got To Do With It?* (1993) for which the lead actors, Angela Bassett and Larry Fishburne, playing the feuding couple, were both nominated for Oscars in 1994. The film generated mixed reactions from the audience, some seeing it as a straightforward, albeit decidedly one-sided version of an important chapter in musical history, while others regarded the film as simply reinforcing stereotypes about crime and violence within black communities and showing gratuitous episodes of black on black violence for white viewers' titillation. That Tina is finally rescued from her drug-taking, wife-beater of a husband and his grasping entourage by a white record producer has aroused controversy. There certainly is a lot of domestic violence in the film and the narrative is bereft of adequate explanations as to why Tina endured the torment for so long, or why most of her family and friends sided with Ike and watched the violence happen over and over. A barely noticed reference to Ike's own violent upbringing and, ergo, the suggestion of a cycle of violence which endlessly repeats itself, is tentatively offered during the film but only as throw-away. While many black men saw the film as self-consciously anti-male, Forna argues that black women also have problems with the depiction of domestic violence since the film offers a highly 'privileged' view of the experience – few battered women can seek refuge in a five-star hotel or have Turner's inestimable talent to fall back on (1993). However, the film was made by Touchstone (owned by Disney), so despite the publicity, it is hardly a 'black' film in any meaningful sense of the word, and the extremely selective presentation of Turner's history ensures that it is indeed (her)story which is dominant. The black filmmaker Linton Mdele comments that the only reason Bassett and Fishburne were nominated for Oscars was because they portrayed black people 'beating up on one another. They are rewarded for portraying the field nigger, the type of role played in the past by Sidney Poitier' (Mdele quoted in Jules, 1994). In other words, they are pandering to the prejudices of the white mainstream, but given the *real* Tina Turner's involvement with the making of this movie, it must be assumed that this particular version of events was one which she, at least, endorsed.

Despite the considerable 'improvements' in typecasting for black actors, while they might have strong roles, they don't have star billing: they might be the buddy but they are rarely the hero. Even in a film like *White Men Can't Jump*, where Snipes's character is allowed to occupy the moral high ground, the twist is that the white anti-hero ultimately proves that white men *can* jump – it is still about white values and preoccupations, it is still a film about being white. But perhaps it is futile to look to mainstream cinema in general and Hollywood in particular, to deliver authentic portraits of black community life, to unsentimentally explore race and racism. If cinema is about escape, spectacle and pleasure and the majority audience is white, it is hard to imagine any producer wanting to make films which place culpability for five hundred years of race discrimination squarely in the lap of white society. It is, on the contrary, to the black filmmaking community where one must look to find an antidote to the historical amnesia which has pervaded the canon of mainstream cinema. It is among black filmmakers that an oppositional and counter-practice has evolved which is successfully challenging the old plantation myths and both restoring black history, culture and traditions but also forging new diasporic identities and hybrid cross-cultural products. It is this vibrant and exciting new cinema praxis which will shape the future for black images, black representations and black narratives. Turn over for the new stories.

2

Black Fights Back Part I: Black Filmmaking and Strategies of Opposition in Britain

> Bhangra music gave us back something for ourselves, it had nothing to do with English people or white society. It also consolidated the debate about whether we are black, British or Asian. . . . What I'm saying is that we're not one thing or the other – we're everything when it suits us and one thing when it suits us, it's not exclusive or mutual.
>
> Gurinder Chadha, Interview

The debates which are now taking place about a specifically black filmmaking practice, and the high profile such debates are enjoying in practitioner, cultural and academic journals, would give the impression that black filmmakers in Britain are an entirely new phenomenon, born out of the struggles of the 1980s. While it is undoubtedly true that a number of black film and video workshops began to operate more consistently and cohesively during the 1980s, black filmmakers have been part of a more general arts movement in Britain since at least the 1960s. Lloyd Reckord, for example, directed *Ten Bob in Winter* in 1963, a film set in 1960s London which considered the experiences of African Caribbean migrants through the eyes of an unemployed student during a Christmas vacation. Three years later, Lionel Ngakane directed *Jemima and Johnny* which was again set in London (Notting Hill) after the 1959 riots, in which the friendship of a black girl and a white boy living in a racially hostile neighbourhood, is explored. At the end of the 1960s, both *Baldwin's Nigger* (1969) and *Reggae* (1970) were directed by Horace Ove and financed largely by the filmmaker himself, repeating the pattern of self-financing set by Ngakane and Reckord.

The relative invisibility of these films and their directors can be understood in terms of their marginalization within the British film

tradition and their limited access to distribution outlets. Thus
although Horace Ove's *Pressure* (1975) was the first black feature
film to be made in Britain, it was not until 1986 that *Handsworth
Songs* (John Akomfrah) and *The Passion of Remembrance* (Isaac Julien
and Maureen Blackwood) completed production and became the
first black films to begin theatrical exhibition at a central London
venue (Mercer, 1988). Throughout the history of black filmmaking
in Britain, the main feature which has characterized the slow process towards establishing a firm base has been an inability to obtain
sustained funding for film projects.

The late 1970s and the early 1980s witnessed significant policy
shifts around 'race' issues and the identification of new priorities on
the part of (potential) funders. Identifiably 'black' artistic endeavours began, suddenly, to enjoy institutional respectability. The BFI's
production of *A Private Enterprise*, a dramatic feature set in the
Asian community co-written by Dilip Hiro in 1975, and *Burning an
Illusion* directed by Menelik Shabazz in 1981, signalled growing
institutional recognition of black filmmaking within the terms of a
so-called 'multicultural' funding policy. Such policy reorientations
were made at a time when outbreaks of civil disobedience were
escalating in scale and volume and it could be argued that the
sudden and unprecedented funding of a large number of black
projects – cultural, social and economic – was the cynical if timely
response of a government eager to provide a sop to an angry and
restless black populace. There was a belated recognition that the
denial of black voices would no longer be tolerated, that protest
would no longer be talk-led (Morris, 1991). At the same time as civil
disturbance made the 'management' of black communities an
urgent priority, 1981 also saw the establishment of Channel 4 television (C4) which, with its mandate to cater for minority tastes and
interests, immediately began to play a significant role in the expansion of the independent film sector. Its brief to commit itself to
'multicultural' programming and develop a new model for public
service broadcasting encouraged high expectations that more appropriate strategies of black representation, both in front of and
behind the camera would be forthcoming, although arguably these
expectations have not, in the main, been fully satisfied.

The black workshop movement

The new commitment to supporting black filmmaking encouraged
the development of a number of different types of filmmaking

organization with varied objectives. On the one hand, there were conventional production companies, competing in the mainstream marketplace for commissions; and on the other, workshops, operating in the public-sector context of subsidized 'independence'. The workshop sector became extremely important as the locus of much of the emergent practice of black filmmaking, and its development as a sector was due largely to the drafting of the Workshop Declaration, drawn up in 1981 in an effort to put film and video workshops on a more secure financial footing. The Declaration was an industrial agreement signed by the Association of Cinematograph Television and Allied Technicians union (ACTT), regional arts associations such as Greater London Arts, the British Film Institute and television companies, which would facilitate grant approval via franchise to film and video workshops which wanted to produce non-commercial and grant-assisted film and video. The rationale for the Declaration was to develop and sustain an independent film sector which might begin to evolve on the basis of a more permanent funding structure than had been possible previously. Whilst the Declaration had not been drawn up specifically with Channel 4 in mind, the relentless reduction in funding from every other source has meant that C4 has become the principal sponsor by default. The workshop concept was, in any case, contiguous with the remit of Channel 4 to produce and showcase programmes for minority audiences and support innovative practice, so it is not surprising that it had (and continues to have) a significant role in supporting the new black independent filmmaking sector. Five black workshops were franchised under the Declaration (including Sankofa and Black Audio Film Collective) which together with the other franchised organizations, were eligible to bid for funding for a term of five years. After this initial period, further funding was provided at the discretion of the Declaration signatories and a number of franchised workshops continued to be sponsored after 1986.

An important part of the activities of black enterprises concerned educational issues, so that practical workshops, screenings and seminars such as the *Black Women and Representation* seminar (organized by the women members of Sankofa) in April 1984 and *Power and Control* which took place in October and November of the same year featured prominently. Such work was 'essential to initiating dialogue and debate around what has been referred to as black film culture' (Julien, 1985: 8). Black workshops have been, appropriately, intimately concerned with issues of marginalization and representation, attempting to disrupt the hegemony of mainstream cinema by providing an authentic counter-narrative to illustrate the reality of being black in Britain and experiencing life at the social margins.

The sometimes uneven quality of workshop products, particularly some of the early output, is associated with an organizational ethos which is political rather than commercial. In addition, many members of the newly created workshops were relatively inexperienced as filmmakers and Head argues that attempts to set up a culturally and politically oppositional sector meant that members were less likely to associate with and learn from peers operating within mainstream, commercial enterprises (1991). The development of the black workshop movement was structured and determined by three inter-connecting features: (1) politics; (2) finance; and (3) culture (Auguiste, 1989). The current threat to the survival of the independent filmmaking sector is as much to do with post-Thatcherite market principles as a failure to support and maintain any sort of British film production base, let alone an independent film sector. In terms of a future for the black workshop sector, the black filmmaker John Akomfrah has outlined three possible routes: 'They can go straight down the commercial line and do what everybody else does, i.e. write scripts and send them around the finance corporations and try to get high-powered producers; or they go to Channel Four and still try to produce their own films with one-off commissions; or they can continue to work in the workshop structure, hoping that there will still be some municipal benevolence left to see them through for a number of years' (1988b: 16). Akomfrah also argued that despite the changing economic imperatives which governed sponsorship of workshops and their output, funding agencies would nonetheless have to continue to support them because if they did not, then such censure would imply a diminishing commitment to the 1980s ideology of defending the dispossessed and giving a voice to the disenfranchised. However, Akomfrah did not reckon with the more ruthless ethos which quickly characterized the decade of the 1990s and by 1992, Akomfrah's third and possibly preferred route was no longer an option.

The launch of Channel 4's policy document *TV With a Difference* in 1989 demonstrated quite clearly that future workshop funding would be linked to single projects and, in addition, that such funding would only be provided for 12 months without an automatic right to renewal if the project had not been completed on time. The official rationale for such a change was the constraining nature of longer-term funding, which both tied up financial resources but also blocked access to funding for new talent. While the argument for enabling newcomers to be given a chance has a certain moral validity, the uncertainty that attends a 12-month contract is unlikely to generate the best possible product or the greatest likelihood of unfettered creativity. The BFI, one of the founding signatories to the original Workshop Declaration, also changed its relationship with the workshops and in 1991 implemented a policy to fund workshops on a commission-only basis, reflecting Channel 4's more general policy of project-specific funding. In addition to the project-based nature of funding, the other significant change was that resources were to be vested in individuals and no longer provided to groups. With the benefit of hindsight, of course, it is clear that a film enterprise which was based upon the creation of a not-for-profit, socially responsible and oppositional film culture was always going to be fighting a losing battle against the more persuasive tenets of commercialization and safe commissions.

Key moments in black filmmaking history in Britain

A number of black narrative fiction films of the 1980s attempted to break out of the strait-jacket of the race relations problematic by incorporating different narrative schemas. Menelik Shabazz's *Burning an Illusion* (1981) achieved critical acclaim for its portrayal of Pat, a young black woman who abandons her colonial identity – straightened hair, trashy white novellas – and begins to search for a more authentic black identity. Her awakened consciousness and newly politicized self-image is prompted by the arrest and later assault of her boyfriend by the police. Although the film was well received, Pat's dependency on the experiences of her male partner has generated some criticism of the film in as much as her transformation is comprehended and predicated upon the politicization of her boyfriend, thus denying her any individual autonomy.

Sankofa's *Territories* (Isaac Julien, 1985) was seen as constituting a radical departure for black film, concerning itself not with the provision of an alternative representation of black community life, but with contesting the very notion of representation itself. The film's style is experimental documentary, exploring the problem of black representation in white media through the creative use of sound and image. Julien wanted to look specifically at the way in which the black subject has been exoticized in white film narratives but also wanted to break with established conventions: 'up to now there have only been linear narrative films and realist documentaries and in a sense they are the modes that have been considered as the natural and accepted types of films for black filmmakers to make. We have to try and break away from that, and try to create space for other kinds of intervention' (1985: 5). For Julien, it is important that the diversity of black experiences and perspectives and interests are reflected in the legitimacy for black filmmakers to produce art works in different styles and with different contents. Julien argues that prior to *Territories*, the only black films which were ever discussed were those funded by the BFI – *Pressure* and *Burning an Illusion* – as if these films constituted the only proper examples of legitimate black film practice. His concern was that a diversity of stories and styles should be embraced under the rubric of black film, so it is ironic to note that subsequently, the films of Sankofa together with those of Black Audio have themselves come to be seen as the significant exemplars of black British filmmaking, particularly outside the UK.

Young Soul Rebels (Isaac Julien, 1983) was the first feature film produced by Sankofa and was set in Britain in 1977, the year of the Queen's Silver Jubilee. The film suggests that that year was particularly momentous because of the particular collision of social and political movements that emerged, charting the passage of anti-fascist challenges, such as Rock Against Racism and the Anti-Nazi League and suggesting that the 1970s were the decade when race and class became key mobilizing themes for a whole generation. Against this political background, issues of sexuality are explored and music, in particular, functions as a conduit through which the main themes develop. The film's use of conventional genre – murder-mystery mixed with buddy movie – its use of glossy cinematography and heavily soul-based soundtrack all contributed to its crossover success. The overt focus of the film is the long-standing friendship (and the strains thereon) between Caz who is black and gay and Chris who is bi-racial and straight, who run a pirate radio station together. Their story is played out in the context of the murder of a young black man during a sexual encounter in a park, a crime for which the police seek a black killer. The actual killer is a white man, known to both Caz and Chris, whose refusal to accept both his homosexuality and his desire for black men becomes his impulsion to kill. The film thus looks at the taboo areas of homosexuality, inter-racial attraction, desire and denial of desire, while retaining the essential motif of a friendship which endures in the face of several adversities. Within the narrative thread are crucial questions which relate to sexuality and, in particular, the valuing of an individual on the basis of her or his sexuality. Is the death of a gay woman or man as important as that of a heterosexual?

Positing this type of question has deep resonances with the other binary proposition of the relative worth of black and white people in the 'postcolonial' period. To a large extent the orientation of the film as narrative rather than experimental can be understood as a response to the diminishing opportunities for the exhibition of black film and the consequent requirement to attract an audience outside the avant-garde: 'I really wanted to make a narrative that played with certain recognisable codes and a particular genre'(Julien, 1990: 18).

During 1986 two films marked a turning point in their self-conscious effort to confound dominant descriptions of black communities: *The Passion of Remembrance* and *Handsworth Songs*. The former was the first feature-length drama from Sankofa to be directed by Maureen Blackwood (with Isaac Julien) and a crucial motivating impulse behind making *Passion* was to demonstrate the danger inherent in speaking *for* rather than *from* a community and the possibility instead, of speaking from the specificity of a particular experience and perspective. More especially, the film was concerned to explore issues of marginalization within the black community, looking, for example, at the ways in which black protest voices have traditionally emanated from the privileged domain of the heterosexual man who felt he had an assumed right to speak for the entire community, virtually excluding the voices of black gay men and black women. The black feminist, Michele Wallace, for example, argues that her book, *Black Macho and the Myth of the Superwoman* (1970), was taken up and then condemned by black sociology simply because it dared to make the 'obvious criticisms about black male leadership' (1989: 51). A similar knee-jerk response was provided in Patrick Augustus's docu-dramatic novel, *Babyfather* (1994), which sought to intervene (on the father's side) in the debate around black sexual relations and parental responsibility. *Passion* unfolds in three distinct registers: dramatic narrative, documentary and allegorical tableau which together produce a contemporary analysis of race, class, sexuality and politics in Britain. The film's delivery at different levels means that the realist drama of the central Baptiste family is bisected by conversations between a man and a woman which take place in imagined space. The film explores homosexuality and feminism from a black perspective, seeking to demonstrate the heterogeneity of black communities. *Passion* avoids the trap against which Hall cautions, of simply reversing the roles of men and women, heterosexual and homosexual, but instead breaks out of the binary stricture by fracturing both the burden of representation but also the narrative thread.

Handsworth Songs was Black Audio's debut into mainstream production. Reece Auguiste of Black Audio was keen to defend the documentary genre through which the film was mainly oriented, suggesting that the film 'was made in a Griersonian spirit with our own diasporic inflection adding substance to it' (Auguiste, 1988a: 7). *Songs* is essentially a political film essay describing the contours of race and civil disorder in contemporary Britain. Filmed in Handsworth and London during the 1985 riots, *Songs* analyzes the legacy of British colonialism. Cutting archive footage from the 1950s and 1960s with news reports of the riots in 1985, the film makes an explicit link between an impoverished and alienated underclass and civil disobedience. The film explores the realities and experiences of race and racism, looking back to the post-war migration from the Caribbean and the Asian sub-continent and considering the poverty of inner-city life today. Answering the criticism of, 'Oh no, not another riot movie', its director, John Akomfrah was moved to say that for many black people, there is very little else about living in Britain, other than issues about race and racism: 'That was precisely the issue which we wanted to foreground – that there isn't more to life, in many ways, and that is the tragedy' (Akomfrah, 1988b: 14).

Also from Black Audio, *Who Needs a Heart* (John Akomfrah, 1991) revolved around the story of Michael X, a British contemporary of Malcolm X who changed his name from de Freitas after meeting Malcolm (and subsequently changing it again to Abdul Malik). The person of Michael X is used as a lens through which to look at 1960s Britain, focusing both on the politics of the day but also the ambiguities surrounding black–white relations. Akomfrah wanted to use Michael X as his point of entry for looking more generally at the British condition because of the complexities which arose around the character when research began on the film. 'He seemed to be a hybrid figure: on the one hand a criminal [he started his career as a brothel-keeper and was hanged in Trinidad for murder], but clearly also an important political figure, a public figure' (Akomfrah, 1992: 30). Two years later, Akomfrah directed *Seven Songs for Malcolm X* (1993) which emerged as the cinematic culmination of his interest in the eponymous black revolutionary. In the same week that Spike Lee's *Malcolm X* was released in London, Channel 4 screened Black Audio's film. *Seven Songs* is documentary in format and combines interviews with friends and family with those of artists and commentators and weaves in reconstructions of events from Malcolm's history in a series of visually interesting tableaux. Akomfrah was keen to explore the intricacies of Malcolm's personality and to remedy some of the omissions made in other dramas of his life, including Malcolm's own autobiography. 'There's no point at all in the autobiography where his hustling life is given a political reading because that's seen by him in the autobiography as a period of darkness not worth evaluating' (Akomfrah quoted in Synmoie, 1993: 3).

A different hunger: black women filmmakers

The work of African American women writers during the 1960s and 1970s began to shift the frame of reference for black politics towards an incorporation of the specific experiences of black women, but Alexander argues that film has been the cultural form which has most resisted black women's participation (1989). However, international black film festivals and British enterprises such as the ill-fated GLC's *Third Eye* and anti-racist film seasons did eventually begin to showcase the work of this most invisible minority. Sankofa members Martine Attile and Maureen Blackwood had solo directorial debuts in 1988 with *Dreaming Rivers* and *A Perfect Image?* respectively: Ngozi Onwurah made her first film, *Coffee-Coloured Children* (1988) while at St Martin's School of Art and Gurinder Chadha's first film, *I'm British But . . .* (1989) was a BFI production, supported by Channel 4. Examining notions of identity, Chadha's film asks four young Asian people their views on being Asian in Britain and their responses are punctuated with bhangra rhythms and rap vocals. Identities are defined in terms of culture and acculturation and the central role of music in forging new identities and generating cultural fusion is a significant message of the film.

> What I've tried to do with all my work is to open up all that stuff – what it is to be British. What I'm doing is making a claim, as well as documenting a history of British Asion People . . . What I'm saying is that there is no such thing as ours and theirs. There is no part of Britain or England that I can't lay claim to. (Chadha in Stuart, 1994: 26)

Putting music at the centre of emerging new identities works to drive the film along and the focus on individuals from Belfast, Glasgow, the Rhondda Valley and Birmingham allows the diversity of their experiences, including their regionally accented speech and the similarities, such as their appreciation of music, to tell their own stories. For Chadha, her aim was to make a celebratory film, a film which showed the possibility of a future in which everyone had a stake and to consider what 'Britishness' meant and would mean for future generations.

Exploring the lives of children who have one white and one black parent, Ngozi Onwurah's film, *Coffee-Coloured Children* (1988) is strongly autobiographical – Onwurah grew up in an area of New-castle where she and her brother and sister were the only black children. Using an assemblage of personal story-telling, photo-graphs and archive-style footage, as well as reconstructions of par-ticular episodes from her history, she paints a vivid portrait of confusion and self-hate. The film retells dramatic private scenes which took place behind closed doors as children scrubbed them-selves until they bled, covered their faces with cleaning detergents and poured bleach over themselves in a vain effort to rid themselves of their black skin. Their wish to be white, like their mother, and therefore to end her (and their) shame is powerfully evoked and skilfully demonstrates the pernicious effects of internalizing racist values.

Dreaming Rivers is the story of Miss T., a Caribbean migrant now facing her imminent death in Britain, who travels on a journey back into memory. A deep sense of history, of identity and of loss per-meates the film and pushes the narrative forward to the future for her three children and backward into historical remembrance. The slow-paced film with its depth of tone, shadows and half-lights is poetic and lyrical and provides an incisive commentary on the black diaspora experience where enthusiastic new migrants soon found that the mother country had little nourishment to offer them. The enduring conflict between the older and younger generation is played out around Miss T.'s deathbed, as her children's talk is fractured by fragments of the St Lucian patois of relatives back home, invading and retreating from the text.

Blackwood's *A Perfect Image?* moves away from the wider cul-tural contexts explored in *Passion* to examine the specific issue of self-images as they are perceived and constructed by black women. This satirical film questions the way in which women collude with stereotypical images of themselves but suggests that women's in-volvement in such self-delusion can also be used as a subversive strategy. Two women with different skin-tones perform a variety of sketches in which they search out the 'perfect' image but at the same time, provide critical assessments of each other, informed by their own views and those of broader society. A blend of originally composed poetry, jazz and humour combine to produce a film which is both celebratory and questioning in tone.

The same but different

More recently, films made by less well-known filmmakers have been successfully exhibited to a wider audience. For example, the 30-minute production *We the Ragamuffin* (Julian Henriques, 1992) was awarded first prize for best black music film and best black independent film, by the National Black Programming Consortium, an organization set up in 1981 to showcase and support the achievements of international black film- and videomakers. *Ragamuffin* is a short, ragga musical which was first screened on Channel 4 in September 1992 but was also part of the *Black and White in Colour* conference screenings in November 1992. The subtitled film celebrates the power and creativity of a popular black music form, and the cult of the ragamuffin – denoting the youth culture of streetwise Jamaica – is embodied in the persons of Shabba Ranks and the controversial Buju Banton. The film is set in Peckham, South London, and follows the fortunes of musician Buckey Ranks who finds himself confronted by gun-wielding 'yardies' in a local nightclub. After this experience, Buckey and the local community begin to work together to rid themselves of this unwelcome presence, with music taking centre stage as the vehicle through which the film's message of the potency of community action is effectively articulated.

While films such as *Passion* and *Songs* are regarded as mould-breaking art works for their experimental style and refusal to conform to the tyranny of the race relations dialectic, Mercer cautions against comparing films of the 1960s and 1970s with those of the 1980s in terms of a simple realist/modernist dichotomy, suggesting instead the existence of:

> a widening range of strategic interventions against the master codes of the race relations narrative . . . brought to bear on the same sets of problems, such as 'identity', but articulated in such a way as to reveal the nature of the problems of representation created by the hegemony of documentary realism in racial discourse. (Mercer, 1988: 11)

Hebdige too argues that films such as *Handsworth Songs* and the earlier *Territories* attempt to deconstruct such master codes by invoking the lived experiences and strategies of resistance (in realist style) as they occur on the street and in the clubs, not in the academy (1987). But Henriques suggests that the conventions which circumscribe the realist paradigm provide the major block to the development of a black aesthetic or artistic perspective (1988). This is primarily because a realist narrative, apart from when it uses parody or irony within the text, assumes a definite link between the presentation and what is represented, that is, that the *reality* is one thing and one thing only. So a character can be happy or sad but not both: the realist tradition cannot portray contradictory forces although that is what real life is actually like. Using the example of *My Beautiful Laundrette* (Stephen Frears, 1985) to illustrate his remarks, Henriques argues that this film was heavily criticized because the audience could not perceive it as anything other than a piece of realism, that is, as an accurate representation of life. On these grounds it fails since the film did not disclose the poverty, overcrowding and racism experienced by many members of Asian communities but instead showed conspicuous consumption and great wealth, transgression of sexual norms and inter-racial infidelity. While this is not to say that such things are any less prevalent in Asian communities than elsewhere, it suggests that neither are they more typical or more usual. The eternal problem with black films is the refusal by many critics to accept them as works of art requiring an artistic response but who insist instead on regarding them as explicitly realist texts. Discussions around this body of work consistently fall into the trap of political correctness, with images evaluated for their positive or negative contribution to the perception of particular ethnic identities. Henriques argues that a film like *Laundrette* was, despite its critics, a significant 'success' precisely because it broke with the realist tradition. 'The souped-up Laundrette and the rest of the film were to me a fantasy expressing the feelings, contradictions and imagination of the characters, rather than any attempt to reflect reality' (1988: 19). Released from the rules of the realist paradigm, film can imaginatively explore the complex nature of real life and it is only when the contradictions inherent in the real world are exposed, that the possibility of struggle and change can emerge. 'Once we break with realism's notion that reality is really just one thing that can be more or less adequately represented, then criticism and progress become possible' (Henriques, 1988: 19). Similarly, arguing against the tyranny of realist techniques, but for slightly different reasons, Mercer suggests that despite the avowed intentions of filmmakers working within a realist paradigm to provide counter-narratives to dominant racist orthodoxies, they are nonetheless compromised by the ethnocentric ideology implicit in such a mainstream technique (1990a). A completely opposite reading of *Laundrette* was made by Jamal who insists that the main utility of the film is to provide a model to other Asian filmmakers of how not to do it (1987). His critique is centred around the notion that the film's writer, Hanif Kureishi, has been colonized by the British university system and he is now incapable of articulating an authentic Asian perspective. Instead, he can only construct a narrative which is littered with caricatures and stereotypes, which relies on improbable liaisons and panders to the racist assumptions made by white people against Jewish and Asian communities. Countering the claim that the film is emblematic of Thatcher's Britain, Jamal argues that, on the contrary, the film exhibits Britain as it has always been, only this time 'seen through the rose tinted spectacles of a liberal offering love between two individuals as a solution to historically based social contradictions' (1987: 21).

The critical acclaim which has accrued to *Laundrette* is dismissed by Jamal as being just so much inverted racism, enabling the white viewer to revel in a confirmation of her own prejudices and, as a bonus, be helped in this endeavour by an Asian supporter, namely, Kureishi himself. Interestingly, while Henriques sees the film offering hope through change, Jamal's somewhat more rigid interpretation is that the film simply views assimilation as the only legitimate aspiration for Asian communities. Jamal's critique exemplifies the problem of applying a realist critique to a film which is something much more. But it is as much for what *Laundrette* leaves out than what it keeps in that Dhillon-Kashyap laments the film, and in particular, its pandering to the appetites of a white audience eager to satisfy its voyeuristic gaze. '*Laundrette* seems to be less interested in exploring issues of class, corruption or sexuality and more in sensationalizing them in order to win a white audience' (1987: 125). Kureishi himself, commenting on Norman Stone's inclusion of *Laundrette* and the later *Sammy and Rosie Get Laid* (Stephen Frears, 1987) in his six 'worst films' list, argues that it is the writer's job to say the unsayable, to disclose the hidden, to hold a mirror to the world in order to show us how we live (1988). Fusco suggests that part of the success of crossover films such as *Laundrette* and those directed by African Americans such as Spike Lee and Robert Townsend is that the issues explored in these films are not unique to black communities, but resonate with a wide range of audiences and reflect the felt experiences not just of *them*, but also of *us* (1989). Of course those films which not only have a controversial content in terms of storyline but also present black communities experiencing the same range of social situations and problems as whites will always be attacked for perpetuating negative stereotypes. As well as *Laundrette* being criticized for showing homosexuality, corruption and greed within the Asian community, both the central love affairs between Omar and Johnny and between the uncle and his mistress are inter-racial, touching on yet another raw nerve, miscegenation. But the way in which to counter the narrow repertoire of stereotypical black portraits invented by white writers cannot simply be to substitute positive for negative images of black people, producing a 'black is good/white is bad' dichotomy in some absurd Orwellian schema. The creativity and inventiveness of black writers cannot be circumscribed by the imperative to always and everywhere show black people in a 'good' light. It is not just about numbers, it is about reaching more than the converted, getting the message across to at least one person outside the chattering classes. As Julien and Mercer argue, the context within which to comprehend race and ethnicity has itself changed, so that the success of *The Cosby Show* or Spielberg's adaptation of Alice Walker's novel *The Color Purple* points to changing conceptions about what constitutes culturally central and culturally marginal texts and practices (1988).

A new wave: British Asian filmmaking in the 1990s

As a crucial part of this changing dynamic of black filmmaking practice, a number of new voices began to break through in the early 1990s, including stories emerging from a British Asian experience. In the same way that African Caribbean filmmakers were providing counter-images to traditional stereotypes, British Asian media workers have been busy subverting the orthodox views of Asian communities as well as exposing the hidden hand of discrimination. The picture of Britain painted by films such as *I'm British But . . .* conflicts strongly with the (re)mythification of Britain's colonial past portrayed in films such as David Lean's adaptation of Forster's *A Passage to India* or Richard Attenborough's *Gandhi*. The few occasions that (white) attempts have been made to survey the Asian perspective/experience in film in the UK have tended to look at the popularity of Bombay cinema – 'Bollywood' – or to extol the virtues of Satyajit Ray (Dhillon-Kashyap, 1988). That much of the debate around 'black' filmmaking practice has concentrated on African American and African Caribbean experiences, has meant that Asian perspectives have been largely obscured. A nascent British Asian filmmaking culture has been present since at least the 1970s but has been largely ignored (Malik, 1994). More recently, though, television has begun to see the commercial possibilities of this new British Asian take on life and both Channel 4 and the BBC have been instrumental in supporting and showcasing innovative work. For example, an original idea from Asmaa Pirzada, the only Asian woman script editor working in BBC2's Screen Two department at the time, was handed over to Meera Syal to write and became *My Sister–Wife* which was broadcast on television in 1992. When the independent and thoroughly Westernized Farah (Meera Syal) marries Asif (Paul Bhattacharjee) she becomes his no. 2 wife: Asif is already married to the timid and subservient Maryam (Shaheen Khan). The subsequent adventures of this extended family, which includes Asif's mother, Sabia (Surendra Kochar), become more and more bizarre as the successful Farah and the unsophisticated Maryam metamorphose into the personality of each other. Despite some plot reservations, serious issues are explored in the film, not least around notions of patriarchy. Whilst the Koran teaches that the gateway to heaven lies at a mother's feet, at the political and sexual level, the lives of women continue to be circumscribed by the whims of men. The film has been criticized for its failure to adequately represent life for Britain's Asian communities, but such criticisms are now an established part of the territory – the paucity of black films means that each one is invested with impossible expectations. Harwant Bains's *Wild West* was funded by Channel 4 and also broadcast in 1992. Bains argues that people need to break free of parochial concerns and embrace uncertainty, to confound the expectations of community and the stereotypes which reside in other people's heads. *Wild West* won the Critics' Award at the Edinburgh Festival in 1992 and follows the fortunes of an Asian country and western band – the Honky Tonk Cowboys – as they lurch from one crisis to the next, taking its title from the parallels that Bains sees between the pioneering settlers of America and the similar impulses behind the migration to Britain of Asian families, particularly to Southall.

> We all have big dreams about achieving big things. Southall is an embodiment of all that because here are people who have come here to achieve their dreams – they may have failed in most cases but the pioneering spirit is there. (Bains quoted in Fareed, 1992: 5)

Wild West does not seek to locate itself strictly within the category of British Asian film in as much as it is not overtly about identity but it does offer a valuable alternative path for British Asian communities to consider – Nashville – against the traditional options of British-ness, Indian-ness or a confused in-between state (Malik,

1994). Its unlikely subject enables its intended mainstream audience
to reflect on majority assumptions of what Asian people are like and
the kinds of things they do, allowing new possibilities to emerge
and rejecting fixed notions of being.

In the early 1990s Meera Syal collaborated with Gurinder Chadha
and developed the story for *Bhaji on the Beach* (1993), Syal writing
the screenplay and Chadha directing. The theme of cultural contradiction and accommodation within a broadly unsympathetic British
milieu is foregrounded in *Bhaji*, Chadha's feature film debut about
a day trip to Blackpool arranged by Simi (Shaheen Khan), the principal worker at the Saheli Women's Centre. Chadha was keen to
continue her interest in notions of identity and hybridity and, as a
filmmaker with a background in television journalism, was particularly interested in media-constructed images of black communities.
'What I'm interested in doing is counteracting those images of how
I – as a black woman – should be, rather than looking at the multi-
plicity and complexity of what I actually am' (Chadha quoted in
Stuart, 1994: 26). The principal characters are briefly sketched out at
the beginning of the film. These include the abused young wife
Ginder (Kim Vithana), Hashida (Sarita Khajuria), a young woman
pregnant by her African Caribbean boyfriend Oliver (Mo Sesay), the
middle-aged Asha (Lalita Ahmed), who questions the sacrifices
she's made for her family, and Pushpa (Zohra Segal), an elderly
gossip. At the beginning of the trip, Simi announces that there are
few opportunities for women 'to get away from the patriarchal
demands made on us in our daily lives, struggling between the
double yoke of racism and sexism'. Although the slightly mocking
nod to political correctness is determinedly ironic, the film deals
with precisely these issues, but in a way which is accessible and
incisive rather than didactic and moralizing.

While *Bhaji* has a lot of humour, its more serious side has generated heated debate about negative portrayals of Asian men and the
blasphemous dream scene in which Hashida is imagined in a
temple, dressed as a harlot and smoking a cigarette. Most of the men
in *Bhaji* are unsympathetically drawn, depicted as either boorish
thugs, in thrall to their families or immaturely reluctant to accept
responsibility. Ginder's wife-beating husband Ranjit (Jimmi
Harkishin) and his bully-boy brother Balbir (Tanveer Ghani) seek
out Ginder to exact revenge, while Hashida's boyfriend Oliver tries
to make amends for his initially callous response to news of her
pregnancy. The climax of the film, when Ranjit attempts to abduct
his son as a way of forcing his wife's return is rather laboured, with
the men reverting to (stereo)type and the older women showing

belated hostility to the violence of the men and ambivalent concern towards Ginder. The only slight problem with the film is that it tries to do too much in its allotted time span, wanting to explore domestic violence, inter-generational conflict, trans-cultural relationships, racism, identity and awakening sexuality all within the confines of a day trip to Blackpool. There are some superbly well-observed and witty scenes, for example, the rendition of 'Summer Holiday' in Punjabi, the confrontation with racist yobs at a service station and a dream sequence where Asha and her elderly white admirer re-enact a typical Hindi film love scene, with him in grotesque blackface. However, there are perhaps a few too many stories within stories to allow the narrative to flow naturally. It tends to veer from slightly heavy-handed issue-based scenes one moment to dissolving into pure pastiche the next, but in many ways this is part of the essence of the film, the simultaneous evocation of English-ness and Indian-ness, where Bombay cinema's overblown colours and characters are juxtaposed with the equally vulgar eccentricities of the archetypal English seaside resort. That the characters make telling asides in Punjabi creates an authentic feel to the film and although such a device excludes the non-Punjabi speakers in the audience, tone and body language provide more than enough clues to enable comprehension. Both *Wild West* and *Bhaji* engage with the debates surrounding identity and points of identification and acknowledge the ambiguities and ambivalences which cross-cut diaspora communities. These films successfully challenge (white) expectations of assimilation and ask pertinent questions about racism and the colonial imperative.

Bhaji is the first feature length film to be made by a British Asian woman and although Chadha resists comparisons with Kureishi's earlier films, she does see parallels with his more recent effort, *The Buddha of Suburbia* (1993). This four-part dramatization of Kureishi's novel was broadcast on BBC2 at the end of 1993. The eponymous Buddha (Rohan Seth) is the contemplative father of the main character, Karim (Naveen Andrews, who also starred in Bains's *Wild West*). *Buddha* tracks the fortunes of Karim, his family and friends as they travel through 1970s Britain replete with disastrous arranged marriages, family conflict and a lot of sex. The Broadcasting Standards Council upheld complaints of bad language and gratuitous sex against the serial in 1994, largely based on a particularly lengthy group sex scene in part III and the use of blasphemous expletives throughout the four instalments. Despite the controversy, the BBC decided to repeat the show in early 1995, scheduling it for prime-time Saturday night viewing. Like all of Kureishi's work, *Bhaji* has also had to bear the full brunt of disapproval from both inside and outside the community, from those who feel they are misrepresented, maligned and misunderstood. Commenting on the mainly negative male characters in her film, Chadha argues that men can't deal with their emotions and it's about time this was pointed out to them:

> What we're saying is that men just aren't confronting the reality of what's going on; women always have. Maybe it's too painful for men to deal with and if you've had it your own way and had it good for a long time, then the last thing you'll want is for it to change. (Chadha quoted in Hussain, 1992: 24)

The theme of family and particularly patriarchal control is again explored in the US/UK film *Warrior Marks* (1993) on which the British Asian filmmaker Pratibha Parmar and the African American novelist Alice Walker collaborated – Parmar producing and directing and Walker working as interviewer and presenter. The film had its premiere on Channel 4 in October 1993 and was also included as part of Birmingham's Film and Television Festival later in that month. *Warrior Marks* explores the myth, history and reality surrounding female genital mutilation (FGM) and was shot on location in Africa, California and Britain. As well as personal interviews with African women about their experiences and thoughts on FGM, the film includes lyrical dance sequences which describe the fear and pain which attend FGM and how these warrior marks (the patriarchal wounds which women carry with them) can be used to resist and fight further subordination.

The burden of representation

Much of the work from contemporary black filmmakers has emerged as a critical response to the historical denial of authority to control images of their own communities and many of their efforts have generated intense debates around both aesthetics and content. While there are continuing arguments over the appropriate use of realist or modernist styles, the broader problematic revolves around the issue of representation and whether texts should only portray 'positive' images and/or deal with the race-relations discourse, or whether they can concern themselves with micro and specific interests and issues which speak *from* a black perspective but not *for* black communities. The relative representativeness of this or that film as truth or fiction has been at the heart of some of the more acrimonious debates around individual films such as *Handsworth Songs* and *My Beautiful Laundrette*. The main problem around this issue of representation and representativeness is that the relatively small number of black art works which are available to a potential audience means that each one must necessarily bear the burden of having to authenticate and typify heterogeneous black communities. No matter what a filmmaker might say about the very particular point being made in a film and the very specific position from which the author speaks, that work will nonetheless be seen as emblematic and typical of the community to which the writer belongs or to which s/he refers. 'If only one voice is given the "right to speak", that voice will be heard, by the majority culture, as "speaking for" the many who are excluded or marginalized from access to the means of representation' (Julien and Mercer, 1988: 4). That black filmmakers must shoulder such a burden is a consequence of structures that have historically marginalised their access to the means of cultural production. But when filmmakers are granted the precious resources to work their craft, the temptation to cram everything into that one project is almost irresistible. As Martine Attile of Sankofa relates during the making of *The Passion of Remembrance*:

> There was a sense of urgency to say it all, or at least signal as much as we could in one film. Sometimes one can't afford to hold anything back for another time, or another conversation or another film. That is the reality of our experience – sometimes we only get one chance to make ourselves heard. (1988: 54)

The constant positioning of the one black voice as the *only* black voice results in a serious double-bind. Firstly, individual subjectivity is routinely circumscribed by the appropriation of her specific experiences as 'typical' of an entire community. Secondly, precisely because that individual voice is perceived as the voice of the many, it is forced to occupy the position of stereotype, where all black people are regarded as the same (Julien and Mercer, 1988). As Hall remarked, it is only by accepting the end of the essential black subject that the burden and 'politics' of representation can begin to be unpacked (Hall, 1988). However, by eschewing racial essentialism and regarding 'race' itself as a social and cultural construction, there is a danger of losing sight of the very real and specifically 'racial' forms of power and subordination which continue to constrain the autonomy of black communities (Gilroy, 1990a).

Exhibition Angst

If it is difficult enough to obtain funding for black film, there are numerous post-production problems associated with distribution and exhibition, notwithstanding the role of television in both financing and exhibiting black film. As Alan Fountain, one-time commissioning editor for independent film at Channel 4 has pointed out, each time an independent film is broadcast on television, it achieves an audience of at least 300,000 (1988) and for some viewers, it may be their first experience of a specifically 'black' film product, speaking with its own distinctive voice. Television is an immensely powerful and important medium for accessing new film works to a mass audience and it thus has a primary role as an exhibitor and not just as another source of funding. As well as trying to secure and maintain a viable audience for black film, other crucial concerns are cash, distribution and exhibition accessibility and there are numerous examples of the kind of battles that black filmmakers experience in trying to get their films to an audience. For example, the Arab Film Festival of Carthage in 1992 asked the Foreign Office in London to provide £5000 to support the exhibition of black films from filmmakers working in Britain, including Isaac Julien and Horace Ové. The Foreign Office refused on the grounds that no one at the FO had seen the films (including *Young Soul Rebels* and *Playing Away*) and they were therefore unrepresentative of British cinema generally and likely to show Britain in a bad light (reported by Derek Malcolm, *Guardian*, 21.10.92). The arguments that Crusz and others were making in the mid-1980s about the struggles to gain continuous funding, recognition and legitimacy on black filmmakers' own terms, continue to find a resonance nearly a decade later and 'while the struggles continue on the financial and business levels, they are mirrored and paralleled on the practical and theoretical levels' (Crusz, 1985). Given the very different practices and funding strategies employed by different production companies, it is clear that the type of exhibition sought by companies to showcase their work will also vary widely. Because of the intimate relationship between funding and subsequent production, the amount of resources available will largely determine how a film is exhibited and therefore the access that a potential audience will have to it. Givanni suggests that funding agencies now require evidence that a film can attract the elusive but increasingly important (both politically and economically) black audience (1988) and as Gerima points out,

Capital in the form of finance, technology and human resources is the foundation of the realisation of any motion picture project. Since the African American community does not control the banking system it is the most powerless segment of the United States, uninvolved in any meaningful fashion in the decision-making process of a film production. (1989: 80)

It is clearly difficult to use cinema as a potent and transgressive mode of expression and resistance without adequate access to funding and without the patronage of the funding authorities, at least not if a filmmaker wants to make a mainstream film with a major studio. Whilst acknowledging the importance of films such as *Bhaji on the Beach* and *Malcolm X* which demonstrate that political films made by black filmmakers can also be popular and commercially successful, Givanni argues that the crossover phenomenon can only have limited potential and should not be seen as a security strategy. She suggests that the success of these kinds of film 'has as much to do with the novelty-value of the plots and characterisation as any other aspect of the films' (1988: 40). But this view is surely a little pessimistic and implies an audience which is both faddish and static, easily seduced by novelty for a few moments but then quickly reverting to the old and familiar. Whilst this may neatly characterize the typical television viewer, it is not so true of the film-going audience. But in any case, given that watching any particular film, for most people, is a once-only activity, the novelty-value can be reinvented endlessly if films are sufficiently different from and between each other. Each one of Spike Lee's films, from his low-budget first film, *She's Gotta Have It* (1986) to *Crooklyn* (1994) have been immediate commercial successes and his docu-drama on the life of Malcolm X (1992) probably received the most concentrated build-up in terms of pre-distribution hype of any film of the early 1990s.

But Givanni is entirely correct when she points to the relatively small amount of work which has emerged from black filmmakers in Britain and which can therefore quickly be exhausted by an eager audience. In 1988, there were approximately 130 films in circulation made by black filmmakers in Britain and available for hire. Two-thirds of these are in documentary format, half are only available on video and the great majority are less than 60 minutes in running time. By 1992, the total number of such films had increased to 204 but the breakdown in terms of format and length has remained similar.

> To be clear about the problems facing those involved in exhibiting
> black film, we have to acknowledge the fact that we are not talking
> about a quantitatively substantive body of work, however innovative
> and challenging it is in qualitative terms. (Givanni, 1988: 40)

One of the crucial tasks, then, is to find a way of building up and
maintaining an audience for black film by accessing more black
production companies to mainstream exhibition venues, including
television, attracting wider and more diverse groups of cinema-
goers/television viewers and giving black films and programmes a
higher profile. Givanni suggests that one possibility for promoting
black film more widely could be by identifying a particular venue
with the exhibition of black film. Gerima has even more radical
ideas about promoting black film, including 'standing on street
corners and in churches distributing leaflets, displaying posters,
etc.' (1989: 89). He argues that the audience-building enterprise will
be quickly achieved by the active participation of film- and programme-makers, producers, directors and other professionals in
community workshops, film festivals and national and international media symposia. 'We need to produce collective handbooks
with information on national and international film festivals, identifying their advantages and disadvantages in terms of promotion
and economic returns' (1989: 89).

The London Film Festival and other regional events such as the
Birmingham Film & Television Festival usually include a discrete
Third Cinema strand of screenings, but such events are only yearly
activities. In response to this particular problem, the Electric Cinema in Portobello Road has been taken over by Electric Triangle
Partners to provide the first permanent home for black cinema in
Britain. The partnership is a consortium comprising the largest
black UK newspaper, *The Voice*, the black radio station, Choice FM
and the Black Triangle Programming group and together they
opened for business in September 1993, the first black-owned cinema in Britain. As a first-run cinema, the Electric will be in direct
competition with the major cinemas for new releases, but will also
function as a media centre, combining screenings with festivals,
symposia, master classes and training in order to further the cultural and educational intentions of the consortium. For example, as
well as being part of the London Film Festival in 1993, the Electric
hosted the Third Black Triangle Festival in November 1993 which
focused on films from the African diaspora which had not previously enjoyed UK distribution.

Although the Electric is the first cinema to be used as a specific venue to screen black-originated films, festivals of black cinema, special screenings and film clubs are also providing much needed exhibition for black art works. There is a general recognition that access to and engagement wifh the audience is crucial to both the survival and the development of black cinema (Givanni, 1993). Nubian Tales, for example, is a black exhibition project set up by Mark Boothe in 1991 to promote, market and distribute the best in black popular culture. In 1994, Nubian were exhibiting at the West End Prince Charles cinema as well as other commercial and independent venues and have been involved in the release of a number of films around the country. Nubian have also put out several films under their own name for theatrical distribution. One of the organization's short-term aims was to build up a loyal audience and by 1993 they had a membership base of 2500 and an extended UK mailing list of more than 6000 people. As well as Nubian Tales, the project is also operating Nubian Vision, a new initiative offering exhibition space for short films, collaboration on scripts, marketing expertise, training and possible co-production opportunities. The team at Nubian want their films to spark off real debates about culture and identity and African American directors such as Julie Dash, Leslie Harris and John Singleton have all hosted discussions at Nubian screenings.

The strategies outlined above are innovative responses by black media practitioners who are tired of being marginalized by the mainstream industry. They are finding ways in which their own particular voices can be heard, spaces in which their own special stories can be told, but they are still few. The particular history and contemporary location of black communities in Britain mean that film products are informed by a variety of influences and experiences which cannot and do not conform to a predetermined format. 'It is only through a process of experimentation that there can be new developments in film techniques, new criteria for visual representation and new voices in cinema' (Auguiste, 1989: 216). In Britain, new black voices are certainly coming through, but only piecemeal and fragmented. While a film like *Bhaji on the Beach* captures the imagination and presents a picture of contemporary British society which celebrates cultural fusions and challenges cultural orthodoxies, it is nonetheless one lone voice speaking in the mainstream. Where is the space for all the other black voices? Where are the other black songs?

3

Black Fights Back Part II: Black Filmmaking and Strategies of Opposition in America

I got interested in the history of the Wild West that we never hear about. Of the first 44 settlers, 26 of them were black. What happens is that you can be convinced that you didn't have a part in building a nation . . . The dominant culture injects itself in the foreground and tends to play everything else as backdrop. But in Westerns, there wasn't even a black background.

Mario Van Peebles, Interview

The history of black filmmaking in America is long and contro-versial and contemporary black filmmakers ignore the past at their peril. There already exists a large body of film works spanning the early decades of this century which demonstrate the ability of black filmmaking pioneers to produce films in Hollywood without the industry's interference (Cripps, 1982). The abundant criticism which has been heaped on the cinematic output of contemporary black filmmakers such as Spike Lee has been fuelled by concern over cultural authority, about which black voices are privileged to speak and for whom and about what constitute the essential differ-ences between traditional Eurocentric film practice and an emer-ging black canon. These criticisms are in many ways updated formulations of those expressed about the pioneering work of filmmakers such as Oscar Micheaux in the 1920s and 1930s. Black movies which were produced from the early years of the century up to the end of the 1930s are often ignored in chronologies of cine-matic milestones although their contribution to the development of a distinctive genre within the industry is significant.

The screening of D. W. Griffith's *The Birth of a Nation* in 1915 and the furore surrounding the film prompted protest and criticism but also galvanized a fledgling black independent film sector into action. Individuals like Emmett J. Scott, George and Noble Johnson and Oscar Micheaux all toiled diligently to find backers for their work and formed their own production companies in an effort to counter the overly negative and misconceived portrayals of black community life which were generated by the Hollywood studios. They also recognized the commercial opportunities raised by the segregation of movie theatres and the hunger of black film-goers for alternative texts. In 1910, Bill Foster founded the Foster Photoplay Company in Chicago and is credited with being the first African American to establish a film production company (Reid, 1993). The company's early productions included *The Railroad Porter* (1912) and *The Fall Guy* (1913), both of which were comedy films but included characters who were not the usual ridiculous caricatures but more realistically drawn individuals. While a number of commentators (cf. Leab, 1975; Cripps, 1977) have forcefully argued that Foster's pictures merely imitated the formulaic devices common to white comedies such as the Keystone Cops-type chase or employed the orthodox range of black stereotypes, Reid suggests that Foster actually had a very different approach and cites three distinctive characteristics. Foster used the social and economic reality of African American life to inform his narratives, so that black characters were not just porters for white folks, but were also waiters in respectable black cafés; his films showed a black middle class thriving in early twentieth-century Chicago; and the pernicious 'Rastus' caricatures which were being regularly rehearsed by white production companies were convincingly subverted by Foster's more realistic portraits of black community life (Reid, 1993).

Early black independent films, such as *The Realization of a Negro's Ambition, Trooper of Troop K* (both 1916), *Birth of a Race* (1918) and *The Homesteader* (1919), attempted to redress the balance of overly negative and stereotypical portraits by supporting and articulating black pride and ambitions. Although these early efforts were low-budget and often technically unsophisticated, their signal importance lay in demonstrating the feasibility of a black cinema which was attractive to a black audience and which showed to that audience realistic and authentic portraits of itself. The insulting stereotypes which were popular in the early years of film, such as *The Dancing Nig* (*c.*1907) and *For Massa's Sake* (1911), were all that black film-goers of the time could otherwise expect to see of themselves. Thus the sight of educated black professionals living a relatively successful American life, albeit with the odd problem of racism here and there, was clearly welcomed by a black audience eager for more positive reflections of itself.

Closely following Foster Photoplay was the Lincoln Motion Picture Company, founded in Los Angeles in 1916 by a group of black film professionals including Noble and George Johnson, Clarence Brooks, James Thomas Smith and Dudley Brooks. As with Foster Photoplay, Lincoln's productions were aimed at a specifically black audience but instead of using comic narratives, Lincoln chose instead to examine serious issues using the concept of individualism and success against the odds as the primary dramatic devices. The first film they produced, *The Realization of a Negro's Ambition* (1916), told the story of a black graduate seeking his fortune on the California oil fields. The film epitomizes the archetypal rural black film which was underscored with good, wholesome, 'American' values such as the importance of family, but also presented a sympathetic if conventional slant on middle-class black America of that period. 'In creating a black, rural family film genre, Lincoln established a new type of black protagonist, a middle-class hero who believes in the puritan work ethic' (Reid, 1993: 10).

Where Lincoln tended to concentrate on the black rural drama, the films of Oscar Micheaux were probably the first examples of the black action film genre. Micheaux founded the Micheaux Film and Book Company in 1918 and his films were situated in an urban setting and often dealt with the kind of race-specific issues which his black contemporaries ignored. He is attributed with making more than thirty films from around 1919 to 1948, many of which were based on his own books (Sampson, 1977). Micheaux's films portrayed the lived experiences of black communities such as lynching, inter-racial relationships, gambling and prostitution and his dramatic considerations of such intimate and controversial subjects were attractive to a newly urbanized and aware black audience (Reid, 1993). *The Homesteader* (1919), for example, described a gentle love story between a black man and a white woman and both *Within Our Gates* (1920) and *The Gunsaulus Mystery* (1921) dealt with the issue of lynching (black and anti-Semitic). *Within Our Gates*, in particular, was the subject of censorship rows because of anxiety that screening the film could incite race riots (Sampson, 1977). If these themes exposed the underbelly of white racism, films such as *The Brute* (1920) looked directly into the depths of the black community with scenes of wife-beating, black dives and gambling joints, provoking numerous protests amongst black spectators. *Body and Soul* (1924) was Paul Robeson's film debut in which he played two roles: a good guy as backbone of local black bourgeois community and a shifty preacher intent on taking advantage of his black flock in general and the demure young heroine in particular. Although the film suffered the usual technical flaws, Bogle argues that it also contained a number of important cultural signifiers, such as a portrait of Booker T. Washington on the heroine's wall and a strong denunciation of manipulative black preachers for dividing and exploiting the black community (Bogle, 1989).

The location of Micheaux's films in an urban environment redolent with tough black men and assertive black gangsters, together with scenes of sex and violence, combined to guarantee Micheaux's place in the Harlem renaissance. Bogle argues that when viewed through the more enlightened, more political and more sophisticated lens of the late twentieth century, Micheaux's films with their technical crudity and artistic clumsiness, have tended to disappoint audiences keen to view these early black works (Bogle, 1989). Hoberman suggests that Micheaux's particular stance in relation to class issues was rooted in his assimilationist desire to be a 'real' American and his efforts to conquer the West through acceptance was a reflection of his attempt to conquer (and rewrite) his own past (Hoberman, 1976). Micheaux's preference for using light-skinned performers (a tendency which is alive and well in contemporary films of the 1980s and 1990s) added further fuel to the criticisms that Micheaux was trying to produce films in which the stories conformed to Western norms and values, including ideas of beauty.

While the ethos of a number of previously all-black enterprises was confounded by the gradual involvement of white people into positions of control, black films during the 1920s continued to show black America a range of images of itself which actively supported a positive identity and belief in the possibility of advancement. This alternative cinema, screening all-black westerns, musicals, comedies and dramas showed black people as doctors, lawyers, teachers – as affluent Americans. Films such as *The Flaming Crisis* (1924) about a tough black journalist falsely accused of murder and *The Flying Ace* (1926) which featured a black aviator, helped to establish new ways of looking at black communities. Black Americans were suddenly incorporated into the American Dream and a new set of archetypes invented as brave black heroes set forth to right the ills of the new world and to subvert traditional notions about the most appropriate position for black Americans to occupy in mainstream (white) society.

In addition to portraying African Americans in non-traditional and aspirational roles, early black films also used specific ideas about race and racism as central motifs. For example, *Scar of Shame* (1927) makes a number of acute statements about the nature of black life in America which includes commentary on racial dynamics and the divisions and tensions within black communities. As with a number of Micheaux's films, *Scar* (produced by the Colored Players of Philadelphia) was crucially concerned with the informal caste system which related lightness/darkness of skin tone to class position. The film convincingly mixes black urban reference points – slang, ghetto scenes, dress codes – with the more traditional Hollywood thematic of class conflict, but this time within the black community (Snead, 1988). Micheaux was eager to provide aspirational material for black audiences, even to the point of creating all-black middle-class neighbourhoods in which to locate the action, insisting that his films should uplift the race, not hinder it. The device of creating a parallel world inhabited by educated black professionals to provide the background to film action has also been used by contemporary filmmakers such as Spike Lee in films such as *She's Gotta Have It* (1986) and in some of the productions with which Eddie Murphy has been associated such as *Boomerang* (1992), in which the film functions both as a vehicle through which to 'normalize' the reality of black professionals but also as a commentary on race and racism more generally. In many of Micheaux's films, however, the narrative stressed the success and culture of the black middle classes and reflected a lifestyle in which the inconvenient facts of racism were subdued or even ignored.

These early black independent film companies suffered considerably during the Depression years and although Micheaux reformed his company in 1929, it was no longer a black independent but a collaborative enterprise which had white financing. During the 1930s when Micheaux was forced into partnership with white backers, he came under ever increasing attack in the black press for the poor production values of his films, the sensational content of narratives and for his 'racism' (Hoberman, 1976). *Daughter of the Congo* (1930) was regarded as yet another example of how Micheaux used skin tone to stand for degrees of civilization, where the lighter-skinned (yellow) characters wore European clothes and were cast as sophisticates while the black actors were all but naked and displayed as barbaric savages. 'Even if the picture possessed no other defects, this artificial association of nobility with lightness and villainy with blackness would be enough to ruin it' (Theophilus Lewis, 16.4.1930, cited in Sampson, 1977: 51). The 'positive' correctives to the more traditional stereotypical representations of black life which characterized much of Micheaux's output are themselves located within a specific cultural context and black filmmakers necessarily operated within the framework of Hollywood's film grammar, constructing their narratives within a culturally mediated context of 'normality'. *God's Step Children* (1937) was probably the most notable of Micheaux's films with a storyline about the wish of a mulatto girl/woman to become white or at least to pass for white and her experiences along the way, including her eventual suicide when her wish is thwarted. The film attracted widespread criticism for the way in which it once again exposed the explicit status hierarchy within the black community which was predicated on shades of blackness. Gerima argues that the ordering of beauty or sophistication on a simple colour-coded continuum with dark skin at one end and light (white) skin at the other is evidence of some early black filmmakers' unchallenged acceptance of the dominant society's norms and values (Gerima, 1982). However, then as now, filmmakers were tied by the expectations of the audience and in any case, writing about the skin tone hierarchy which existed in the black community was to describe a real preoccupation, not a constructed invention, notwithstanding the racist provenance of the value system it venerated.

Throughout the 1940s and 1950s, numerous black performers starred in black films and because the dimension of racism was largely removed from film narratives, the resulting portraits of black community life were celebrations of a particular black style rather than accurate descriptions of life for most African Americans. Between 1910 and 1950 more than 150 independent film companies were organized for the specific purpose of producing black-cast films for black audiences and of this number, slightly more than one-third were owned and operated by black individuals and partnerships (Sampson, 1977). Many whites involved in 'black' film production were highly cynical about their products and their audiences. In a 1942 interview, film producer brothers Jack and Bert Goldberg who had made a number of these 'black' films, said of the audience for their films: 'All they know is that they want plenty of singing and dancing or drama depicting Negro life in typical Negro spirit. They are wonderful audiences, too: there's nothing sophisticated or cold about them . . . they definitely know what they want' (Goldbergs cited in Kagan, 1970: 6).

One step beyond

The 1960s saw a renewed interest in black-produced films and some of the most significant challenges to the traditional white images of African Americans were made during the 1960s by black (and white) independents producing low-budget, limited-distribution

films. These films, such as John Cassevetes' *Shadows* (1960), Shirley
Clarke's *The Cool World* (1963) and William Greaves's *Still a Brother:
Inside the Negro Middle Class* (1968) all dealt with the reality of the
black experience, including the destructive aspects of an impoverished existence such as crime and drug addiction, but without sentimentality and without piety. These films did not attempt to
answer the question, 'What are black people like?' but rather documented the experiences of black communities living under pressure
and strain. But despite the (limited) progress that had been made in
rehabilitating the black individual as something other than mere
stereotype, black actors were rarely allowed to show the sensual
aspects of their characters. The great majority of roles played by
Sidney Poitier in the 1950s and 1960s, for example, denied him any
kind of sexual life, either excluding romantic interest from the narrative completely, as in *The Defiant Ones* (1957) or *The Blackboard
Jungle* (1950), or else forcing him into an unbelievable celibacy as in
The Long Ships (1964), in which he took the part of an African prince
who, despite his large harem, had taken an oath of chastity. Even in
the extremely successful *Guess Who's Coming to Dinner* (1967),
Poitier is denied a screen sexuality despite the film's claim to deal
with an inter-racial relationship (between him and Katherine
Houghton).

The radical political context of America in the 1960s with a renewed black militancy campaigning for Civil Rights led to the production of a new movement in independent black filmmaking,
exemplified by Melvin Van Peebles's now seminal film, *Sweet
Sweetback's Baadasssss Song* (1971). This film, together with Gordon
Parks Snr's *Shaft* (1971) and Gordon Parks Jnr's *Super Fly* (1972),
constituted a renewed attempt by black filmmakers to portray their
communities for themselves. Out of these films emerged a new
urban hero who was rough, tough and out to win, and the success
of these films led to the production of a number of similar, formulaic
films which are often described under the banner of 'blaxploitation'
(see chapter 1). While some commentators regard all those macho-
type films, including *Sweetback*, *Shaft* and *Super Fly* as well as the
white-produced fare, as blaxploitation (see, for example, Michener,
1972), others suggest that the films of Van Peebles and Parks were in
fact mould-breaking examples, and all the rest simply crude imitations. Cripps argues that films which seriously attempted to describe the authentic black experience should more properly be
identified as 'black genre' films (Cripps, 1978). Those films which
were explicitly about exploiting a black audience for mere profit
and were generally made by whites are therefore left to constitute

'blaxploitation'. But although films such as *Super Fly* and *Sweetback* were serious attempts to develop a black film genre replete with black heroes, the attempt to subvert or at least challenge the ortho-doxies of mainstream cinema narratives is inevitably constrained by their continued use of the Hollywood model of 'the cult of the hero' (Yearwood, 1982a). Instead of questioning the very idea of the hero as a narrative device, such films mimicked the formulaic violent-action-hero film, but with a funky new black twist. Where the black genre movie-makers chose 'hyperbole as a mode of celebrating the combination of triumph over adversity, fellow feeling and moral superiority of the oppressed known most recently as "soul"' (Cripps, 1978: 12), blaxploitation on the other hand was typified by 'stylised, choreographed violence and a new set of stereotypical images of blacks who lived by their fists and loins and whose vocal utterings were intended to outrage rather than inform' (Miller, 1980: 61). Commenting on *Super Fly*, Patterson argues that, regardless of the generally poor standards of film which typified blaxploitation movies, *Super Fly* did attempt to break new ground by identifying the abject failure of American society to provide legitimate oppor-tunities for its bright but impoverished black citizens (Patterson, 1975). Commentators have tended to focus on the more sensational aspects of this film and therefore missed the vital message of denied opportunity. Wesley, for example, bemoaned the existence of the so-called blaxploitation films for having such a low regard for black audiences. 'The black film, as a genre of cinematic art, is degenerate, debased, and an insult to the integrity of audiences of black people, who, starved for the sight of *anything* black on the silver screen, flock to see these manifestations of celluloid prostitution' (Wesley, 1973: 65). Wesley does in fact identify *Super Fly* as the pinnacle of the black 'style' movie, where the eponymous hero not only outwits the crooked cops, the double-crossing villains and anyone else who crosses his path but gets the woman as well. *Sweet Sweetback's Baadasssss Song* was a significant film of the early 1970s, dramatizing the experiences of its inarticulate black hustler/hero which was written, directed, produced and starred Van Peebles. The film's reception ably demonstrated that it was possible for a black filmmaker to retain editorial, financial and distribution control over a film product and still produce a box-office success. *Sweetback* was the first black action film to attract a large, black, teenage audience, with Van Peebles arguing that in order for a black film work to be meaningful it had to speak to a wide audience and this meant that black film had to abandon any tendency towards the didactic. 'If Brer is bored, he's bored. One of the problems we must face squarely is that to attract a mass we have to produce work that not only instructs but entertains' (Van Peebles, 1972: 15).

The critical is political

But the sensationalist action film was not the only genre of film being produced during the 1970s and early 1980s and an important group of black filmmakers began to make their mark during this period, many of whom were active in Los Angeles and had been trained at the UCLA film school. Filmmakers such as Julie Dash, Larry Clark, Haile Gerima and Charles Burnett explicitly criticized the orthodox film conventions which they had been taught, reshaping the conventional cinematic language of cuts, fades and frame composition in order to produce a different view of black cultural experiences (Snead, 1988). The new wave of black film from the 1970s included Gerima's *Bush Mama* (1975), Burnett's *Killer of Sheep* (1977) and Clark's *Passing Through* (1977) and these films signalled a new direction in black independent filmmaking. *Bush Mama*, for example, describes the story of Dorothy whose husband is falsely imprisoned and who comes home to find a white police officer attempting to rape her daughter. As Dorothy kills the policeman, she is liberated from her politically unconscious state and though her violence empowers her relationship with her daughter, it does little to change her economic condition. The film uses archive material intercut by sharp black and white photography. The savage sexual assault on the daughter and the subsequent murder of the white perpetrator articulate the oppression and hopelessness of ghetto life which inflects Gerima's work. *Sankofa* (1993) explores the history of slavery from an uncompromising black perspective, when Mona (Oyafunmike Ogunlano) an African American fashion model goes on a photographic assignment to Ghana, falls under the spell of an African drummer and is transported back to an eighteenth-century sugar cane plantation.

Charles Burnett's *Killer of Sheep* uses a non-linear narrative style to describe the everyday life of an American inner-city area (Watts) and like other black independent filmmakers working in this period, Burnett's film shows the problems and frustrations of black families. *Killer of Sheep* is a bleak and pessimistic portrait of black urban life which is not lightened by a sudden change in fortune or a happy interlude but continues relentlessly to show the audience the devastating effects of poverty on family life. For filmmakers like Burnett and Clark, the action of their work focuses on black urban areas and on families and individuals who never escape their background, although sometimes characters are allowed to develop political awareness if not financial security. Unlike the black action film genre, these films tend to describe ordinary events of ordinary people and Reid suggests that their use of non-linear techniques, unknown actors and unconventional devices set them apart from mainstream products in both form and content (Reid, 1993).

Spike Lee comes to town

While still a student at the New York Film School, Lee's short, *Joe's Bed Stuy Barbershop – We Cut Heads* (1982) won a student Oscar and put him in the public gaze for the first time. His production company, 40 Acres and a Mule (named after the provisions made for black slaves when they were granted their freedom), has gone from strength to strength and *Malcolm X* (1992) was probably the most hyped film of the early 1990s. Reid suggests that films such as *She's Gotta Have It* (1986), *School Daze* (1988) and *Do the Right Thing* (1989) are examples of what he describes as 'urban black folk comedy' which are studio-distributed works rather than independent productions (1993). '*She's Gotta Have It* typifies the urbanized black comedy film in which the absence of white characters prevents the film from reflecting a racially dualistic world' (1993: 94). The misogynistic and homophobic sub-themes which underlie much of Lee's work contribute to the perpetuation of derisive forms of black subjectivity. By positioning the narrative in an all-black world, as in *She's Gotta Have It*, the action can concentrate on the development of male–female relations within a film structure which supports patriarchy and heterosexuality as the norm. Although the Nola Darling character (Tracy Camila Johns) in *She's Gotta Have It* is drawn as a supposedly independent, sexually liberated woman, she is routinely manipulated in a narrative which arouses male fantasies of a masochistic and insatiable sexual (m)other who seems to 'ask for' sexual violation. Where Lee was fêted as a visionary, Jones suggests that looking back at the opening sequences of the film, which feature a 'litany of sexual slander and macho posturing' (Jones, 1991: 38), it is hard to conceive of the film as revolutionary, either cinematically or any other way. The objectification of black women in popular film exposes the writer's use of patriarchal forms to amuse the largest audience and in *She's Gotta Have It*, sexism masquerades as female independence. Lee himself says of *She's Gotta Have It*, that it stands as an antidote to how the black man has been perceived elsewhere in film, citing specifically the male characterizations in *The Color Purple*.

> See, nobody is saying that black men haven't done some terrible things and what Jamie does to Nola at the end of the film is a horrible act. But Jamie is a full-bodied character, unlike Mister in *The Color Purple* and the rest of that film's black men, who are just one-dimensional animals. (Lee, 1986: 48)

The film's 'heroine', Nola Darling, is entirely defined by her three male lovers and although she is independent in as much as she lives in her own apartment and has the lovers she wants, she is nonetheless denied sustaining relationships either with women (mother, sister or friends) or platonic friendships with men: she is only really alive through sex. Despite her relative autonomy, the eventual assault on Nola by one of her partners demonstrates the ultimate inability of male filmmakers to allow of a strong and capable heroine who is not at the mercy of her physical frailty or at risk from the violence of men. The film's central theme ostensibly revolves around Nola's decision to have three partners simultaneously, but her apparent independence and sexual freedom is continually compromised by the narrative's preoccupation with promiscuity. The beating/rape Nola sustains as a result of her insistence on having as many partners as she wishes is in some way seen as justified. 'The idea, "... serves her right!", has already been spread through the film copiously. Even other women hated Nola, except the lesbian' (Baraka, 1993: 147). hooks argues that she first began writing film criticism as a result of watching this film and wanted to contest Lee's mimicry of Hollywood's practice of presenting women simply as objects for the phallocentric gaze (hooks, 1993). For hooks, Lee's eagerness to embrace a patriarchal orientation which precisely reflects that of mainstream (white) practitioners, makes him the ideal black candidate for entrée into the Hollywood canon. His straightforward substitution of black women's bodies for those of their white sisters to function as objects of male desire, may be an act of transfer but it is certainly not one of change.

Lee's second film, *School Daze*, is set in a black southern college and examines colour-consciousness amongst college students and the friction between two groups of students – the wannabees and the jigaboos. The political over- and undertones which are present within the film are articulated through the positioning of the campus activist, Dap, fighting both the college establishment to relinquish its financial ties with South Africa and the male 'leader' of the wannabees, Julian. But whereas the men are allowed to be explicitly political, the women are destined to remain locked in a destructive domestic conflict, arguing spitefully about the merits of darker or lighter skin, straight or nappy hair and who has authority to claim an authentic African ancestry (Perkins, 1990). The focus on the politics of hair is particularly interesting in the contemporary context where hair style has once again become the site for expressing black identity and pride.

In *Do the Right Thing*, Lee's third feature-length film, the main tension in the narrative is delivered through the development of racial and ethnic hatred played out against the background of a local pizzeria. While the older generation, personified by the Italian pizzeria owner, is content to stay in the black neighbourhood, the younger family members (his sons) are less sure and their overt and covert racism eventually leads to an explosive confrontation with the predominantly black clientele. Lee plays the central character, Mookie, a gofer in the pizza parlour, and although Mookie is relatively self-assured, his character remains undeveloped and his inadequacy as a father and indifference as a lover evoke no sympathy from the audience. Once again, Lee's ambivalence towards women is underlined by Mookie's use of the young mother of his child as simple sex object (Johnson, 1991). The women in the film are sisters, stand-in mothers, friends and lovers of the male characters, defined by their men rather than autonomous characters in their own right, forever relegated to the sidelines. They function as women on the edge of male violence, if not always the manifest victims (Kennedy, 1990). Rather than operating as active agents of their own lives, the women in *Right Thing* are circumscribed by a narrative which explores the rather too familiar territory of men and 'their' women, a preoccupation which has now been wrung rather dry.

> *Do the Right Thing* fails to provide either visualizations or intelligent hearings of creative, culturally resistant black women. The women's portrayals in the film do not go beyond stereotypes of the cantankerous shrew (Tina), the passive watcher-with-an-attitude and a gender-specific chip on her shoulder (Mother Sister) and those blandly neutral seekers after male company (Jade and Ella). At the moment of uprising against Sal's, women do not provide revolutionary counsel or energy; they only scream. (Baker, 1993: 175)

The final explosion of anger in *Do the Right Thing* which leads to the destruction of the pizzeria unfolds to the rap rhythms of 'Take the Power' and burning down the pizza parlour is a symbolic and actual act of revolt, but for Lee, the revolution is cultural not political. 'Lee's portrayal of cultural oppression as unconnected to political and economic structures is as illusory and utopian as the liberal view that racism can be dispelled by reasoning and goodwill' (Kelemen, 1992: 25). It is hardly unintentional that class relations do not figure in Lee's narratives, since his plotlines depend on a racism which is entirely determined by cultural difference and the desire to preserve cultural identity and community through violence against 'outsiders'. But in the real world of scarce resources, the shared interests of class compatriots often result in the aligning of groups along class rather than race lines in order to take some of that 'power' for themselves.

Critics lamenting the lack of 'positive' black characters, and outraged by the depiction of intra- and inter-community conflict in *Do the Right Thing*, are, for Muwakkil, missing the point. Instead of keeping the less desirable aspects of black community firmly within the domain of the private, Muwakkil argues that Lee's iconoclastic insistence on showing the diversity of black experiences is the only way in which the actions of the image police can be subverted (1990). But though Lee is amenable to showing the harsh realities of a black urban existence and he is not particularly judgemental, his very ambiguity leaves a certain dissatisfaction with this film. The viewer is never allowed to know what the 'right thing' is, nor who should be responsible for doing it. The dual images of Martin Luther King and his insistence on resistance without violence together with those of Malcolm X and his more pragmatic 'by any means necessary' message filter through the text, and ending the film with words from both MLK and Malcolm X enables Lee to sit neatly on the fence.

Mo Better Blues (1990) is set within the jazz milieu but is disappointing to those audiences who expect the film to explore musical themes associated with jazz and jazz musicians. The film concerns the coming of age of Bleek Gilliam (Denzel Washington) who has been encouraged from boyhood to play the trumpet. As with other examples of Lee's work, the hero shuffles uneasily between two lovers, while the women function as sexual objects and also provide the locus for a consideration of colour codes – Indigo is dark-skinned and Clarke is fair. The theme of inter-ethnic hostility between the Italian and African American communities is again explored in *Jungle Fever* (1991) in which the brief romance between the African American architect Flipper (Wesley Snipes) and his Italian American secretary Angela (Annabella Sciorra) provides the backdrop for an exploration of historical cultural antagonisms. The dynamics of racism which have shaped the black experience in

America is the structure through which contemporary racist discourse is examined as the respective families of Flipper and Angela
and their communities counsel against the ill-fated union.
Interestingly, the American dream is exemplified by Flipper with
his middle-class values, house, wife and clever child, whereas
Angela's domestic situation is set against a background of strong
patriarchal values and macho racist posturing in a motherless environment.

When *Malcolm X* was released, Spike Lee, ever the astute director,
publicly encouraged young people to miss school in order to see the
film, guaranteeing big box-office returns and maximum publicity.
Adding to the spectacle, Lee was reported to have said that he
would only be interviewed about the film by African American
journalists, although he subsequently said that he merely wanted
to give preference to black interviewers (Lee cited in *The Weekly
Journal*, 3.12.1992). The suggestion by Lee that only black journalists
would have the necessary 'insight' to discuss the film raises the still
unresolved issue of who is allowed to criticize black art works and
the extent to which the legitimate interrogation of black film is
determined by the reviewer's ethnicity. The docu-drama charts the
(selected) life and times of Malcolm X from his early hustler days as
Malcolm Little, through to imprisonment and enlightenment where
he discovers religion in the form of the Nation of Islam, and his
subsequent disaffection for the black Muslim movement and murder in 1965. Making explicit the contemporary currency of
Malcolm's struggles, the film's opening sequence shows the
American flag burning into an X which in turn dissolves into archive footage of the Rodney King beating. Once again, Lee has
made a film which is thick with political significance but somewhat
lacking in its development as a coherent whole, particularly (again)
where female characters such as Betty Shabazz, Malcolm's wife, are
concerned. Alexander suggests that even with Denzel Washington
giving a masterful performance as the eponymous hero, his presence is not enough to unify the various diverse elements of the
narrative. 'At times it seems as though Lee has simply lost control of
the genres at his disposal, especially when he slips into sentimental-
pedagogical mode at the end with nauseating scenes of "one world"
cuteness' (Alexander, 1993a: 47).

Criticism of the film abounds, with some commentators suggesting that it will incite racial hatred through its implicit support for a
struggle-through-violence ideology, a claim which has been made
about nearly all Lee's films. Until his departure from the Nation of
Islam, Malcolm X believed that not only was violence justified – as

a means of self-defence against endemic racism – but constituted an intelligent response. However, it is the rewriting of black history which has caused outrage, with the deification of a man who had an ambivalent effect on social and political events in his lifetime and whose petty criminal history (albeit later reformed) does not appear to offer a positive role model to young black people. Other critics suggest that Lee has cynically exploited the life of a great hero to indulge the vulgar pleasures of Hollywood and the masses and the opening of his boutique – Spike's Joint – in the legendary Macy's department store, stuffed full of X baseball hats and other X-branded merchandise, seems to lend some credence to complaints about Lee's enthusiasm for publicity and cash. Lee's preoccupation with examining the role of white racism in subverting black success ignores equally important aspects of the black experience such as drug abuse, sexism and violence and, more generally, the class dimension. Reid is highly critical of the 'misplaced' plaudits which Lee's films have attracted because the success of these productions necessarily contributes to their reception as truthful portraits of black community life and continuously sustains Lee's mythic world (1993). Women in Lee's films are poorly drawn and usually unsympathetically described, and his failure to treat adequately with gender issues and sexism across the range of his work has been heavily criticized. In his world, it is always men who are used as spokespeople for the black community, who are central in the affirmation of black culture. Dyson suggests that because of his particular take on the meaning of blackness and his desire to display the full complexity of his characters, Lee is confronted with a conflict. 'How to present the humanity of black folk without lapsing into an ontology of race that structures simplistic categories of being for black people and black culture that are the worst remnants of old-style black nationalism' (1993: 23, 24). One of the most radical stances that Lee takes in his films is the refusal by him/his characters to accept a reconciliation with white American society, marking a significant fracturing of liberal accommodationist discourse (Kelemen, 1992). Lee's work has also been condemned for its preoccupation with a black working-class urban environment and an insistence on the pervasiveness of white racism, when Lee himself is the product of a rather more privileged background. It sometimes seems that Lee is more interested in getting the idiomatic references correct – hairstyles, mannerisms and clothes – than in describing an authentic black milieu. Lee invites his black audience to share in his insider jokes and cultural cues while encouraging them to vicariously enjoy the sight of their own normally private community being exposed to the scrutiny of outsiders. But whereas early films promised the possibility of developing a discourse through which divisive issues within black communities such as sexism, homophobia and colour caste divisions could be articulated, such themes emerge briefly only to disappear again (Gilroy, 1991b). In support of Lee, Perkins suggests that the corpus of the filmmaker's work has tended to be attacked on the basis of individual characters, plotlines and his own defensiveness, whereas the larger messages they contain have been largely ignored (1990). His films have been condemned for perpetuating various kinds of black stereotypes and, in the case of *Mo Better Blues*, for being anti-Semitic. In response to this latter charge, Lee prefaced his next film with an address to camera where he says, 'All you enlightened beings who feel that I'm anti-Semitic can kiss my black ass.' Lee's ability to generate controversy is matched only by his outstanding ability as a self-publicist.

Out of the ghetto and into the 'hood

The late 1980s and early 1990s saw a clutch of black-produced and directed films emerge from out of the shadow of big-time Hollywood. At a time when hip-hop music had come to dominate popular cultural expression, films such as Mario Van Peebles's *New Jack City* (1990), Ernest Dickerson's *Juice* (1991), John Singleton's *Boyz N the Hood* (1991) and Matty Rich's *Straight out of Brooklyn* (1991) all provided naturalistic portraits of black urban/ghetto life and, if not quite glamorizing the casual gun culture which scars the daily existence of many black communities, certainly placed violence at the centre of their narratives. The motif of violence which characterizes all these films has sometimes spilled over into the real world with rioting attending at least two openings. In March 1990, when overbooking meant many black cinema-goers were unable to see the newly released *New Jack City* for which they had queued, the disappointed crowd vented their frustration through violent action. The American cinema at which this happened responded by withdrawing the film. The following July, the US opening of Singleton's film provoked a burst of racial violence which ended in the death of two people and injuries to a further thirty-five individuals (Winokur, 1991).

Because of the violence contained within these new gangster movies and their potential to incite violent reactions on the part of the audience, advocates of a boycott against films such as *New Jack*

City made a call for a 'national alert' to be brought against such films for their perpetuation of negative imagery (cited in the *Hollywood Reporter*, 3.7.1991). The call came during a news conference held by the Coalition Against Media Racism in America (CAMRA) which claims to represent leading black religious and media organizations. *New Jack City* came in for particular criticism for its portrayal of African Americans as violent, sexually promiscuous and obsessed with drugs. In his defence, Van Peebles later argued that his film portrayed both negative and positive characters and that, in any case, it was inappropriate to insist that black filmmakers only produce films which are upbeat and glowing. *New Jack City* has a 'just say no' message where the macho gangster Nino (Wesley Snipes, again) is humiliated in a violent beating towards the end of the film at the hands of the tough black police officer, although the casting of Ice T as the cop and the use of Ice T's rap rhythms as the film score send out contradictory messages about who are the good guys and who are the villains. Is each the other also? Dyson argues that the film is full of fusions of attitude and style which function as a replacement for political discourse and which provide alternative choices for young black men, particularly those for whom drug-dealing is a lucrative, albeit short-lived career (Dyson, 1992). But the exaggerated contours and characteristics of the ghetto as defined by Van Peebles appear to have more in common with the urban landscape of blaxploitation movies of the 1970s than with contemporary America. 'This action adventure film depicts frenzied, vulgar Americanism run amok in Hollywood's new fantasy land: the crime-infested black ghetto' (Jones, 1991: 34). *New Jack City* functions as a piece of propaganda in which the problems affecting black communities are easily explained by the indolence of individual members in effecting change, the persuasiveness of the drug culture and a general refusal of community members to take charge of their own lives. Instead of an incisive analysis of how the dual oppressions of racism and poverty impact upon the daily experiences of black communities, *New Jack City* concentrates on violent and savage confrontations both within the black criminal fraternity and between them and the police. Ultimately, the film's insistence on focusing on the here and now of violence and crime, rather than attempting to unpack its cultural and historical significance, reduces it to simple genre, just another gangster movie.

A same but different tack is adopted by John Singleton in *Boyz N the Hood*, where a significant message of the narrative is that the active involvement of black fathers is vital to the satisfactory upbringing of black sons. The central characters – the 'Boyz' – are three young black men, two of whom are half-brothers, Ricky (Morris Chestnut) and Doughboy (Ice Cube), being raised by their mother (Tyra Ferrell). The other, Tre (Cuba Gooding Jnr), has been handed over to his father since his mother is no longer able to cope with him, telling Tre's father that she cannot teach Tre 'how to be a man'. Both Ricky and Tre yearn to escape the bondage of the ghetto but while Ricky dreams of a footballing career, Tre is determined to pursue his academic studies. But what is really different about the two young men is their family arrangements. Ricky's family comprises a loud-mouthed half-brother and an ineffectual mother, neither of whom give him support or encouragement. Tre, on the other hand, safely delivered into the arms of the man, is fully supported by his black nationalist daddy and encouraged to follow his father's lead down an exceedingly straight and narrow path (Jones, 1991). Years later, the three meet up again as young men but, after various (mis)adventures, the end of the film finds Ricky and Doughboy dead and Tre leaving the 'hood to start a new life with his girlfriend. Tre's survival has been guaranteed by following his father's dictum that violence between black gangs is a tool of white oppression. The familial messages, at least, are clear: father knows best and mother knows nothing.

Matty Rich's *Straight out of Brooklyn* is a desolate rejection of the liberal view that an individual can transcend her/his background and circumstances by positive agency and collective action (Dyson, 1992). The pervasive force which is the ghetto is shown to exert an irresistible influence over its inhabitants, even while they attempt to escape its embrace. As with other ghetto films of the early 1990s, the narrative thrust of *Brooklyn* is centred around the experiences of the three black male characters and is specifically related to the general hopelessness felt by black men which turns inwards to the family and results in the subjugation of female family members, including physical assault. The main subject of the film is teenager Dennis (Lawrence Gilliard Jnr) and his friends Kevin (Mark Malone), Larry (Matty Rich) and girlfriend Shirley (Reana Drummond) to whom he turns increasingly for help and succour in the face of an alienating domestic environment. The beatings of Dennis's mother by his father are filmed as both literal events but also as allegory, where the husband/father's rage at the weight of social oppression and racism is played out through his brutal domination of the wife/mother. For Rich, the source of hopelessness which underlines the drama is to be found in the racism endemic in white America and the encircling rope of poverty which defines the ghetto existence. When Kevin and Larry decide to rob a local drug-dealer in order to get 'out of Brooklyn', Dennis is less keen but he is carried away by his friends' insistence on the success of the theft and is then let down by them at the end. His father is murdered in a revenge killing at the same time as his mother dies in hospital.

A more vicious gang association forms the basic unit of male bonding in Ernest Dickerson's *Juice*, where friendship and support is offered to each gang member as protection against the incursions of rival gangs. While most of the gang are content to play relatively safe, one member, Bishop (Tupac Shakur), wants to move them up a level, to play in the big league. To this end, he secures possession of a gun and embarks on a macho course of mayhem and destruction, killing foes and friends alike. Unlike other contemporary black films, the stable black family unit is actively articulated in *Juice*, where mothers and fathers do normal parental things such as exhort their offspring to get up in the morning and remind them to take their books to school. When the film's 'hero' Q (Omar Epps) is nearly murdered by the psychotic Bishop and is then involved in a struggle with him on a rooftop during which Bishop plunges to his death, others on the scene whisper to Q that he's got the 'juice', at which point Q shakes his head sadly and walks away. As with the other young men and guns dramas, the basic anti-violence message which inscribes *Juice* tends to get buried under the weight of music and thrills.

The theme of black male friendship links all these films, such friendships sometimes operating within the context of a group of adolescents who simply hang out together (as in *Straight out of Brooklyn* and *Boyz N the Hood*) or else filtered through gang life (as in *New Jack City* and *Juice*). Friendship (and love) for each other is the only nourishing force which appears open to black men in these films, since women are routinely abused, both physically and verbally and rarely emerge as credible or creditable characters. Women are constantly described as whores and bitches and while occasionally allowed to adorn a bracelet-encrusted male tricep, are entirely peripheral to the lives of the male protagonists and usually completely ineffectual as wives, mothers and partners. Commenting on *Boyz N the Hood*, Dyson argues that,

> Singleton's moral premise, like so many claims of black male suffering, rests dangerously on ideas of black male salvation at the expense of black female suffering; black male autonomy at the cost of black female subordination; black male dignity at the cost of black female infirmity. (1992: 19)

Tracy Camila Johns who played Nola Darling in *She's Gotta Have It* is seen once again stripping down to her underwear in *New Jack City* and these two roles are representative of the narrow repertoire of character types which are allowed to black women in most contemporary films made by black men. The 'bitch' role in *New Jack City* is occupied by Vanessa Williams as Keisha, the bloodthirsty female member of Nino's gang who was presumably recruited by the film's director to demonstrate gender even-handedness in the killer instinct. But her character is so one-dimensional that she is difficult to distinguish from other gang members, apart from her obvious sex.

In 1993 the winning combination of drugs and violence was again used to good box office effect when *Strapped* (Forest Whitaker, 1993) and *Menace II Society* (Allen and Albert Hughes, 1993) were released. These two films continued with the 'hood theme, providing more cautionary tales about being young, black and male in America and the way in which the culture of the gun exerts a demonic influence over the young and hopeless. Once again, black on black violence provides the primary focus for these films although here, as elsewhere, the respective 'heroes' attempt to avoid being drawn in to the casually violent and often murderous activities of their gang friends with little eventual success. In *Strapped*, meaning 'to carry a weapon', the hero Diquan (Bokeem Woodbine), wants to do the right thing by his pregnant girlfriend Latisha (Kia Joy Goodwin) but when she is arrested for drug-dealing, he turns police informer to avoid his girlfriend being prosecuted. In *Menace*, a particularly nasty thug, O-Dog (Larenz Tate) claims that he is America's worst nightmare 'young, black and doesn't give a fuck'. Both films offer opening sequences in which the hero witnesses a gratuitous killing by a friend and is horrified, but over the period of the film, comes to understand that this is the way of the world, that violence is the only route left for the alienated and that they have no other choice but to follow their unfortunate and often fatal destiny.

In *Menace*, the central character Caine (Tyrin Turner) tries to avoid the obligatory descent into violence which typifies the brief lives of many young male 'hood dwellers and is lectured by his mentor Parnell (Glenn Plummer) to make a better life elsewhere (Parnell delivers his sermon from behind bars). Parnell's erstwhile girlfriend, Ronnie (Jade Pinkett), and her child seem to offer an alternative way of living but Caine quickly finds himself teaching her son to hold a gun in the same way that Parnell had taught him. It is all quite hopeless for Caine who inevitably gets drawn into taking part in a revenge killing. The content is what the audience have come to expect from films made by young black men in urban America but the extensive and gratuitous use of violence, where the smallest slight to a gang member's sense of self provokes an instant

extermination, numbs the senses. While drugs and guns have become an integral feature of the black urban landscape, the violence
generated by hopelessness seems to be accepted rather than questioned in films such as *Menace*. The one-dimensional portrayals
of drug-addicted parents, God-fearing elders and plucky single
mothers trying to battle against their circumstances cannot compete
with the more thrillingly shot sequences of guns and killings.
Taubin argues that for the films' directors to 'fetishise the representation of the macho violence they critique is merely to place them in
a worldwide tradition of great film-making' (Taubin, 1993: 17). But
Menace is not filmmaking at its greatest; it is a cynical attempt to
exploit the very real problems facing urban black (and white)
America without offering a critique beyond futility.

A different view

Most of the discussion around black American film has tended to
centre on African American and Caribbean work but, as Roy points
out, Asian American film and media have begun to emerge as a
major instrument in shaping Asian American identity even if it is
still not that widely exhibited (1993). With some notable exceptions,
such as Mira Nair's *Salaam Bombay!* (1988) and *Mississippi Masala*
(1991), Wayne Wang's *The Joy Luck Club* (1993) and the various film
enterprises of Ishmail Merchant, Asian American film practice remains almost entirely hidden from view. The 'hood is not the only
setting for contemporary stories of America's various diaspora
communities and in mapping the contours of trans-cultural relationships, Mira Nair's *Mississippi Masala* offers a fresh approach to
this particular taboo subject. The film shows the development of a
relationship between Mina (Sarita Choudhury) a young East Indian
woman who emigrates to America with her family when they are
expelled from Uganda, and Demetrius (Denzel Washington) the
hard-working owner of a carpet-cleaning business. While the main
focus of the film is the way in which their romance affects and
concerns their respective families and communities, it is also about
Mina's father, Jay (Rohan Seth), his relationship to Africa and how,
after years in exile, he comes to terms with his lost homeland. Jay
may be only a secondary player in the narrative, but it is he who
goes through the most profound changes.

Providing an entirely different setting, Mario Van Peebles's
sequel to *New Jack City*, *Posse* (1993) is, if not quite the first black
western, then certainly the first for a very long time. The narrative

follows the conventions of the 'western' genre with good guys and bad guys and the film demonstrates Van Peebles's affection for and knowledge of the genre. When Van Peebles decided to make *Posse*, it was as much a political decision as an excuse to play at cowboys and Indians.

Van Peebles himself, as the anti-hero Jessie Lee, provides a passably good Eastwood-ish brooder, with flashback sequences telling the story of Lee's pain. The film makes use of every western cliché yet constructed and manages to fit them all in, although the fact that all the (anti)heroes are black and all the bad guys are white, lends a certain metaphoric quality to the proceedings. *Posse* is ostensibly a corrective to the historical amnesia over the existence of black cowboys and highlights the fact that several all-black towns were built and occupied during the frontier days, notwithstanding their subsequent casual destruction by the Ku Klux Klan and their followers. Twists and turns in the plot have been appropriated with a touching fidelity from Eastwood's formula westerns with generous sprinklings of John Ford, but the specific ethnicity of the cowboys remains largely unexplored territory. That this is an essentially 'black' story is somewhat subordinated to the demands of the western genre and sometimes weak editing, together with an attempt to provide humour as well as pathos, leaves the film looking and sounding a little caricatured. While the project of rehabilitating black history is laudable, the film 'puts its heroes into a milieu where the only history that's relevant is the genesis of TV shows such as *Gunsmoke* or *The Virginian*' (James, 1993: 50).

Bill Duke's work has managed to avoid some of the worst excesses of the guns 'n' violence genre and both *Rage in Harlem* (1991) – based on a Chester Himes novel – and *Deep Cover* (1992) are clever and multi-layered texts. *Rage* is a love story wrapped up in a gangster movie but love wins out, albeit with the unlikely pairing of Forest Whitaker as the innocent hick and Robin Givens the streetwise hustler. Here, at least, is a black woman who is something more than mere cipher. Here is a black woman who is both cunning and loving and whose greed is, in the end, confounded by her love. *Rage* could have been mawkish but isn't, instead transcending the limitations of the genre and being more complex and involving. The film was selected as an official entry in the 1991 Cannes Film Festival. *Deep Cover* is an action thriller which draws heavily on the real-life exploits of various South American business people and politicians. Like *Rage*, the film manages to extend the possibilities of what action thrillers can be, bringing a strong moral authority and asking, by way of the black cop protagonist (Larry

Fishburne), what remains for decent folks in the post-Reagan aftermath.

Locating itself in the world of black urban violence but turning it on its head, Tamra Davis' *CB4* (1993) is a spoof rap film about a trio of middle-class young black men who reinvent themselves as a gangsta rap band and take on the world. Albert (Chris Rock, who together with Nelson George wrote the story and screenplay and co-produced the film), Otis (Deezer D) and Euripides (Allen Payne) who comprise the band CB4 (standing for Cell Block 4), are the subjects of a documentary film being made by a sycophantic TV director named A. White (Chris Elliott). En route, the real genesis of the band is revealed and the film traverses the various adventures of the three heroes, including Albert's forced involvement in an armed robbery, the dissolution and reformation of the group and their final break with gangsta rap and return to the less violent lyrics of 'traditional' rap. The introduction of real-life rappers Ice T, Ice Cube and Public Enemy's Flavor Flav provides an authentic endorsement of CB4 but, beneath the parody, the film explores very real issues. The way in which gangsta rap is venerated as *the* only genuine articulation of the pain of black communities is overtly challenged in *CB4* and the easy identity offered by an affiliation to outlaw chic is examined through the group's initial celebration and endorsement of gangsta values and their subsequent descent into confusion and crisis. The perception of a homogenous black community who share an undifferentiated enthusiasm for the messages and modes of gangsta rap is held up to scrutiny in the film and found wanting. Nelson George is critical over the increasing number of 'bad records, whose only virtue is how nasty and violent they are' (George quoted in Spencer, 1993: 4). Through well-judged parody, the film manages to question both the assumptions which underpin the lyrics of gangsta rap itself but also the alleged support of a loyal black community who blindly subscribe to its values. Rusty Cundieff's *Fear of a Black Hat* (1993) lampoons hip hop in a similar fashion, 'tracking' the band NWH (Niggaz with Hats) as they take to the road on their latest tour.

Sistren

While Hollywood continues to court those black filmmakers willing to work in the 'guns 'n' crime' genre, notwithstanding the films discussed immediately above, the subversive hand of black women filmmakers such as Leslie Harris and Julie Dash is beginning to show that there are a range of other black stories waiting to be told from a differently gendered perspective. As Mario Van Peebles points out 'I hope to see black filmmakers move outta the 'hood and I think it's the sisters that will take us there' (Peebles quoted in Ross, 1993: 18). But Dash is quick to own that her first feature-length film, *Daughters of the Dust* (1992), was fifteen years in the making and on completion stayed in limbo for a further twelve months waiting for a distributor. If it had incorporated the more saleable ingredients of sex, drugs and violence, it would have had a ready market. As it is, the story, set at the turn of the century in the distinctive Gullah culture of the rural Sea Islands off the South Carolina–Georgia coast, does not seem to be instantly commercial. But at a time when most black films embody a gang-related motif, this textured portrait of a unique and largely unknown society has found an interested audience (Turan, 1992). *Daughters of the Dust* explores Gullah culture in intricate detail as the central characters – the extended Peazant family – celebrate a last supper before most of its members leave for a new life on the mainland. Women, as the keepers of the family's African heritage, are the focus of the film which languidly explores rootedness and migration. The film exemplifies the enterprise of African 'retention' which seeks to revive and retrieve lost cultural remnants for the spiritual nourishment and wholeness of contemporary African Americans (Rich, 1992).

The dreamy style and acute attention to cultural details such as costume, language, food and music, together with the slow pace and rhythm of the film, have combined to afford considerable opportunity for criticism for reasons similar to those put forward against Isaac Julien's evocative and sensuous portrait of the Harlem renaissance poet, Langston Hughes (*Looking for Langston*, 1989). But as Alexander points out, although the film is criticized for its emphasis on historical detail, knowledge of the past provides the only context in which to understand the present (Alexander, 1993b). The critics apparently want their prejudices reinforced, not challenged by these different and unapologetic texts whose narratives are far removed from the urban 'hood. Black films must not, apparently, be too lyrical and the black aesthetic must not be too beautiful. Although Dash had already made ten films, including *Illusions* in 1982, which won Best Film of the Decade from the Black Filmmakers' Foundation, *Daughters* is the one which has placed her in the mainstream public eye. The film is extremely personal to the filmmaker as Gullah culture is part of Dash's own history and the narrative style of the film, which Dash describes as 'griot', is a direct take on the West African story-telling tradition which has a multi-layered rather than linear rhythm and structure. Dash is aware that her texts are often difficult to read for an audience which is more used to having plotlines explained to them and that she faces opposition in presenting these alternative black images.

> People can't conceive of seeing black people outside of the images that are on television or the way that they think we look. When I first became involved with film, I was interested in correcting certain distortions about black people, distortions that I had been bombarded with by the media since my childhood . . . I decided to investigate various means of correcting what I viewed to be the intentional misrepresentation of what was happening. (1986: 17)

Working out of a rather different tradition, Leslie Harris's *Just Another Girl on the IRT* (1993) showed that life for women in the 'hood was not just about hanging out with the local gangs and being constantly described as bitches and whores. The film was publicized as the first popular film (as opposed to 'arty' film – *Daughters*) made by an African American woman and provides a cautionary tale about aspirations, attitude and accidental pregnancies. (Interestingly, the 'first popular film made by an African American woman' label has recently been claimed for Darnell Martin's *I Like It Like That* (1994) as if studios constantly need to reinvent the 'first ever' pitch in order to market films made by black women.) The rationale for *IRT* was the fact that Harris had been unable to find any portraits of herself or women she knew in films about contemporary black America. The film's hero, Chantel (Ariyan Johnson), tells her story directly to camera and punctuates the narrative with first-person overlay and asides. Her story is that of an intelligent and streetwise teenager, determined to become a doctor and escape the poverty of her environment, who becomes pregnant and then denies the fact of her increasingly obvious condition. Chantel is bright, energetic and funny with a bad attitude, disrespecting all authority figures because she knows, intuitively, that she has what it takes to leave the projects far behind. Harris shows that young women who find themselves in such situations are not always irresponsible junkies but often ordinary teenagers who get trapped by their ignorance. Although the film was panned severely for its inconsistency, didactic narrative and general lack of credibility, it perhaps deserves a more thoughtful analysis as the first African American pop film to have a determinedly female subject (Taubin, 1993). There certainly are problems with the film, including a pro-choice bias which goes unacknowledged when Chantel first finds out that she is pregnant and a ridiculous birthing scene towards the end of the film, but it is the lack of gun-toting violence which probably sets the seal on *IRT*'s fate. Although there is a heavy rap soundtrack à la mode, there are no killings and, as has already been pointed out, violence, crime and bad language are what the mainstream audience wants. The feel-good ending, where Chantel realizes that having her baby was the beginning of 'getting her shit together', is really a cop-out since going to community college instead of medical school is portrayed as an equivalence. But maybe that's the point.

Black and white Hollywood

The interest that Hollywood studios show in black films and black filmmakers is largely determined by their potential to succeed at the box office. Spike Lee's demonstration that black-oriented films can appeal to a mixed audience and make serious money led the way for filmmakers such as John Singleton, Ernest Dickerson and Robert Townsend to build up a range (albeit limited) of images and stories which have specifically black themes. However, Hollywood's embrace is not unconditional and even very successful filmmakers like Spike Lee still have to struggle to secure adequate budgets for their films. Reid argues that although black filmmakers are often seduced by white-owned studios' offers of funding, such projects often receive very low production budgets, narrow race-specific marketing strategies and limited distribution (Reid, 1993). The appeal of white studios, though, despite the above shortcomings, lies in the fact that such companies will shoulder all the pre- and post-production and distribution costs, that filmmakers and artistes will receive automatic publicity and if the film is financially and critically successful, the filmmaker is then in a very good position to take more control over future projects. But Hollywood is extremely conservative and will only support the formulaic projects which guarantee success, hence the spate of ghetto, guns and violence movies which characterized black filmmaking in the early 1990s. Black male filmmakers' fascination with the 'hood represents, to some extent, an opportunity for them to work on their own particular versions of African American life and make a lot of money in the telling. They are astutely responding to Hollywood's propensity to sell an old story in a new way and convince the audience that what they are seeing is a completely new truth. The unexpected success of Spike Lee's low-budget films provided a tempting new treat for the major studios. The ambiguous relationship between black filmmakers and their sponsors raises issues about the politics of representation and the intentions of black filmmakers to either integrate themselves into the existing codas of film production or to forge a new cinematic language which embraces the diversity of the African American experience (Jones, 1991).

The emulation, by some black filmmakers, of the gangster/crime thriller genre with which Hollywood and its audiences are already familiar and comfortable, replaces white hoodlums with black but does not subvert traditional cinematic conventions nor posit alternative strategies for the future. The preoccupation with ghetto contexts and the violence they necessarily connote may circumscribe, by their very success, the possibility of other black voices being heard. While such films are valuable in providing insights into the experiences of urban black communities and particularly those of young black men, they are largely desolate in their conclusions. It is still open to question whether such films function to force an examination of the condition of African American communities or whether they simply/also pathologize black communities for the voyeuristic pleasure of the majority white audience.

Gilroy suggests that the reason why the voices of more innovative and oppositional filmmakers such as Norman O. Bland, Bill Gunn and Wendell B. Harris have been largely ignored, is that their stories do not fit neatly into Hollywood's perception of what African American film should look like, that is, that they should portray African American communities as a permanent underclass without a sustaining culture or heritage (Gilroy, 1991a). But the ubiquitous 'hood theme has been partially subverted by the (limited) success of alternative black visions such as Julie Dash's *Daughters of the Dust* and Mira Nair's *Mississippi Masala*, together with the more upbeat films which have just been made by Spike Lee and John Singleton (*Crooklyn* and *Poetic Justice* respectively, both 1994).

However, despite the (partially) successful penetration of black workers into the media industry, their access is restricted not only by the whim of commissioning editors and studio managers, but by the potential marketability of their product. Unless black production companies are willing to give the market what it wants then they are unlikely to be given contracts unless they already have a good track record or are known to be bankable and even then, there are no guarantees. Those filmmakers who have attempted to subvert Hollywood's orthodox conventions on both story and structure, for example, Charles Burnett, Julie Dash and Haile Gerima, have generally struggled to attract mainstream funding although such films have achieved significant critical success. The irresistible tension between market forces and artistic integrity continues to occupy the film industry and it seems as if even the critics have descended to the shallow depths of the commercial. Despite the excellent list of contenders for the Critics Prize at Cannes in 1994, including Kieslowski's *Three Colours: White*, the judges, led by Clint Eastwood, decided to give the Palme d'Or to Quentin Tarantino for his formula blood and guts film *Pulp Fiction*. The future for films which dare to be different seems bleak indeed.

PART II

Television

4

Small but Imperfectly Formed: Small Screen Portraits of Otherness

We can get to know only a few kin and friends intimately as individuals. Others we have to categorise through stereotypes.
Jonathan Benthall, Director of the Royal Anthropological Institute

Since the beginning of the 1950s when the ownership of television sets became more common, researchers have tried to assess the influence and impact of television on the viewing public. This research has tended to follow either of two broad paths: one examining the links between the media and the powerful in society and the other looking at the relationship between media messages and the audience. The former perspective looks at media organizations at the institutional level and examines issues around ownership, control and the relative autonomy and independence of different forms of media. Currently, much media research at this institutional level is concerned with the proliferation of terrestrial and satellite/cable networks together with computer nets, and the way in which media are moving from the local, regional and national arenas towards an increasingly global media environment. The other strand of media research which is of more relevance to this text is concerned with the images and messages of media texts and seeks, among other things, to understand how viewers receive and perceive broadcast material. Much of the early research work in this area took a largely deterministic perspective, suggesting that television functioned as an agent of social control, feeding its audience with establishment propaganda. More recently though, research interest has turned towards an exploration of the audience as a heterogeneous amalgam of individuals and in particular, has asked questions about the viewer's relationship with the text and what she does with it, rather than the other way round.

Whilst the precise relationship between the television text and

the audience remains elusive, it is clear that TV viewing is a significant social activity and the billions of pounds spent on TV advertis-
ing provides at least partial corroboration for the view that the
medium has the potential, at least, to raise people's awareness and
change opinions if not absolutely alter their behaviour. In the
specific context of the black 'other' then, mainstream television has
tended to represent black communities in very specific ways. Media
portraits do not develop in a vacuum but are products of their
particular time and deal with the social, economic and political
concerns of their day. Key moments in contemporary history such
as the break-up of Empire, the Civil Rights movement, migration
flows from the Caribbean and South Asia and more recently the re-
emergence of racist and fascist social movements, can all be tracked
through their representation in televisual output. A preoccupation
with discussing the 'problematic' aspects of the black presence in
Britain, for example, can be clearly seen in much of the social conscience programming which dealt with aspects of 'race' in the 1950s
and 1960s, focusing more or less exclusively on the (racist) attitudes
of white people towards black people.

The early years

The ways in which television programmes cover black issues are the
result of deliberate policy and programming decisions about what
is included or excluded, who is allowed to speak and who is not, as
well as the language and imagery used. The pre-existing iconography of blackness used in cinematic portraits provided an extremely
convenient store-house of images which could easily transfer to the
nascent medium of television. During the early years air-time was
scarce so those programmes which *were* broadcast were often endowed with more authority than would have otherwise been the
case. One important contribution to the early demise of more positive images of black groups, at least in America, was the preference
among white audiences for the traditional familiar stereotypes.
Miller argues that the early promise for realistic black representations was short lived because the racist formulae used in cinema
were irresistible to the new industry.

> The structure of television simply could not prevent older images
> from spilling over into the new medium . . . television adopted many
> of the storylines and stereotypes already successful in radio and
> film . . . stereotypical and demeaning roles entered the medium and

compromised the many positive images of blacks in early television.
(1980: 70)

In America, most appearances of black actors/characters in television programmes of the 1940s and 1950s mimicked the types of
roles and characterizations which were already present in film and
radio. In the immediate post-war period, when racial segregation
was still a routine part of life in many Southern states, the imperative for less pejorative race stereotypes was rarely articulated. It
was, arguably, during the 1960s and the Civil Rights movement that
black communities began to win some of the representation ground,
albeit hard-fought and piecemeal. One programme which provided
the focus for a deal of hostility on the part of African Americans was
Amos 'n' Andy, a show which had transferred from radio to television with relative ease, the main difference being that the television version featured black actors whereas the radio show stars
were white. Amos and Andy were two lazy, bumbling and essentially stupid African Americans (Spencer Williams as Andy Brown
and Alvin Childress as Amos Jones) who represented straightforward reworkings of the black fool type. As with other programmes
which had serious racist undertones – for example, *The Black and
White Minstrel Show*, *Till Death Us Do Part* and *All in the Family* – the
criticisms levelled against *Amos 'n' Andy* were largely ignored since
it was extremely popular with the predominantly white audience.
The show was the first prime-time programme to feature a predominantly black cast and was sued by the National Association for
the Advancement of Colored People (NAACP) because of the
negative imagery surrounding its characters. Generally, black TV
characters were imbued with characteristics which made them appealing to the white audience and which confirmed for that audience their perceptions (and prejudices) of what black people were
and how they should behave.

American entertainment programmes have consistently peddled
the myth of the dream family, where Mom and Dad's strong moral
values provide a tough but fair framework in which to bring up the
kids. While black artistes were sometimes the 'stars' of their own
show, for example *Benson* and *Beulah*, most only really existed in the
context of and in relation to white folks. The eponymous Beulah,
notwithstanding her 'sassy' role, was little removed from the stereotypical mammy figure of an earlier era. In many ways, then as now,
the television portrayal of black people and their apparently successful assimilation into mainstream American culture was and
remains in sharp contrast to their position in the real America. The

race riots which gave rise to the Civil Rights movement in the late 1950s took place against the background of a gently serene Nat King Cole singing 'When I Fall in Love' on his own show in 1956. Comparable ironies can be seen in the juxtaposition of live reports of the LA riots in 1992 set against the cosy homilies and domesticated dramas experienced by Bill Cosby's have-it-all family.

If 1950s America was intent on turning its face against its own very real problems and pretending that life was sweet and fair for all its citizens, the post-war years saw Britain attempting to re-establish itself as a major power in the world and to bolster the confidence of the British public. These dual concerns were reflected in television's preoccupation with all things colonial. In the early to mid-1950s, much of the programming which dealt with black issues was concerned with looking at black communities as they existed outside the British context, often as the exoticized 'other'. For example, in 1954, the BBC began to generate its own news service on television instead of using radio news reports and this led to a shift in emphasis particularly in relation to its ability to show powerful visual images. The comparative expense involved in television production meant that a number of programmes went out on to the streets to canvass opinion about social issues of the day – the vox pop approach – and this innovative form of programme-making coincided with the recruitment of a number of media practitioners who were interested in making 'socially responsible' programmes such as *Does Britain Have a Colour Bar* (1955) and *People in Trouble: Mixed Marriages* (1958). The insistence on 'honesty' as far as discussing crucial social problems such as poverty, delinquency and racism were concerned, often resulted in rather stagey 'reconstructions' of situations played out in studios (see for example, *This Week: The Negro Next Door* – 1965) intercut with newsreel footage which gave a strange drama-documentary feel to what should have been a straightforward factual piece.

Many of the social responsibility television plays of the 1950s such as *A Man from the Sun* (1956) and *Hot Summer Night* (1959) can be seen, with hindsight, to be grossly patronizing. However, there are dangers in looking at these artworks of the 1950s with a 1990s sensibility and ignoring the fact that all artefacts are necessarily of their own time and speak with that voice. *The Colony*, for example, broadcast in 1964, had a white director and producer but was nonetheless ground-breaking in that it enabled black views to be articulated directly through personal narrative, rather than using the convention of a (white) interpretative voice-over. But media images are always constructed by the practitioners working on them who privilege some voices over others, allow some stories to be told but not others. Control over production is seldom in the hands of 'ordinary' people and even within those genres which purport to give editorial control to the community, such as the BBC's Community Programmes Unit, production is still in the hands of the experts, not the amateurs. Even as *The Colony* facilitated the articulation of genuine black voices, the agenda was still a white construction and the stories described were those which fitted a white-defined problematic.

Programmes which were firmly centred around a black-as-problem discourse nearly always presented the issue as one of working-class racism. In dramas such as *A Man From the Sun*, the problem of race relations (racism) was rooted in the irrational prejudice of the white working class towards the black community in general and specific black individuals in particular. The more pervasive and damaging forms of institutional racism and the prejudice of elites were rarely documented. By the 1960s, the race-relations problematic had taken a solid hold in Britain, providing both an explanatory framework within which to analyse 'society' and identifying race as a social rather than political problem requiring social solutions (Ali, 1993). However, subsequent legislative responses to the 'problem' of race have largely been oriented towards restricting further migration into Britain, thus taking a very obvious political solution to the societal 'problems' facing black communities. It was arguably Powell's 'rivers of blood' speech in 1968 which proved the turning point for both press and broadcasting in Britain, at last opening up the public debate on race which had been raging beneath the surface of polite society. The reality of white racism had to be finally acknowledged and for news media at least, blackness became inextricably linked with an internal conflict which needed to be contained (Tulloch, 1990). This equation of black = problem continues to be an abiding theme in both fictional and factual programming in contemporary media.

In America, television's fascination with the family and in particular its interest in promoting 'good' family values did not confine itself to celebrating the kinship and solidarity of white family networks but began, in the 1960s, to show African Americans in their own domestic series. *Julia*, starring Diahann Carroll was first broadcast in 1968 and constituted a breakthrough in American portraits of black communities in that black people were seen as *relatively* ordinary. Julia was not only the first black woman to head a household on television, she was the first black woman to star in her own series since *Beulah* nearly fifteen years before, although, as was often the case with black stars, the supporting cast of *Julia* was white (see also *Benson; Diff'rent Strokes; Beulah*). The possibility of black actors appearing in programmes other than sitcoms began to gain a firm foothold during the 1970s and the decade saw a number of family-drama series such as *Sanford & Son, Good Times* and *The Jeffersons*, all produced by Norman Lear. All these shows featured black families, sometimes middle-class and sometimes working-class, but all shared a prevailing ethos of hard work and 'family values'. In *Good Times*, a working-class family struggle to ascend the economic hierarchy but as Eliot so eloquently argued, nothing struck a falser chord than the sight of a poor black family enjoying their poverty (Eliot, 1981).

One of the first and perhaps most popular British programmes to discuss race themes was *Till Death Us Do Part* which was originally broadcast from 1966 to 1974 on BBC1. As well as constant repeats since the mid-1970s, the programme's main character, Alf Garnett (Alf), saw a 1980s revival with a follow-up series, *In Sickness and in Health*. Although Alf's creator, Johnny Speight, argued at the time of the original broadcasts and since, that his intention was to expose racist bigotry through the exaggerated utterances of Alf, such an intention has back-fired for many commentators. The enormous popularity of the show signified that there was something about it which appealed to a significant proportion of the viewing public.

> Wherever the series has been shown – in Great Britain or in the United States or Germany (the last two in local adaptations) – the effects have by no means been what the author intended. If racism is widely spread in a society, as it is in ours [Britain], such shows will be seen by a considerable part of the audience as validating their views. (Hood, 1980: 26)

Many viewers found their own opinions being expressed by Alf, opinions which they probably kept hidden, even from themselves. The attitudes of ordinary men and women, worried by the 'immigrant avalanche' constantly reported on in the media, found a certain resonance in the racist bigotry espoused by Alf. 'A whole repertoire of anxieties and prejudices was being expressed for the first time and with such bravado and forcefulness that the response was instant and massive' (Medhurst, 1989: 18). Although Alf was challenged in his more ludicrous diatribes by his daughter and son-in-law, there was a degree of complicity with his views on the part of the audience, observing the old maxim of no smoke without fire. Medhurst argues that the overt language of racism contained in the show has never been rivalled and has in fact been toned down for more contemporary audiences. 'The sheer virulence of Garnett's prejudices (racial and otherwise) was startling and far stronger than anything heard on television today' (1989: 17).

When first broadcast in 1971, *All in the Family* (the American equivalent of *Till Death Us Do Part*) was considered ground-breaking, upsetting the traditional pattern of inoffensive and bland situation comedy through the depiction of its principal character, Archie Bunker, as a boorish, racist, bigot (Cantor and Cantor, 1992). Archie openly used racist language, for example, 'jungle bunny' and 'jigaboo', to describe African Americans and this was a signifi-cant component of his unpleasant personality. While early episodes intended to lay the foundation of Archie's character as essentially dimwitted and reactionary, there were mixed views over the extent to which Archie was actually seen in this way by the audience. On the one hand, some commentators such as Cantor and Cantor argue that 'although some viewers may have misunderstood the pro-ducer's intent, to most it was obvious that Archie was out of step with his family and neighbors' views about racial, ethnic and sexual equality' (1992: 29). Similarly, Greenberg and Atkin argue that only a small percentage of viewers believed that Archie's views were valid and a substantial number of viewers felt that the programme helped them to identify their own prejudices (1982). On the other hand, Woll and Miller suggest that research studies carried out on the show demonstrated that

> Archie's behaviour actually reinforced prejudice, for racist viewers could not see that the show was intended to satirise prejudices . . . hearing the words 'coon', 'jungle bunny' and 'spade' regularly on network TV gave such slurs a currency of legitimacy no amount of disclaimers and counter humour could match. (1987: 78–81)

Again, Vidmar and Rokeach's survey in 1974 found that 62 per cent of their adolescent respondents admired Archie, with 35 per cent unable to see anything amiss with his use of racist language. The authors suggest that the operation of selective perception occurs so that 'prejudiced' people view Archie as 'telling it like it is', while non-prejudiced people perceive the programme as satirical with Archie regarded as the bigoted fool (1974). At the end of the first year of broadcasting, *All in the Family* had attained the top position in the audience ratings and remained the most popular series, in terms of gross audiences, for five consecutive years. The success of such shows confirms to some viewers that their own private opinions are shared by others who are more willing to articulate them than they are themselves. Programme producers and writers cannot really substantiate their claim that mixing humour with bigotry will automatically illuminate the stupidity of the latter and lead to its reduction. If bigots do not perceive such programmes as satire, and much of the research effort so far seems to indicate that a satirical reading is by no means universal, then they are rather unlikely to become *less* prejudiced as a result of watching these shows. At the end of the 1980s, an Alf Garnett exhibition was staged at the Museum of the Moving Image in London, where visitors pressed buttons representing particular social problems and Alf appeared on video to opine on the selected subject. It is a strange idea and exemplifies the ease with which TV characters can make the transition from one media to another, mutating from demon to sage along the way. Although *Till Death Us Do Part* did not contain a permanent black cast member, its successor, *In Sickness and in Health*, regularly featured a young black man cast as Alf's homosexual home-help, Marigold. It is difficult to understand the reasons behind this particular casting, except perhaps to enable Alf to rehearse both his racist and his homophobic rage on a single, all-purpose target. Although Marigold did his best to show Alf the error of his ways, it is again open to question whether Speight's explicit intentions for the viewing public – to expose racism and homophobia – have been realized.

Three notorious British comedy series of the 1970s to feature black characters were *Love Thy Neighbour* (Thames Television, 1972–5); *Mind Your Language* (BBC1, 1976); and *It Ain't Half Hot, Mum* (BBC1, 1973–81). All three used standard sitcom formulae such as double entendres, quarrels, underdog cleverness and so on, and all were seen at the time as harmless fun. The African Caribbean actor Rudolph Walker who starred in *Love Thy Neighbour* now argues that the show was never intended to find answers to the race question but rather was made as 'entertainment and to make money' (Walker quoted in Pines (ed.), 1992: 78). The fact that his black character was 'allowed' to respond to the white neighbour's verbal and physical assaults in like manner – a feature that Walker had deliberately written in to his contract – meant that the show broke new ground in featuring an attractive black couple who were positive and assertive and most definitely not victims. However, *Love Thy Neighbour*, as well as the other sitcoms around at the time which incorporated a specific 'race' theme, were seldom able to transcend the limitations of the genre and although bolder than the shows of the 1960s, they nonetheless peddled the same stilted range of character types. Another series of that time, *Mixed Blessings*, attempted to bring a humorous air to the issue of black–white relations and featured a married couple where the wife was African Caribbean and the husband white. Commenting on the show in which she starred, Carmen Munroe argues that the series had the makings of a good sitcom with some hard-hitting social commentary thrown in, but ultimately it simply didn't work. 'I don't think we were really versed in the art of making social comment without it becoming just that, and without it losing the comedy of the situation. We weren't able to do that very well then' (Munroe quoted in Pines (ed.), 1992: 63). Possibly the worst of the 1970s 'comedies' about difference was *Mind Your Language*, a series set in an English language class which exploited every racist stereotype imaginable in an effort to turn a cheap laugh. Michael Grade who presided over *Mind Your Language* when he was at London Weekend Television now accepts that the show was racist, but the Channel nonetheless profited by its 12-month run at the time (Wadsworth, 1986). In 1986, the show's American equivalent, *What A Country!*, was created and constituted the first British sale made directly to US syndication.

In 1976, London Weekend Television launched *The Fosters*, the first comedy series to feature an all-black cast: the show ran for a second season in 1977. *The Fosters* was the first series to describe an 'ordinary' black family and their life without constantly privileging their problematic blackness and was a British re-working of the very popular American show, *Good Times*. Following quickly on the heels of *The Fosters* came *Empire Road*, the first black soap, which ran for two seasons between 1978 and 1979. The series had a predominance of African Caribbean and Asian characters and included storylines which were concerned with mainstream issues such as parental discipline and difficult relationships. North suggested that the main strength of the series lay in the fact that black communities were seen as ordinary and normal, containing the same quota of capitalists and delinquents as in the white population. He argued that the trivialization of the black community had finally been achieved (through its celebration as soap) whereby the minutiae of life could be explored without constantly relying on the play of black–white tensions (Richard North, *The Listener*, 16.11.1978).

A review of British programming broadcast during the 1950s to 1970s period would not be complete without a brief look at the notorious *The Black and White Minstrel Show*, one of the BBC's most popular series which ran for twenty-one years, between 1958 and 1978. In today's more enlightened social climate, it would be

unthinkable to broadcast such blatant caricatures but even in the
show's infancy, dissenting voices were heard.

> The Black and White Minstrels might as well abandon its ebony
> pretences . . . I can see no point in white singers putting on a gro-
> tesque make-up which has nothing to do with the natural good looks
> of an African, in order to sing popular songs which have nothing to
> do with the coloured world. (Ivor Brown, television critic in *The
> Listener*, 19.3.1959)

However, the show was extremely popular, regularly attracting
audiences of 12 million and sometimes as high as 18 million viewers
(Woffinden, 1988). It is unclear precisely what it was about the show
that made it so successful although the variety genre was extremely
popular at the time in other entertainment media such as theatre
and film. Woffinden suggests that part of its appeal lay in its vitality, since the minstrels mimed to pre-recorded tapes and were
therefore free to indulge in dynamic and energetic dance sequences
which gave the shows a lively and fresh appearance (1988). The
television shows were also mirrored by stage revues so that the
minstrels phenomenon soon had a large and devoted following. In
May 1967 a petition backed by the Campaign Against Racial Discrimination (CARD) was taken to the BBC, insisting that the show
be taken off air. But the BBC had to weigh its social conscience
against its millions of satisfied viewers and licence payers and,
ironically, the arrival of colour television in the same year gave the
show a new lease of life. However, the campaign and the mounting
criticisms in the quality press began to sound the death knell for the
show which was eventually taken off in 1978 although the live
theatre shows have continued: even in 1994, the Black and White
Organisation Limited auditioned for men and women to sing and
dance in the 'Minstrel Spectacular' for the summer season at the
Princess Theatre, Torquay (*The Stage*, March 1994). Jim Moir, as
Head of Light Entertainment at the BBC, talked with pride about
The Black and White Minstrel Show winning the Golden Rose of
Montreux award in 1961 and reported that even at the end of the
1980s, his postbag was still full of letters requesting repeat showing
of those 'wonderful' programmes (Moir, 1989). When the BBC celebrated fifty years in broadcasting in 1986, *The Black and White
Minstrel Show* was left out of the reminiscences and there was some
hostility towards Bill Cotton, then BBC Director, for taking such a
decision. The great loyalty that the series provoked and still com-
mands is difficult to understand until Robert Luff, former impre-

sario at the Minstrel Shows suggests an 'alternative', non-racist reading, with the now ubiquitous disclaimer to justify that view.

> [the show] was – and still is – incredibly successful and popular. It is not racist and never has been. We have just completed a 14 week sell-out tour around Britain and no one came out of a theatre complaining about it. (Luff quoted in *The Daily Mail*, 23.10.1986)

Television's love affair with the 'family' and its widespread insistence on family values, consumerism and individual problem-solving is exemplified by the medium's treatment of history and particularly, the history of colonialism. The 1977 mini-series, *Roots*, taken from Alex Haley's novel on the experience of African Americans from slavery to the present day, was ground-breaking in content and record-breaking in ratings. What was a little surprising about its popularity was its deliberate black-oriented focus on the horrors and brutality of a practice inflicted on black people by whites. When the series was shown in America over eight consecutive nights, 130 million viewers watched some or all of the programmes, representing 85 per cent of all households which owned a television (Rapping, 1987). But maybe its popularity is not really that surprising since, as with *The Cosby Show* which came several years later, the crucial feature of *Roots* was that, having clearly laid out the evils of slavery and encouraged the white audience to feel guilty about its notorious past, it then spelt out that with hard work and a supportive family, anyone could achieve the American dream. Thus within one short series, white people could not only salve their collective conscience by admitting their historical sins but also celebrate their contemporary humanity and goodness by 'allowing' the hardworking black to have a slice of American pie. It should also be remembered that the series was liberally soaked in blood, violence and sex and smoothed over the rough edges of inconsistency for the sake of a good dramatic story. Although at the time of the transmissions there were some small criticisms about historical inaccuracies which Haley brushed aside by saying that blacks as well as whites needed a hypothetical Eden (cited in Rapping, 1987: 156), more recently, the entire project of Kunte Kinte's history has been exposed as a rather fanciful fabrication. But historical licence or not, the pivotal role of the family in achieving social, economic and political success had clear and reactionary messages for white, and particularly black viewers: do not look to political movements for liberation but look instead to yourself and your family to achieve personal success. When *Roots* was broadcast in Britain in the same year, it was during a period in which the children of migrated parents were beginning to challenge various forms of institutional racism and it was also an era in which cultural identity movements began to achieve a following, particularly amongst disaffected young African Caribbean people. The retrieval of the past in order to restore black pride and self-esteem which were pivotal to the back-to-Africa movements found special resonances in Haley's story. The images of black communities shown in this epic also provided significant counter-portraits, particularly in the British context, to the stereotypes which characterized black representations in mainstream programming. Here was something new, here was something different, here were images of enterprise and fulfilment, the quintessential rags-to-riches story which could hold for black communities as well as white. The awesome power of television is its ability to gloss over or ignore inconvenient truths in order to present a more hopeful scenario, where hard work can overcome every disadvantage, even endemic racism.

The history of television's treatment of black and other ethnic minority communities has paralleled society's treatment of these groups in the real world: 'Exclusion or, at best, marginalization, ghettoization, stereotyping; these are the key processes that distinguish that treatment' (Cashmore, 1994: 110). Whilst African Caribbeans and African Americans were the most frequently seen black minorities on British and American television during the 1960s and 1970s, other minorities have also featured, for example Desi Arnez who played Lucille Ball's husband in *I Love Lucy*. Jay Silverheels was the first Native American to appear in a network series when he played the role of Tonto in the 1950s *Lone Ranger* series. But as Cashmore points out, the crudely etched characters in series such as *The Cisco Kid*, *Charlie Chan* and *Hawkeye* were often scarcely more than simple cartoons and were, in any case, often played by whites (Cashmore, 1994). No black community was exempt from racist stereotyping although series in subsequent decades became more polished in their representations, albeit that the vein of racism still runs close to the surface in many contemporary programmes. If portraits of black communities suffered from narrow-casting during the early years of British television, the initiation of a fourth channel in 1981 (Channel 4) was heralded as the breaking of a new dawn: here was a channel set up specifically to cater to minority interests which would also have a positive knock-on effect on the other television companies. At the very least, Channel 4 *has* expanded independent television production and encouraged more

black practitioners into the industry (Mercer, 1990c), but the real
and enduring changes in black images have been slow in coming.

I laughed 'til I cried

The location of black actors on television has been, as already
suggested, extremely narrow and the popularity of 'race' themes in
comedy continued into the 1980s. Jim Moir suggests that in the field
of light entertainment and comedy, there has always been a sense of
exaggeration and the use of both ethnic and social categories as foci
for humour (1989). Similarly, Medhurst argues that comedy cannot
function without resort to stereotype, since jokes need victims and
such victims must be accepted by the audience in some way as
constituting an appropriate butt. 'Comedy can never be inoffensive.
Attack and hostility are built into its very structure and the skill in
producing good, successful, political comedy lies in finding the
right targets' (1989: 17). In other words stereotypes are an integral
and requisite aspect of humour, provided they are rooted in the
correct ideological background. At one level, Medhurst's argument
seems quite plausible, but it is a moot point whether a consensus
exists on what constitute the 'right' targets. Televised comedies help
their audiences to adjust to the social order as preferred codes of
behaviour are reinforced through the transmission of favourable
myths and ideologies. In comedies which feature black actors, the
twin themes of mainstream white xenophobia and concomitant
black subservience are irresistibly played out. In the same way
that prime-time television panders to the achievement of the American dream with mythically constructed examples of what the
American way of life should be, so too have black communities
been absorbed into the unreal culture of television fiction with
greater or lesser degrees of success. One recent and relatively challenging comedy-drama, *Frank's Place*, has been a (prime-time) casualty of the mass audience's predilection for 'feel-good' television.
Henry Louis Gates comments that for many people, *Frank's Place*
was the best programme about African American life for a very long
time, largely because it portrayed a diverse, interesting and believable range of black character types, but it was quickly brought off
air by its low ratings (Gates in Riggs, 1991). The show, which was
produced by and also starred Tim Reid, mapped the adventures
of a university professor – Frank – after he inherits a restaurant
from his estranged father and decides to run it. The regular cast of
characters included various waiting staff and black professional

women representing an authentic multicultural society which at
the same time provided an accessible way into discussing issues
relating to multi-ethnic America (White, 1991). Although the ingredients for the show were promising in that the stories were situated
in a realistic working(-class) environment, it only lasted for one
season on prime-time US television and was subsequently broadcast on the black cable channel, Black Entertainment Television
(BET).

> It was precisely because the show attempted to show a realistic
> portrait of black community life and the relationship between black
> and white Americans that marked its downfall: *Frank's Place* was too
> real for Americans. It was the closest thing to the reality I experienced
> growing up and the reality I now experience as a person of color in
> American society . . . and I don't think that the average white
> American is prepared to encounter the full complexity of that reality.
> They want to encounter fictions of that reality which are palatable to
> them. (Gates in Riggs, 1991)

Tim Reid reports on the constant tension between the show's
writers and the network, with the former wanting to write realistic
dialogue and the latter insisting on a more formulaic sitcom text
(Reid quoted in Riggs, 1991). White argues that *Frank's Place* was
essentially domesticated into just another ordinary sitcom because
television is simply unable to handle the issue of racial difference
(1991). Despite the limitations on more challenging storylines and
the lack of sufficient (white) audiences to ensure continued air-time,
the show was highly successful with black viewers, largely due to
its inclusion of people, locations and circumstances which are rarely
represented on television (Gray, 1993a). But the success or otherwise of a television series is largely dependent on audience ratings
and if *Frank's Place* did not offer a mass audience exactly what it
wanted, *The Cosby Show* suffered no such defect. If television fictions
normalize the universe and package it in such a way as to make it
palatable and pleasurable to the majority audience, *The Cosby Show*
was and continues to be adept in giving the audience precisely what
it wants. The show has been one of the most successful in America
and has also had a relatively good reception in Britain, although its
transmission on Channel 4 has meant that it never attracted the size
of audience that a mainstream comedy programme screened on the
two major channels would have managed. However, in America,
Cosby has been extraordinarily popular to the point where entire
academic texts have been dedicated to exploring and explaining the
phenomenon. *Cosby* is unique in that it is a show about an African

American family which has also achieved a large and loyal following amongst white Americans and its star, Bill Cosby, is reputed to be the highest paid television comedy actor in America.

The paradox of *The Cosby Show*'s success is, how can a show about wealthy African Americans become so popular with white Americans at a time when racial tensions in America are on the increase? Surely there is a clear contradiction between white America's past (and continuing) discriminatory treatment of black communities on the one hand and the popularity of *The Cosby Show* over the past decade on the other, a show moreover which contains none of the more common racist stereotypes which have usually guaranteed popularity with white audiences? There are two broad ways that commentators have deconstructed *Cosby* and which are essentially polarized positions. On the one hand is the favourable response which sees the normalization of black family life through the show as a brave and progressive step forward (cf. Hartsbough, 1989). The opposite view is that the Huxtables are fantasy figures, masquerading as 'ordinary' people and therefore denying the reality of racism and oppression which is the normal and routine experience of most African Americans.

The history of black media images in both Europe and America has been largely stereotypical, racist and derogatory so the portrayal of a successful, affluent African American family which eschews the safe stereotypes for a more risky 'normality' can be seen, to some extent, to hail a significant victory for the liberal left. The show allows black and white audiences alike to relate to the Huxtables, perhaps even aspire to their lifestyle. Its narrative emphasis has always been on describing and inculcating good American family values: teaching the younger members the difference between right and wrong, respecting Dad and listening to Mom. The great trick was to show that African Americans as well as whites believed in these values, to encourage all members of the audience to relate to *Cosby* characters as daughters, sons, mothers and fathers in a story where ethnicity is of little importance. It was clear from the start that the show's portrayal of the Huxtables as an ordinary American family was never a remotely representative portrait of the lives of African Americans. The saccharine sweetness of Huxtable family discourse never acknowledges racism, never mentions poverty, never speaks of violence, drugs or police brutality and its overt message of wholesome, *American* values subverts any positive non-stereotypical effects the show might have. Indeed, the happy, smiling positive images can be seen as grossly counterproductive since they peddle the myth that hard work will bring its own rewards so that under-achievers have only themselves to blame. Cosby's comic vision repackages the egalitarian beliefs of the Pilgrim fathers so that cries of 'racism' then become an excuse for laziness, because if Cosby can do it, and he's black, then so can all the rest. The fact that Bill Cosby/Cliff Huxtable are one and the same and that Bill Cosby, the person, is enormously wealthy in his own right, proves the point even more since it's not just acting, it's for real.

> As long as all blacks were represented in demeaning or peripheral roles, it was possible to believe that American racism was, as it were, indiscriminate. The social vision of 'Cosby' however, reflecting the minuscule integration of blacks into the upper middle class, reassuringly throws the blame for black poverty back onto the impoverished. (Gates, 1989 cited in Lewis, 1991: 160)

As America again witnessed race riots in the early 1990s provoked by the brutal police beating of Rodney King in Los Angeles and the controversial court case which followed, the disparity between the privileged lifestyle enjoyed by the Huxtables and the lived experiences of real African America becomes more extreme. While a programme devised to sit squarely within the sitcom genre cannot at the same time be expected to behave as if it were documentary, the conspicuous lack of any discussion of race and racism in a series about black family life is a naive omission, although it is easy to see why such a device is used if the target audience for the show is white. Forcing white viewers to face up to their complicity in continuing to keep African Americans at the bottom of the ladder would clearly be commercial suicide. Suggesting that black people can achieve the American dream allows white America off the hook of racism, relieving them of the burden of their history, flattering to deceive.

Although *Cosby*'s shortcomings may be considerable, particularly the way it functions as almost an apologia for an inherently racist system, its refusal to rely on stereotypical characterizations for its humour enables the show to be viewed with some sympathy. Downing, for example, argues that the cultural climate of conservatism militates against the production of any sort of black image, so that to have been good enough to leap this most basic discriminatory hurdle was in itself an achievement (1988). In addition, one of the great strengths of the show is that not only does it counter the more prevalent racist stereotypes of black communities, but it does so by showing black people as human beings (Dyson, 1993). It is also the case that while didactic messages about race/racism may be absent from the dialogue – most of the moral points relate to sexism rather than racism – black culture is quietly celebrated in subtle ways. The Huxtable children attend black colleges and complete assignments on black heroes. Significant points in black history, such as the Civil Rights movement and the shooting of Martin Luther King have been introduced into the narrative at various points. When the eldest Huxtable daughter, Sondra, decides to name her children Nelson and Winnie, the reference is obvious.

The Huxtables are sanitized and safe, providing no threat and issuing no challenge and the show has received significant praise. Hoggart comments that the widow of Martin Luther King said of the programme '[it is] the most positive portrayal of black family life that has ever been broadcast . . . it is inspiring to see a black family that has managed to escape the violence of poverty through education and unity (Coretta Scott King cited in *The Listener*, 31.3.1988). But Real usefully summarizes the programme's internal contradictions, arguing that in its general implications, *Cosby* functions to 'resolve' America's racial failures by successfully recoding *black* in positive terms and therefore countering a history of negative stereotyping (1989). But at the same time, the show ignores other problems and solutions by its selection of particular storylines, thereby subordinating real social conflict and its potential resolution to the economic demands of the mainstream populist TV format. *The Cosby Show*, notwithstanding its limitations, does provide a significant landmark in the history of black images but the price has been very high.

> We cannot blame Bill Cosby for playing by the rules of network television. Only by conforming to . . . cultural limitations [portraying the Huxtables as upper middle-class] was he able to make a black family so widely acceptable – and respected – among the majority of TV viewers (who are white). The consequence of this intervention, however, this 'readjustment of the rules' to include black people is to foster damaging delusions. Television, having confused people about class, becomes incomprehensible about race. (Jhally & Lewis, 1992: 135)

In Britain, other types of 'black' humour were broadcast in the 1980s such as *No Problem!* (London Weekend Television 1983–5), *Tandoori Nights* (Channel 4, 1985 and 1987) and *Desmonds* (Channel 4, 1988–94). Although all these series have been quite popular and have run for a second season in most cases, none of them has approached the phenomenal success of *The Cosby Show*. As shows like *No Problem!*

have got cheap laughs from parodying and parading aspects of African Caribbean life, the Asian community has been exposed to similar ridicule in so-called comedy series like *Tandoori Nights*. This latter series was written by Farrukh Dhondy who was also co-writer on *No Problem!* and centres on the goings-on at a local Indian restaurant, The Jewel in the Crown, and its rival establishment, The Far Pavilions. Whilst the naming of these eateries is obviously Dhondy's little joke, there is precious else funny about the series. It would be slightly more acceptable for Dhondy to insist that comedy should not be subordinated to mere soapbox, if his subsequent effort at comedy writing actually hit the mark. All the usual stereotypes are there for our enjoyment, including the grasping and unscrupulous restaurant owner whose keen desire to become 'acceptable' includes dating white women; the excruciatingly servile would-be waiter desperate for a job; and the bumptious Indian film star expecting fainting maidens at every turn. This is ethnicity as farce.

One of the few British comedy series to have received almost universal acclaim has been *Desmonds* (Channel 4) which completed a fourth series at the end of 1994. The show won the Best Channel 4 Sitcom award in 1992 and the series producer, Humphrey Barclay, attributed its success to the warm and friendly atmosphere of the family (cited in *The Voice*, 15.12.92). As this chapter has amply demonstrated, scriptwriters' interest in 'the family' as a site of normalization seems never-ending and is again in evidence with the framing of the Ambrose clan as a happy (and intact) family unit with only the most pedestrian of 'problems' allowed to intrude on familial bliss. In more recent series, however, the typically domestic narratives have been occasionally interrupted by more political observations, usually delivered by the eponymous Desmond himself. Unfortunately, these reflective pieces do not ring true because political discourse has not been a constant theme within previous series, so although these orations are pithy and pertinent in themselves, they do not sit comfortably in Desmond's mouth.

Humour has been particularly successful in challenging stereotypical images in the area of British-based alternative comedy with personalities such as Lenny Henry, Ben Elton, Harry Enfield and black troupes such as the Bibi Crew, They Wouldn't and The Posse all performing counter-cultural routines. Shows such as *Spitting Image, Saturday Night Live, The Comedy Store, The Real McCoy* and *Get up, Stand up*, have done much to highlight and explore issues of racism and sexism. Although new stereotypes have sometimes emerged as a consequence, they have not carried the same weight of invective and hostility which pervaded their predecessors. Lenny

Henry in particular has been a controversial figure in television and his detractors claim that he often reinforces negative stereotypes of black people by the various caricatures which constitute his stock-in-trade. The character of 'Delbert Wilkins' as a loud and brash entrepreneur has angered critics who suggest that Henry is simply pandering to the stereotypical images that white people have of the black community, with associations of criminal activity, sharp clothes and a pseudo-'black' linguistic style. But does Delbert represent the same old clownish stereotype or a fresh and witty representation of black British identity as understood by whites? (Mercer, 1990c). Henry himself has countered his critics by saying that he is attempting to show the ludicrous nature and pernicious effect of such stereotypes. He has branched out into production and his company, Crucial Films, produces *The Real McCoy*. At the beginning of 1994, Crucial produced a series of 10-minute dramas for BBC2, including one written by and featuring Henry, which showcased black writers and went under the generic title of *Funky Black Shorts*. He has also begun to work in other comedic forms and in 1993, starred in a new sitcom, *Chef!* in the lead role, modelled on a composite of the new wave of visible and risible chefs who have become the enfants terribles of the food world. Whilst Henry acknowledges his comedy roots in the traditional stand-up (racist and sexist) comedy routines of the 1970s, his 1993 tour, *Loud*, was an attempt to demonstrate that both he and his work have evolved into more consciously black territory. As if to underline his new black awareness, Henry presented a South Bank Show special in 1994, journeying through America to find the roots of African American comedy. The subsequent programme, *Darker Than Me*, broadcast in February 1994, was Henry's homage to stars such as Richard Pryor, Dick Gregory and Redd Foxx and the programme also looked at the work of more contemporary artists such as Thea Vidale and Keenan Ivory Wayans. Personal interviews intercut with archive footage successfully showed the pain and humiliation which underlies much black humour as a consequence of the ubiquity of racism. While *Darker Than Me* is less formally 'entertaining' than his previous effort, *Lenny Henry Hunts the Funk*, and lacks some of Henry's wit, it exemplifies the emerging requirement that Henry wants to be taken seriously.

If British comedy shows such as *The Real McCoy* are still being gentle with their caricatures of black British life, the show's American counterpart and forerunner, *In Living Color*, pulls no such punches. Whereas *The Real McCoy* is still reticent about knocking black heroes, *In Living Color* spares no one and is fearlessly offensive

(Jivani, 1991). For example, Sammy Davis Jnr was shown singing *The Mandy Man*, a spoof song about Nelson Mandela, and another sketch featured Mike Tyson and his then girlfriend, Robin Givens, as a mismatched couple on a blind-date game show. The producer of the show, Keenan Ivory Wayans justifies his burning of sacred cows by suggesting that the more people know about you, the less afraid they are. That the show is popular is not in doubt and it picked up an Emmy award for outstanding comedy show in 1991, but popular with whom and at what cost? Wayans argues that popular shows such as *Saturday Night Live* have been satirizing black stars for many years but from only one perspective and what his series offers is a whole range of different views (Wayans cited in Rense, 1991). For Wayans, the fact that he is a black producer means that he instinctively 'knows' the bounds of acceptability when it comes to lampooning black heroes:

> Now for the first time, you have black creators behind works that represent black people. So when it's coming from the source, you don't have to worry about the criticisms and uproars from the community. I know what's offensive. I know how far to go . . . I have the pulse of the folks that I'm having fun with. (Wayans cited in Rense, 1991: 33)

For Wayans, humour is what is important and the fact that the community might be offended is secondary to his insistence that raising a laugh never hurt anyone and that indeed his targets should be flattered that they are well-known enough to warrant caricature. That he is the self-appointed arbiter of what is offensive and what is not offensive to the black community would not be so important if his show was one of many black satirical comedies on prime-time US television rather than being the only one. Whilst black performers should no more be censored than their white counterparts, it is naive of Wayans to suggest that he can constitute a fair barometer of black opinion simply because he *is* black. It would be more honest of him to say that he will caricature anyone and do a sketch of any situation if it raises a laugh and encourages a larger audience. Responding to a question relating to his (unintentional) reinforcement of racial prejudice amongst whites, Wayans suggests that 'My intentions are not to give those people [racists] something to gloat over, just to do this parody and hope it will be funny to people with the right sense of humor' (Wayans quoted in Rense, 1991: 36). His concern for offence is exemplified when he says of himself and his co-writers 'We certainly don't aim to reinforce any stereotypes, but I don't think we worry that much about it: we worry about what's funny' (Wayans quoted in Rense, 1991: 37).

Soapbox

The most popular (in terms of viewing figures) genre in television is arguably the soap opera and every week across Britain and America, the top-rated slots are dominated by soaps. Despite the 'realist' philosophy which underpins soaps, including the glitzy *Dallas* and *Dynasty* which purported a realism of their own, very few soaps have introduced significant black characters into their main narratives. On the British scene, a producer and writer for the extremely popular *Coronation Street* explained that the reason the series had hitherto excluded significant black characters had been because of the problems which would be created for storylines.

> We would . . . be forced to put unhelpful comments into the mouths of fictional men and women who command a wide following among the serial's millions of viewers with potentially dangerous effect.
> (Harry Kershaw quoted in Daniels and Gerson (eds) 1989: 121–2)

It is difficult to imagine what kinds of dangerous effect might be envisaged unless the assumption is that *Street* characters would, by their very nature, make racist or otherwise derogatory remarks about minority groups. While it is true that most soaps, including now defunct examples such as *Crossroads*, have regularly introduced black characters into storylines, they have mostly been fleeting and specific to particular situations. It is also true that the same actors stay on the soap circuit, being reinvented as the standard stern Asian father, the dutiful Asian mother, the rebellious black teenager and so on in a never-ending cycle of typecasting. *EastEnders'* producer Julia Smith reports having made a conscious decision that when the new soap was launched, it would be a working-class series which would reflect the cultural diversity of the *real* East End. The soap began broadcasting in the autumn of 1984 amid a welter of publicity for this new, home-grown soap which was the BBC's answer to Channel 4's successful *Brookside*. Smith claimed that the series would deal with controversial topics and would be 'drama which could encompass stories about homosexuals, rape, unemployment, racial prejudice, etc. in a believable context . . . we had a Bengali shopowner, a Jewish doctor and

Caribbean father and son, a Turkish Cypriot cafe-owner married to an English girl' (Smith quoted in Buckingham, 1987: 16). Five years later, all the original black and minority characters had left the series, some in the glare of publicity. The African Caribbean actor Judith Jacobs who starred as Carmel is quoted as saying,

> I've been so deeply offended and angered by the way EastEnders scriptwriters have treated black people that I was prepared to pack my job up if they refused to make the changes I asked for. (Jacobs quoted in *News of the World*, 19.6.1988)

Shreela Ghosh who played downtrodden wife Naima Jaffrey left the cast in 1987 and also made critical comments about the soap for its placement of her character as the eternal outsider and the cynical use that Julia Smith made of the soap's multiculturalism: 'I keep playing scenes week in, week out which have no substance . . . in one scene . . . I come into the launderette and Pauline's supposed to show me how to use a washing machine. I haven't just stepped off the boat, for chrissakes! We're a political football for Julia Smith, a trump card over all the soaps' (Ghosh cited in Daniels and Gerson (eds), 1989: 128). But despite the shortcomings of most soaps on British television, *EastEnders* and *Brookside* at least try to represent black communities in ways which are not simply ciphers and when black characters and even entire families leave the series, they are usually replaced with a different mix of black characters quite quickly. The genre of soap dictates that relationships flourish and fail, marriages begin and end, characters come and go, because soaps demand an internal dynamic which constantly confronts the viewers with new situations and new people. Flagging interest can be revived with a judicious injection of disaster, intrigue, marriage, infidelity or murder. The dynamics of change are only really successful when viewed against a background of constancy. The majority of (white) soap characters are ordinary and often dull, and sometimes disastrous things happen to them, but these events are countered by the relentless mundanity of their existence otherwise and by the stolid presence of the other cast members. The occasional forays into abnormal behaviour by some characters are overwhelmingly compensated for by the uneventful boredom of the lives of the majority. Such diversity of behaviour and occupation is not, however, the lot of the black characters, so each individual or family must bear the continual burden of representing their entire community at the whim of the writers' imagination.

In June 1991, the first British Asian soap – *Family Pride* – was broadcast, directed by David Vaughan-Thomas and produced by Central TV for Channel 4. The serial, originally conceived as a 26-parter to be broadcast twice a week, centred on the rivalry between two successful Asian families, the Bedis and Rizvis and was devised as an antidote to the stereotypical portraits of Asian life found in most other popular programmes. 'Our characters are mostly achievers . . . they are successful and relatively affluent, now they're looking at how best to provide for their children in a society which has come to accept the Asian input' (Zia Mohyeddin cited in Smurthwaite, 1991: 23). If this is a rather optimistic assessment of white Britain's response to Asian communities, the fact that an Asian soap was made at all is still noteworthy. The soap returned for a second run in December 1992 with the introduction of two new families, the Doshis and the Alis. The newcomers were less affluent than the original characters and presented a balance to counter the criticisms that Asian family life had been portrayed as unrealistically wealthy in the first run. There has been very little discussion of this groundbreaking soap, largely because many commentators simply failed to see the series. It was broadcast at 4.00 pm on weekday afternoons which is a time usually reserved for children's television and although it was not particularly controversial, its positioning in such an unfavourable slot in the schedule more or less guaranteed its invisibility. The reasoning behind commissioning the serial in the first place and then burying it in a slot where few people would watch it remains unclear.

Dramatic tensions

Peter Ansorge, Commissioning Editor for Drama at Channel 4, argues that the main complaint about the way in which black people are represented in drama is that minorities are usually placed in ghettos. 'The Asians are always in shops and the daughters have always got arranged marriages and the blacks are always about to mug people' (1989). However, the simple exercise of exchanging negative characters for positive ones will not necessarily achieve a better level of understanding since the viewer has to believe in the characters before she can be influenced by them. The dramatist has a role to play in suggesting how things ought to be but must at the same time acknowledge how things actually are. The 1980s saw a number of black artistes in plays and drama series acting in significant and sometimes leading roles. Some programmes appear to have consciously set out to create 'positive' black characters, for example, African Caribbean and Chinese police officers (*Wolcott*, Thames Television, 1981; *The Chinese Detective*, BBC1, 1981–2), an African Caribbean (male) barrister (*Black Silk*, BBC1, 1985) and an African Caribbean (female) private detective (*South of the Border*, BBC1, 1988). Though *South of the Border* and *Wolcott* had black lead characters, most appearances of black actors are in the more mundane roles of petty criminals, victims of crime and occasionally as police officers. While black villains are very much in evidence in ordinary crime series, if a black policeman is featured, he (and it usually is a he) is normally brought in to deal with the villainous black community, as in *Wolcott*. The criminalization of the black community thus undermines any positive image which might have accompanied the portrayal of a black person as law enforcer. 'The "realism" invoked in such drama of the black criminal milieu relies heavily on popular racist images of "black crime" which is represented in an unquestioned manner for dramatic effect' (Pines, 1989: 64). With a series like *Wolcott*, which has no black technical input other than the lead actor himself, the black hero conforms to white notions of blackness and appears synthetic and one-dimensional, a desperate attempt to show that black people are just like whites really. The producer of *Wolcott*, Jacky Stoller, suggests that drama can often influence attitudes to a greater extent than more straightforwardly factual works.

> I think that sometimes drama can educate more effectively than documentary. Certainly it has the opportunity to educate more people because its audience is wider. But it also has the facility to make people identify with characters from an alien and previously misunderstood group and that can lead to sympathy for the group. (Stoller quoted in the *Guardian*, 31.1.1981)

Stoller is correct to suggest that fictional programmes reach a larger audience than documentaries and therefore have the greater potential to inform, but it is arguable whether the white audience will readily identify with black actors, heroes or not. It is ironic that if black communities were misunderstood before *Wolcott* appeared on television, they were better understood as typified by villains and occasional police officers after it. As in other programme genres, the main difficulty with drama and specifically crime and police series is that of representativeness. Although it is obvious that both black and white people commit crime, it is the habitual casting of black people as villains in television fictions which perpetuates the black-as-criminal stereotype. Many crime series also use a variety of white stereotypes, but for the predominant white audience these stereotypes are recognized as caricature, something not afforded minority characterizations.

> We don't have to be . . . concerned about these (white) misrepresentations . . . because the majority of white viewers won't be fooled by them as easily. They have a wealth of certain knowledge that all whites are not like that. About blacks they know nothing but what they are told and what the camera shows them, interpreted through their ignorant fears and their racism. (Caesar et al., 1981: 82–3)

If Caesar et al.'s remarks can be considered a little sweeping, it is nonetheless true that the diversity of black experiences on mainstream TV is largely proscribed by the limited imagination of (white) writers which then encourages the continuation of racist imagery. However, the ethnicity of writers is no guarantee of acceptability as many black writers and producers have discovered. Hanif Kureishi has been heavily criticized by minority and mainstream audiences for his portrayal of homosexuality and corruption in the Asian community in two of his films which were later broadcast on Channel 4, *My Beautiful Laundrette* and *Sammy and Rosie Get Laid*. Farrukh Dhondy, Commissioning Editor for Multicultural Programmes at Channel 4, attracted considerable hostility for his drama serial *King of the Ghetto* (BBC2, 1986). Protests against this latter serial culminated in a demonstration outside BBC Television Centre by angry Bangladeshis claiming that the drama reinforced racist stereotypes through its portrayal of corrupt Asian businessmen. Again the difficulty with programmes of this kind lies in the tension between positive versus realistic characterization. Programmes which explore those aspects of community life which fall outside what is considered to be acceptable codes of behaviour are often condemned by a conservative audience. When the community under scrutiny also happens to be African Caribbean or Asian then such programmes are doubly attacked both for promoting (at least covertly) deviant behaviour but also fuelling the fires of racism whereby all black people are regarded as perverts/homosexuals/ criminals and so on. However, the criticisms of *King of the Ghetto* were not made by assimilated Asian communities anxious to reflect only positive images but by individuals who were exasperated at Dhondy's apparent hijacking of a community which he apparently spoke for but knew nothing about. Abdul Shukur of the Federation of Bangladeshi Youth Organisations argued quite pointedly that Dhondy, does not come from the community, and he doesn't understand it, which is why King of the Ghetto misrepresents us so badly. And why did he make us look so thick? In one scene, a Bangladeshi woman was being shown how to use a teapot. Bengal is one of the biggest tea-producing regions in the world. Don't you think a woman from there would *know* how to use a bloody teapot? (Shukur, quoted in the *Sunday Times*, 11.6.1986)

The burden of representativeness unfortunately afflicts much of the work originated by black authors and playwrights and Dhondy himself has argued on numerous occasions that it cannot be artisti-cally desirable, still less realistic, to expect black writers to proscribe or limit the activities of their characters in order to present them as always good, honest and conformist. Thus the artistic freedom and integrity of the writer is won at the cost of alienating some parts of the audience, but it was ever thus.

And so, to the 1990s

The 1990s have not brought forward any great innovation in the representation of black communities on television. This is not to say that black actors have been absent from the small screen and there has in fact been a marked increase in the number of black 'back-ground' or minor characters which now populate mainstream drama programmes. But it is to argue that there have been very few leading roles or series which have revolved around a black charac-ter in British drama so far this decade, although the Channel 4 series *Little Napoleons* was a notable exception. As with film, the most common way in which television includes black actors (outside comedy) is through the crime genre and this is true of both American and British television series, from *Miami Vice* to *Prime Suspect II*. Series which feature either police officers or private detec-tives invariably cast one or two professional characters as black, notwithstanding the usual gamut of black villains. Black characters in police dramas are either introduced as permanent members of the cast, such as in *The Bill* which has had three black officers including a black woman detective inspector (Sally Johnson played by Jaye Griffiths) or as temporary squad members, brought in for their first-hand knowledge of 'the black community'. But it should also be said that black media professionals are beginning to obtain a slightly more visible presence outside the restrictions of the crime genre. For example, hospital-based dramas and comedies have usu-ally recruited at least one black actor as a health care professional (see for example *Casualty, Surgical Spirit, Cardiac Arrest* and *e.r.*). Similarly, a number of current affairs and news programmes have become less self-conscious about recruiting black media personnel and now regularly feature black newscasters and presenters: Zenab Badawi on *Channel 4 News*; Carmen Pryce on *Tomorrow's World* (BBC1); Sankha Guha on *Here and Now* (BBC1); and of course veteran news presenters such as Connie Chang and Moira Stewart. Mainstream documentaries are also taking up 'black' themes as part of their routine fare and prestige documentary strands like *Arena* and *Without Walls* have, in 1994, been notable in this regard. The black filmmaker Isaac Julien presented *The Dark Side of Black* for *Arena* (BBC2) in February 1994, taking a critical look at rap lyrics and their misogynistic and homophobic sentiments; in March, the rapper Ice T introduced an exploration of the so-called blaxploitation movies of the 1970s for *Without Walls* (Channel 4); and *Extreme Asia* was a late-night programme, also on Channel 4, which examined modern youth culture across Asia, highlighting musicians, filmmakers, dancers and painters who are popular in their own countries but still largely unknown in the West.

However, it is arguable whether the representation of black communities is significantly 'better' now than it has been in the past or whether the climate of political correctness simply gives the appearance of being so. In March 1994, the first ever episode of the very popular *Minder*, originally screened in 1979, was shown again and it is salutary to note that, with an ear to the new 1990s sensibilities, the original episode was censored. An unidentified spokesperson for the show said that references to 'dopey spades' had been cut from the original because they were offensive, although no comment was made on how offensive the phrase might have been in 1979 (quoted in the *Today* programme, BBC Radio 4, 17.3.1994).

Watching the detectives

Notwithstanding the 'improvements' in images of black people in television over the past decade, the small amount of research which has been undertaken in the area of television and ethnic imagery suggests that while some gains have been made during the 1980s in terms of less offensive caricatures and more rounded characterizations, the picture of black communities is far from perfect. Between 1978 and 1979, Anwar and Shang carried out a monitoring study of British television and found that 22 per cent of actors were black (Anwar and Shang, 1982). Given that the black population in Britain is less than 5 per cent, this would seem, on the face of it, to be good news. But the point at issue is not about the volume of black characters but the roles they are assigned to play. Research undertaken by Barry in 1986 found that the three black stereotypes which she believed characterized black media portraits – trouble-maker, entertainer and dependant – still had currency in terms of television images and she concluded that 'on occasion [the myths] were . . . traces, but elsewhere, they continued to flourish just beneath the new skin of change' (Barry, 1988: 101). In another study, Ross found that during a monitoring exercise of prime-time television, none of the black characters had leading roles, none had strong leadership roles and few featured regularly in the series in which they appeared (Ross, 1992). Black characters tend to operate at the margins of the social world they inhabit, peripheral to the main storyline but adding a bit of realism to the scene, particularly if the social milieu is a deprived, inner-city area. The vast majority of black characters on television are forced to act with constant reference to their skin so that black actors are only allowed to play specifically defined 'black' characters. The notion of integrated casting, whereby black actors are simply cast in roles which are not defined as 'black' has long been argued for amongst black media practitioners and organizations such as Equity's Afro-Asian Committee but it still remains tantalizingly elusive.

On American television, a similar picture emerges, with black people more likely to appear in programmes about sport, entertainment and beauty. A number of American studies have highlighted the failure of television to reflect the diversity of black experiences. One investigation into television 'minorities' suggested that 20 per cent of characters covered during a monitoring exercise were black or ethnic minority (cited in the _Hollywood Reporter_, 7.2.1992) and this finding is remarkably similar to Anwar and Shang's more than a decade earlier (Anwar and Shang, 1982). The 1992 study, carried out for the Media Image Coalition of Minorities and Women evaluated 569 characters in 56 dramas and situation comedies across the main networks during October–November 1991. The proportion of African Americans was relatively high (17 per cent) but the study found that they were more likely to appear in comedies than drama. Another study, undertaken by the American Psychological Association, was a five-year project which concluded that a steady diet of television that misrepresents minorities and women while glorifying violence can lead to antisocial behaviour and a warped view of reality (cited in the _Hollywood Reporter_, 4.3.1992). While black people are rarely called in as experts on current affairs issues, they often feature both on American and British news programming, as

newscasters and reporters. Rapping suggests that black professionals are allowed to occupy these particular roles for two main
reasons: firstly, as symbols of the media's commitment to equal
opportunities; secondly, as news moves from the field of information to that of entertainment, appearance becomes more important than ability (Rapping, 1987). While the first reason is relatively
unproblematic, Rapping's second justification seems strange. Does
she mean that black people have achieved greater visibility in news
broadcasting because they are more attractive than their white
counterparts or that their lower abilities are compensated for by
their physical features? Ambiguity notwithstanding, the point being made is clear – black people who are allowed into the industry
are tolerated within carefully defined boundaries.

While the television industry has attempted to respond to discrimination in terms of access into the industry, such strategies still
constitute extremely tiny steps forward. Government agencies set
up to monitor and regulate broadcasting output, such as the Federal
Communications Commission in America and the Broadcasting
Standards Council in Britain, have signally failed to secure significant improvements in the representation of black people. Commenting on the FCC's attempts to 'promote racial diversity', Fife
argues that despite the apparently laudable aims of FCC policies,
they still emerge as being 'consistent with mainstream majority
cultural understanding about race and minority status in US
society . . . This society sees Black Americans as a minority race that
is subject to acculturation, rather than an integrated element that
participates as an equal in the formation of American culture' (1987:
497). Similarly, the BSC's 1992 report on the portrayal of 'ethnic
minorities' on television found that most (white) viewers believed
that the representation of black people on TV was generally satisfactory and more than half the survey respondents believed that programmes made specifically for 'ethnic minority' communities
should only be screened outside prime-time transmission hours
(Millwood Hargreave, 1992). Thus there is no real acceptance by the
majority culture that minority communities have an equal right to
see themselves, their interests and their concerns reflected by television programming and certainly not on prime time.

It is certainly the case that the incidence of black people on
television has increased throughout the 1980s but the reasons for
their greater visibility are likely to be rooted in economic imperatives rather than social consciousness. In America, the greater availability of black roles coincided with the emergence of a more
economically active black viewing population and the rise of a black

middle class which was becoming increasingly attractive to adver-
tisers (Atkin, 1992). Other commentators (see, for example, Tulloch,
1990; Cashmore, 1994) echo Atkin's sentiments and argue that the
sudden penetration of the industry by African Americans during
the 1980s, after decades of fruitless lobbying, was largely a consequence of an emerging black polity and a recognition by the industry of the purchasing power of the black audience. As McDonald
notes,

> In essence, improved African American representations in modern
> television is the result of a simple equation: first, there are more
> stations and consequently greater competition for viewers and
> profits; second, there are sizeable minority audiences, the most
> prominent of which is the black viewership, whose loyalty is now
> highly desirable; and third, each minority audience appreciates posi-
> tive depictions of itself on TV. (1992: 255)

But if the representation of black communities is better in the mid-
1990s than was the case in previous decades, the issue cannot be
said to be fully resolved. The more obvious and offensive stereotypes may well have been consigned to the dustbin of history, but
new and more subtle forms have taken their place. Some programme-makers appear to be using black images to demonstrate a
more contemporary 'take' on the subject under discussion (Daniels,
1990) so that the inclusion of black presenters or experts now demonstrates a programme producer's right-on credentials. But if the
range and diversity of roles available to black performers in television has undoubtedly increased over the past decade and black
comedy programmes such as *In Living Color* and *Desmonds* are
appreciated for both their humour and their witty social commentary, are they enough? And more importantly, do such 'positive'
shows gloss over or ignore the true condition of black and ethnic
minority communities in the real world. Both these shows and the
definitive *Cosby* present fictions of black people in almost exclusively black milieu, untainted by the terrifying realities of racism and
discrimination. As Jhally and Lewis point out 'the social success of
black TV characters in the wake of The Cosby Show does not reflect
a trend towards black prosperity in the big, wide world beyond
television' (1992: 132). On the contrary, black communities in both
Britain and America are no further forward and more overt forms of
racism, both structural and personal, are increasing. The cosy colour-blind and class-unconscious world of television peddles the
myth of the American way, the work ethic and honest family
values.

Norman Beaton who played the eponymous barber in *Desmonds* admits that the show is really 'where we ought to be at, if we're playing light comedy [but] not where we ought to be, if we're talking about the seriousness of our lives' (Beaton in Pines (ed.), 1992: 118). The point is that black people and comedy have always been inextricably linked and if shows like *Fresh Prince of Bel Air*, *A Different World* and *Desmonds* are perhaps a more authentic entertainment because they are written by black writers for a black cast, they are still located within the comedy genre. Where are the black dramas, the black soaps, the black thrillers? Where are the representations of anything approximating real life for black communities on both sides of the Atlantic?

> There are very serious black people about, but those roles are not being written. This is either because the white man does not understand where black people are coming from and, therefore, doesn't know how to write about black people; or it's because we black people don't have the confidence in our own existence and destiny, so are not writing that kind of material for ourselves. (Beaton in Pines (ed.), 1992: 118)

But of course Beaton has missed a more fundamental point in his analysis which is that it is less a problem of black writers not creating material so much as black writers being unable to get their scripts accepted. Much black talent is thwarted by the invisible but very real phenomenon of the 'one only' syndrome which demands that only one black comedy/drama/soap programme can be broadcast at a time. So, while *Desmonds* is an excellent series, it is not broadcast at the same time as, say, *The Real McCoy*, which is another black comedy series, although very different in style. Similarly, where the cops and robbers series *The Bill* has introduced a black woman detective, no other crime series includes black women as professionals, although they all consistently feature black people as criminals and victims rather than ordinary members of the public going about their business. One of the newer writers on *Desmonds*, Joan Hooley, who is herself an actor, suggests that although black characterizations are more diverse than in the past, and soaps do feature more authentic black families: 'the writing and what black artists are expected to do in these programmes is still very stilted' (Hooley, in Pines (ed.) 1992: 101). Echoing Beaton's sentiments, Hooley asserts that black writers themselves must start making demands for their work to be recognized and valued, but in order for this to be effective, recognition needs to be made that a problem exists: it is precisely this next step that the industry has so far failed to take. It is salutary to consider that the distinguished career of one of the few African Caribbean actors who was constantly in work in Britain was cut prematurely short by Beaton's untimely death in December 1994, weeks after he was told that *Desmonds* was being dropped from the schedule to make way for new material. Where is it?

5

Minority Interests: British Television and the Multicultural Agenda

I . . . speak within this historic enclave, because, hidden by the dim mists of history, there is also the reality that, from here, there issued decisions which imposed on my own country and people a condition of existence which condemned us, as South Africans, to seek to resolve our conflicts not through peaceful means but by other than peaceful means. Your right to determine your own destiny was used to deny us to determine our own.

Nelson Mandela addressing the British Parliament

In December 1953, black viewers were formally addressed by television as a discreet viewing entity and given their first show, *Asian Club*. The programme which began life as a radio broadcast was televised because it was thought that the vitality of the people and their clothes would make attractive television (Daniels, 1992). The show was structured in the form of a debate between an Asian studio audience (consisting largely of 'professional' people) and an invited Asian speaker, although the ethnicities included under the inclusive term 'Asian' were considerably more fluid then than now. Interestingly, the programme's content did not confine itself to the discussion of exclusively Asian themes but rather debated a wide range of topics including literature, science and politics. In this sense, the programme was more innovative, flexible and non-problem oriented than many of the discussion and magazine format programmes which have followed.

The specific needs of black viewers were thought to be largely linguistic and related to information about integrating successfully into British society. Programmes such as *Apna Hi Char Samajhiye*, which began broadcasting in 1965 was an English language educational series and together with programmes such as *Nai Zindage*

Naya Jeevan, was less about giving black communities a voice and more concerned with providing a service (Daniels, 1994). As a result of pressure from black media practitioners through organizations such as the *Equity Coloured Artists Committee* and the *Campaign Against Racism in the Media*, programmes for black audiences began to move from the regional to the national stage in the late 1970s and early 1980s (see, for example, Cohen and Gardner, 1982). The demands which emerged from black communities and campaigning organizations related to issues of poor representation and lack of access to the means of media production. Public service broadcasting, so-called, became the target for dissatisfaction and viewed as part of the same oppressive structure which operated against black autonomy in the real world. Although there was a marginal visibility of black performers on television, black practitioners working on the other side of the camera were almost entirely absent and there were very few opportunities for programme-makers who wished to make a more radical assessment of black issues.

If the BBC had been broadcasting programmes for Asian viewers in mother tongue languages (usually Hindustani) for a number of years, the late 1970s saw the independent ATV produce three films in 1978–9 under the generic title of *Here Today, Here Tomorrow* which provided realistic portraits of what it was like to be Asian in Britain at that time. These three shows were presented by Zia Mohyeddin, an actor turned presenter, and built up an incisive portrait of black Britain including the insistence on the part of the Asian participants that despite their negative experiences, they were determined to stay (Robinson, 1985). The reception of these films was sufficiently enthusiastic for Central TV to agree to broadcast a weekly 'multicultural' programme – *Here and Now* – also hosted by Mohyeddin. In the same year (1979), London Weekend Television (LWT) broadcast *Babylon*, a six-part serial aimed at young black people and hosted by Lincoln Browne. The series looked at the experiences of and problems affecting 'second generation' black British people who, as far as Browne was concerned, were an entirely different constituency to their migrant parents because they had greater expectations. 'We're putting the emphasis on saying what's possible, what can be done using your own methods to solve your own problems' (Browne, 1979). A year later in 1980, with John Birt running factual programmes at LWT, the Channel set up the London Minorities Unit (LMU) in response to the Birtian view that all television audiences are a minority because no programme is watched by a majority of the public and that television should begin to address minority concerns instead of remaining obsessed with

the mythical mass audience. 'The London Minority Unit's programmes are neither exclusively by or for their particular communities (although they are in part both these things) but they are
emphatically about these communities' (Birt, 1980). Birt considered
that some minorities were being less well catered for than others,
including young people, the gay community and black people, and
the LMU began producing *Skin* and *Gay Life* in 1980. The way in
which television responded (and in fact continues to respond) to the
supposed needs of black communities must be understood in the
specific historical context in which they originated, in this case, a
policy atmosphere which was dominated by the race-relations
issue. It is also true that these new discursive spaces were opened
up to the black community because independent television companies were changing the structure of their schedules in the run-up to
the franchise reallocations in 1980. For a London-based company
such as LWT, the decision to fill off-peak slots with programmes
which would resonate with Londoners' experiences would be related to a consideration of the future programming needs of the
capital's black populations.

Skin was a 30-minute magazine series designed for a black audience but also aiming to attract passing white interest and was probably one of the most important of LMU's broadcasts since it
addressed the largest and most significant minority group in
London at that time (T. Phillips, 1992). Whilst *Skin* was criticized
from the very start for its low production values, amateurish presentation and lack of balance (see, for example, Gardner and Merck,
1980) the very existence of a programme targeted specifically at the
black community meant that at least some of the criticisms about
television's preoccupation with white, male, middle-class values
were being addressed (Gilbert, 1981). However, the documentary
format as well as the formulaic style of the series in which each
programme would be built round a particular issue (problem) encouraged an overriding preoccupation with examining black–white
relations.

> I think that was a problem . . . because it meant that the agenda for
> *Skin* was constantly about conflict between the races. But we had to
> do that because the programmes had to be of interest to both blacks
> and whites, and the dominant characteristic of the relationship be-
> tween blacks and whites at that time was one of conflict. So that gave
> the series a slightly unhappy, whining feel. (T. Phillips, 1992: 147)

The deliberate appeal of *Skin* to a crossover audience led to considerable tension within the series, with self-evident truths (for

black people) laboriously articulated for the benefit of (the imagined) white viewers whose experience of racism and discrimination would be nil. The fact that the series collapsed the interests of
both African Caribbean and Asian communities into one and
treated them as the same not only led to problems of viewer identification but also meant that black minorities only became visible in
relation to the white majority, that minorities only existed when
considered against the majority (white) culture. Such an orientation
necessarily resulted in programmes which emphasized only the
problematic aspects of being black in Britain and an unhelpful and
restrictive focus which viewed racism as the only defining feature of
life for Britain's black diaspora communities. The small amount of
research which was undertaken at the time with black viewers suggested that although the audience enjoyed 'minority' programmes,
they also wanted to see a greater diversity of topics covered (Anwar,
1978) and the focus on race and racism in many programmes was
clearly cause for concern. Although Anwar's study looked at 1970s
television, minority programming strands remain guilty of playing
to largely the same preoccupations now as then.

   While most commentators were fundamentally in favour of a
programming strand which responded to the particular interests of
Britain's black communities, the very notion of 'ethnic' programmes
was attacked by some media watchers because of its potential for
division. The critic and newspaper correspondent Chris Dunkley
was highly sceptical about the value of minority programmes, describing them as 'benign fascism' (cited in *Broadcast*, 2.12.1982).
Dunkley's main worry was that such programming strands produced a kind of 'cultural apartheid', but this fear could only be
expressed by someone whose own viewing needs were being satis-
factorily fulfilled and who takes a somewhat naive view of a happy
and harmonious multicultural society. It is entirely inappropriate
for Dunkley to liken black broadcasting to apartheid or fascism and
demonstrates the myopia invoked by his privileged position as a
white, middle-class male.

Competing for the black viewer

In response to the development of Channel 4 in 1982 with its remit
for innovation, the BBC developed a new series, *Ebony*. Where the
BBC's pre-existing 'multicultural' programme, *Asian Magazine*, had
always occupied a ghetto slot, often broadcast at unpopular times
during the weekend schedule, the new series had a much higher

profile and was also supported by a level of financial and human resource which was unprecedented for a minority programme series, although it was still extremely modest compared with the budgets allowed for other mainstream series. *Ebony* was also trans-mitted when the potential viewing audience was actually awake, unlike its Channel 4 counterparts, *Black on Black* and *Eastern Eye* which, going out at 10.50 pm on Tuesday nights, catered for a very exclusive sub-group – African Caribbean and Asian insomniacs (Anderson, 1988). Like *Asian Magazine, Ebony* also had a magazine format and went out as a 30-minute programme every two weeks. When the *Ebony* team moved from Bristol to Birmingham at the beginning of 1985, they became part of the general programmes unit at Pebble Mill. Derek Nelson, an original member of the *Ebony* production team, argues that before *Ebony* was set up, the black community felt distanced from the BBC by the lack of black images on mainstream television and part of *Ebony*'s function was to begin to break down viewer alienation (Nelson, 1985). Two years later *Asian Magazine* which had been broadcast in mother tongue languages was replaced by a new magazine-style programme, *Net-work East*, broadcast only in English. Members of Asian organiza-tions in Scotland made national news when this programme change was announced, threatening to withhold their TV licence fee if *Asian Magazine* was not immediately reinstated. They didn't and it wasn't. In 1989, the *Ebony* production team became the African Caribbean Programmes Unit (ACPU) and, together with the Asian Pro-grammes Unit, comprised the BBC's response to meeting the pro-gramming needs of Britain's black communities.

It was also in 1989 that the Mosaic project was launched as a five-year BBC TV Continuing Education and Training Initiative. The project was concerned with examining discrimination against mem-bers of 'visible' minority groups and identifying appropriate strat-egies which would establish equal opportunities for such groups and also aimed to respond to Britain's cultural diversity (Mosaic publicity literature, 1993). Although all the programmes were aimed at a general audience, they incorporated a strong educative element to enable their use as training materials by teachers, trainers and community groups. The project produced a number of anti-racist training programmes which have been accompanied by print mate-rials and also broadcast the *Black and White Media Shows* (1 and 2) and *Racism and Comedy*, both of which explored issues of race and racism in the media. The programmes and videos which were spe-cifically produced for education broadcasting included titles on topics such as equal opportunities at work, racial harassment, the

Children Act and attitudes to Islam. This latter video was supplemented by a six-part series – *Living Islam* – which was broadcast on prime-time television and, like other titles in the Mosaic project, sought to provide a counter to the generally negative views about Islam. Other Mosaic programmes which have been concerned with exploring the richness of Britain's cultural diversity have been broadcast under the *Birthrights* heading and there have been three series of *Birthrights*, one series broadcast during the summer schedule each year since 1991. Each of the six programmes which made up any one series were produced by different black independent film companies so that each took a fresh and individual perspective. Not only did this enable a variety of views to be screened but also provided crucial access to emerging black media talent. Where *Birthrights* programmes differed fundamentally from others broadcast under the 'black programming' banner was in their refusal to engage with the race relations problematic looking instead at the great variety of 'other' black stories, for example black MPs (*Honourable Members*, 1991) wealth distribution in Asian and African Caribbean communities (*Black Gold*, 1992) and the role of black women in the war effort (*Reunion*, 1993). Although all three series have included programmes which have looked at black–white relations – for example, the 1993 series included one programme on dual heritage children (*The Colour of Love*) and another looking at cultural fusions narrated by Benjamin Zephaniah (*Crossing the Tracks*) – they have managed to avoid the ubiquitous 'black as victim' scenarios. (This latter programme won the Commission for Racial Equality's 1993 Race in the Media Award for best current affairs programme.) Instead, these programmes have focused on the diverse experiences of Britain's black communities and looked at the positive ways in which black individuals and communities enrich the cultural life of Britain, notwithstanding the external pressures of racism and discrimination which regularly inflect their lives.

From 1989, with a change of Managing Editor (Colin Prescod taking over from Vastiana Belfon), the BBC's African Caribbean Programmes Unit began to cut loose from the magazine format imposed by *Ebony* and started to produce different kinds of black programmes. *On the Road* was the first new series to emerge from ACPU in 1989 and allowed individual black people to tell their own stories of life in British cities. The series broke with the tradition of the studio-based discussion items and described the lives of black Britons in a more direct, accessible and realistic way than was possible within the confines of the studio. *On the Road* mixed individual narratives with local culture and music, providing a dynamic and vibrant picture of black community life. *Black on Europe* used the same idea of articulating individual stories which had become so successful in *On the Road*, but took the show to Europe. *Ebony People* and *Hear Say* were both studio-based talk shows which followed the tradition set down by *Ebony*. The *South Africa under the Skin* series comprised six programmes which investigated the diverse experiences of black people living in South Africa and, like *On the Road*, sought to make sense of the larger political context of that country by focusing on the experiences of individuals living within it.

In 1992, ACPU produced the *Out of Darkness* series, a six-parter looking at the changing circumstances in six African countries and this highly acclaimed series became the final one for ACPU which was dissolved later in that year. In November 1992 the African Caribbean Programmes Unit and the Asian Programmes Unit were disbanded and were replaced by the single Multicultural Programmes Department (MPD). The move was, notionally, a result of the BBC's anxiety about apparently privileging the programming needs of the Asian and African Caribbean communities in Britain at the expense of the needs of those other minority communities which are also a part of multicultural Britain. Interestingly, however, since its inauguration, the Department continues to produce *Network East* (targeted at the Asian community) and in 1993–4 its output included a programme on the Notting Hill Carnival, two series of a current affairs strand looking at issues in the African Caribbean community in Britain (*All Black*) and a series on African Caribbean sport stars (*Will to Win*). It remains to be seen whether, in subsequent years, the output of the MPD will indeed extend to programmes on other minority communities: currently (1995), the Department does not have a regular weekly slot scheduled for its output other than a sub-titled Hindi soap on Saturday mornings.

After Scarman

Following closely behind the BBC initiative to set up specific minority programme units came the launch of Channel 4 with its remit to provide programmes catering for a diversity of minority interests. The underlying rationale for providing a channel geared towards minority audiences was complex but was partly a result of political tensions at the time – for example, the 1981 riots – and partly in response to the growing frustration of independent production

companies which wanted both access to television and also control
over their material and were unable to achieve either because of the
stranglehold exerted by the BBC and ITV network (Seaton, 1991).
For the first time a major channel had instituted a policy which was
openly geared towards creating new access opportunities into the
industry. The potential was there for black media practitioners to
finally get a foot in the door of the industry with the Annan Report
on the future of broadcasting arguing that the new fourth channel's
output must be substantially different to that which was currently
being offered by the BBC and the independent sector (Annan, 1977).
That the new channel would be a commissioning rather than a
producing channel fuelled further hopes that the way would be
clear for the involvement of media practitioners who were outside
the usual mould of white, middle-class male. That the channel had
black programming built into its structure from the very beginning
inevitably meant that it would be the focus of considerable and
possibly unrealistic expectations. The appointment of the first ever
commissioning   editor   for   multicultural   programmes   (Sue
Woodford) was a significant milestone in the history of black programming, but when Woodford promptly commissioned London
Weekend Television rather than a black production company to
produce the department's two new multicultural series, *Black on
Black* and *Eastern Eye*, there were immediate denunciations of the
channel's hypocrisy. The producers of these two programmes,
Trevor Phillips and Samir Shah, who had both previously worked
on LWT's *Skin* dismissed their critics, arguing that only an experienced production team with sufficient resources would be able to
deliver the kind of programmes envisaged. Woodford, for her part,
insisted that a lack of experienced black media practitioners was the
only reason that a white production company was being commissioned to produce black programmes (1983). But her argument
falls a little flat since even in the early 1980s, the Black Media
Workers' Association Book included numerous entries from professionals experienced and trained in all aspects of media production.
Phillips and Shah were keen to avoid the shortcomings of *Skin* by
ensuring that *Black on Black* and *Eastern Eye* would adopt specific
cultural perspectives which would resonate with their intended
audiences. The crucial change would be away from a format which
collapsed all minorities into one and tried to explain black people to
whites – the *Skin* formula – towards providing programmes *for*, not
about black and ethnic minority communities. Trevor Phillips suggested that he wanted to get away from an unrelenting focus on
black–white relations and move towards an exploration of black

people's lives and interests which did not necessarily include issues of racism:

> the dominant consideration in my mind was that the programmes had to be about our community's experience speaking in its own terms. They were not about explaining 'us' to white people. They were not primarily about our conflict or our relationship with white people. They were about our lives, part of which was to do with relationships with other people, but a lot more was to do with the things we were interested in, such as our art, music, the places we came from, where our ancestors came from, and so on. (1992: 149)

The result of such considerations was the development of two distinctive series and a move from the single-issue documentary format of *Skin* to a more diverse magazine-style programme, where serious items and lighter stories could be fused into a single 30-minute session. Acknowledging the heterogeneity of different black communities instead of seeing black Britons as sharing identical experiences, was part of the emerging trend of multiculturalism which had replaced the race relations problematic as the framework for understanding contemporary British society and through which appropriate policy responses would be developed. Unlike earlier integration and assimilation models, multiculturalism celebrated difference but still looked to education and an understanding of and between different cultures as the appropriate route out of racism. If we only got to know each other, we could all live together as one big happy multicultural family. Multiculturalism became the new anti-racism but, like all other policies which try to treat the symptom rather than the cause, the concept has now fallen out of favour, condemned as inadequate and superficial. The principles of multiculturalism however, such as the positive articulation of difference and an identification of different diaspora experiences, were enthusiastically incorporated into the programme structure of LWT's new strands. An overriding preoccupation with racism was replaced by a more diverse exploration of black community life. Samir Shah effectively took over the production of *Eastern Eye* and suggested that the experience of British Asians was much richer than problems over immigration and that a series geared towards this group had to reflect the community's own internal interests such as Indian film rather than externally imposed concerns (Shah, 1992). With *Black on Black*, the production team decided to use a black studio audience to give the programmes a more 'live' feel and encourage a sense of identity and solidarity between the programme and its intended black family audience. While it was expected that white people might want to watch some parts of the programme, the imagined audience was very definitely black, with the white audience being regarded as interested outsiders (T. Phillips, 1992).

A year after Farrukh Dhondy replaced Sue Woodford as commissioning editor for multicultural programmes at Channel 4 (in 1984) he decided not to recommission *Black on Black* or *Eastern Eye*. Dhondy, who came to Channel 4 as a fully-fledged writer and producer, did not believe that black communities could spontaneously produce media professionals, suggesting that good black investigative journalists, for example, had to be created rather than recruited, since such a profession was outside their usual experience (Dhondy, 1984). This rather harsh view of black talent has characterized Dhondy's stewardship of the department and has been the source of considerable disquiet among black writers and production companies who have complained about his gate-keeping proclivities, which enable only certain types of black project to be commissioned. Instead of retaining *Black on Black* and *Eastern Eye*, Dhondy approached a newly established black production company, *Bandung Productions*, run by his co-politicos Tariq Ali and Darcus Howe, to produce something different and *The Bandung File* subsequently became the Channel's pre-eminent black programme. The orientation of *The Bandung File* was precisely the same as *Skin* in that it claimed a 'Third World' perspective rather than any specific ethnic identity and as with *Skin*, this fusion of African Caribbean and Asian interests served to alienate some audiences. Dhondy stated, in defence of *Bandung* and its deliberate appeal to a wider audience, that once the public gets used to the idea that black people are a permanent part of the British population, then they will also get used to the fact that black people will be doing mainstream programmes (Dhondy, 1988). Dhondy argued that he was living up to the remit of Channel 4 by providing more work to black production companies and that he commissioned over thirty companies to produce programmes for the channel in his first year, notwithstanding his subsequent refusal to continue with *Black on Black* and *Eastern Eye*. Although *Bandung* was well received by some observers, it was regarded as rather too highbrow by many black viewers who had enjoyed the magazine-style format of the programmes which *Bandung* replaced (Daniels, 1994). In 1991, *Bandung* was replaced by *Black Bag* which has had a number of companies working on it and was intended to be a series devoted to investigative journalism, highlighting controversial issues facing African Caribbean and Asian communities. In the 1992 series, the subjects for programmes included the plight of Asian newsagents who were being unfairly treated by the big newsprint wholesalers, the traps involved in seeking asylum under the new Asylum Bill, the conversion of African Caribbean people to Islam and an examination of the elections then being carried out in the Punjab.

> *Black Bag* tries to fulfil a very specific purpose – namely to instigate investigative journalism which is fearless, to breed real investigative journalists rather than people looking for racism in every corner of British society. Again, we want to get away from grievance programming, though if there is a grievance and it can be well substantiated in investigation, fine, let's go for it. (Dhondy, 1992: 171)

Despite Channel 4's stated responsibility to respond to the needs of minority viewers, criticisms over the essential tokenism of 'black' programmes were quick to develop. Wadsworth, for example, suggests that the setting up of Channel 4 in the first place reflected the consummate failure of mainstream television to take the reality of a multicultural society seriously (Wadsworth, 1986). Wambu argues that from their first steps, black programmers had difficulties with notions of identity and identification, tending to locate most discussions within the conflict model of ethnic interaction, so that 'rarely did the programmes attempt to engage the wider society on any other level' (Wambu, 1989). However, as Wambu himself acknowledged when he joined the BBC's *Ebony* team in the late 1980s, the practitioners involved in black programming were beginning to acknowledge that their output had to diversify out of the magazine format and Wambu was responsible for producing a series of one-off specials – *Ebony People* – in which black communities had space to tell their own stories. Phillips makes the entirely valid point that at the very least, *Black on Black* began to constitute a regular slot, a programme space which was available every week at the same time, which was a quality production and which spoke directly to Britain's black communities (T. Phillips, 1992). Notwithstanding the considerable problems which the series had, and in particular, the uneasy positioning of both serious and lighter items in the same thirty minutes, such difficulties could have been overcome by splitting into two separate strands rather than stopping the series entirely. Phillips himself agrees that there were seldom sufficient resources available to do the 'entertainment' topics well and that he would have liked to have seen a separate broadcasting strand which was more overtly about entertainment than information. To some extent his wish has been fulfilled by series such as *Desmonds*, *Us Girls*, *The Real McCoy* and *Get up, Stand up*.

Criticism over the Channel's handling of black issues has been voiced from the very beginning and barely a year after its inauguration, Gilroy had scant regard for the Channel's early offerings to black viewers, suggesting that the separation of ethnic identities, as in *Black on Black* and *Eastern Eye*, exactly paralleled the marginalization of black communities in everyday life (1983). Presuming that African Caribbean people are exclusively interested in policing practices and Asian people with immigration law, further distances minority groups from any involvement with mainstream society (Gilroy, 1983). He also suggests that a concentration on adverse relations with white people at a variety of levels encourages the perspective of black as the problematic 'other'. But then Narendhra Morar, Managing Editor of the BBC's Multicultural Programmes Department, suggests that ethnic stereotypes are being broken down by the very existence of 'multicultural' programmes like *Network East*. He argues that the format for the now defunct *Asian Magazine* which began in 1965 and went out in Hindustani was old fashioned and inappropriate for the new generation of British Asians and that *Network East* is broadcast in English to appeal to a younger and more diverse audience, tackling important social issues as well as celebrating artistic endeavours. Morar is adamant that both positive and negative aspects of Asian life should be dealt with in a magazine programme in order to more realistically reflect the life of the community.

> My view is that, as programme makers [we should] reflect both what I call the enthusiasms and the concerns of the community. Immigration, racial attacks, racism and things internal to the community that are problems, dowry abuse, sexual abuse, gays and lesbians, whatever. I think it is incumbent upon us as journalists to dig the dirt both ways. (1989)

Unfortunately, though, all of Morar's examples explore negative aspects of life for Britain's black diaspora communities. If investigative journalism must always pursue the deviant subject, then multicultural programming should incorporate other genres in its menu so that other voices may speak of other stories.

Black broadcasting into the 1990s: sex sells

If the 1980s saw a shift in the way in which black communities were represented, away from an inappropriate preoccupation with the black conflict model towards more diverse issues, interests and images, the 1990s look like returning full circle to precisely the same old race-relations problematic. If early black programmes such as *Skin, Ebony, Black on Black* and *Eastern Eye* provided a forum in which issues of interest and relevance to black communities could be discussed but which did not always involve problems of racism, a number of more recent black programmes appear to have shifted back to a focus on the 'black as problem' discourse. There seems to be a definite and discernible trend in documentary programming at least, whereby filmmakers invade and exploit particular communities for the sake of 'good television' rather than for the purposes of genuine understanding.

The early to mid-1990s spate of series which concentrated on problems within black communities and on inter-racial sexual relationships provoke a consideration of their intended audiences. The more diverse and celebratory tenor of black broadcasting in the 1980s seems to have given way to a programming strand whose purpose is altogether more questionable. The concentration on negative aspects of black community life which characterizes a significant segment of black broadcasting suggests a shift from engaging with a politics of representation to a more cynical move which speaks to a politics of exploitation. For programmes to have any currency in the contemporary television market, they must apparently appeal to the baser viewer instincts such as a prurient and voyeuristic interest in the more deviant aspects of black community life, and it is likely that the audience for these products are intended to be white. This shift in emphasis can be seen most clearly in two series which were broadcast during the summer and autumn of 1993: the BBC's *All Black* series, which was a seven-part series which began broadcasting in July 1993, and Channel 4's *Doing It with You . . . Is Taboo*, which was a three-part series which began transmission in October 1993.

For seven weeks during the summer of 1993, the newly formed Multicultural Programmes Department of the BBC exposed the soft underbelly of black British life to the voyeuristic gaze of the television viewer. Week after depressing week, the 'high quality journalism' which programme-makers insisted underpinned their stories, probed and prodded and dished the dirt, with a damaging concentration of black blues as the producers sought to provide new insights into issues concerning the African Caribbean community in Britain today. The series led on what was described as the 'now' story which no one else had covered, namely, the phenomenon of black rent boys, and closed with the familiar tale of racism along the thin blue (police) line. In between, we learnt that more black people

than white are killed in London each year, that black pupils are four
times more likely to be excluded from school than their white peers
and that black people are disproportionately represented in psychiatric units and as clients of psychiatric services. Throughout the
series, more disconcerting facts and statistics emerged about the
way in which black Britons have differential experiences from white
in a variety of contexts, from the criminal justice system to education, from the killing streets to sweat labour. In most programmes,
black individuals, standing in as signifiers for their communities
more generally, were shown as incapable of exerting autonomous
agency, unable to alter their material circumstances, in thrall
to a racist society which wanted them kept in chains or else terror-
ized by members of their own communities. Whilst these basic
premises of a routinely racist society and an escalation of black
on black violence are undoubtedly true, the conspicuous lack of
analysis throughout the series detracts from the series producer's
claim of programme values comparable to the high quality
Panorama.

The opening programme in the series, *Boys on the Game* provided,
potentially, a unique opportunity to explore not only the reasons
why young black men go on the game, but also better to understand
the particularity of black male (as opposed to white male) prostitution. Unfortunately the programme barely managed to get past first
principles. Although a number of factors were implicated such as
the recession and unemployment, their stifling embrace is not restricted to young black men. The differentiating feature of black rent
boys' experiences as opposed to those of their white counterparts is
surely the consumption, metaphorically and literally, of black
bodies by whites. Black male prostitution is, among other things,
about the objectification of the black man by the white, about feeding those fantasies that have evolved through four hundred years of
Empire, about ownership, possession and control. The nature of the
colonial gaze and the subsequent requirement for black people to
decolonize their minds have been effectively described by a number
of scholars (cf. Fanon, 1970; Said, 1978; Bhabha, 1983) but was sadly
absent in this sorrowful story. The slave experience has meant that
the recent history of black masculinity has been bounded by sexual
repression and private property rights: strongly implicated in the
white man's desire for black male bodies is the enduring myth of
black male potency. 'One is no longer aware of the Negro, but only
of a penis: the Negro is eclipsed. He *is* turned into a penis. He *is* a
penis' (Fanon, 1970: 12).

The interviewed subjects in *Boys on the Game* and the agency workers who regularly patrol the scene offering advice and condoms all point to the disturbing fact that the great majority of, if not all, the clients who purchase these black services are white. But interpretative analyses were unforthcoming. Black masseurs who advertise in the gay press stress their ethnicity and physique in the text of their messages, only too aware that what they are offering is a qualitatively different service and one which has a ready market. But the real story of the endurance of the vast imperial project is rendered invisible here. The camera pans lazily to black limbs, oiled and sweaty, flexing in the gym as another service provider explains the importance of having a good body: it's what the customer expects and good money can be made only for as long as you remain 'young, cute and not too hairy'. But apart from a rhetorical enquiry about supply and demand – as in, are black rent boys responding to a market demand or are they creating it? and a reference, en passant, to the priapic expectations of the customer – there is precious little analysis of the particularity of black experiences or why the number of black rent boys has risen so dramatically over the past few years or what precisely is going on when white men pay to use black men's bodies? The appropriation of black male (and female) bodies by white consumers is a grotesque re-enactment of traditional slave relations, but those obvious historical links were never made.

The second programme in the series, *Sons and Lovers*, looked at absent black fathers and interviewed a number of women about their experiences of bringing up children on their own. The programme was clearly woman-centred, suggesting that the propensity for thoughtless and routine fornication was an integral and inevitable aspect of the black male psyche while at the same time seemingly relieving women of any involvement in the act of procreation and of responsibility for the care and upbringing of any resulting progeny. Whilst women complained that men 'had babies all over the place', in order to consolidate their vision of their own machismo, discussion of women's collusion in feeding this vanity and their reasons for doing so, never materialized. Instead, a faulty black male pathology was paraded for criticism: a group of young black offenders traded anecdotes about the terrible irresponsibilities of (some) black fathers and black school children were lectured about the evils of hitting and running. As with the *Boys on the Game*, this second programme failed to make any meaningful analysis of the lives of its subjects either in the context of the black communities in which they live or, more generally, their functioning in a predominantly white society. Both programmes called for an acknowledgement on the part of black communities to recognize the fact of 'the problem' and both appeared to locate the resolution of such problems squarely in the lap of black communities themselves. What these programmes implicitly signify is the reduction of black humanity to an essential sexuality, bodies to be used and abused to feed the fantasies of others. What they don't identify is the context in which such behaviours occur nor the history of black subjugation which finds a contemporary resonance in new slave forms.

The programme on education, *Bad Behaviour*, focused on the growing number of black pupils who are being excluded or expelled from school and looked to educationalists and researchers to explain this trend. One 'expert' who has been researching into exclusions offered the finding that African Caribbean children are four times more likely than their white peers to be excluded from school but was reluctant to relate it to racism. The curious language with which race/racism is often discussed means that various kinds of double-speak and euphemisms are uttered so that in this instance, the researcher suggested that although the exclusion procedure is not of itself racist, the excluded black child often feels that her/his excluding school has been racist. So is race/racism a factor or not? Other programme contributors suggested that white teachers are intimidated by black pupils and therefore have certain expectations of them which then feed the insecurity and negative feelings which already reside in pupils to create precisely the kind of confrontational experience that teachers anticipate. Thus teacher anxieties become self-fulfilling prophecies as black pupils act up and out of the classroom. It should be said, though, that this programme was one of the few in which the black community, continually exhorted to do something for itself elsewhere in the series, had taken up the challenge, in this case by setting up an all-black primary school in which the teachers respond more appropriately to the educational (and other) needs of black children. Explicitly, this school provides a sympathetic black environment where children can learn about and be proud of their history. Implicitly, white teachers fail their black pupils by refusing to recognize and acknowledge their cultural distinctiveness whereas black teachers are necessarily empathic and supportive because they share the same culture as their pupils and are not burdened by inappropriate expectations. This separatist approach was not welcomed by all and the programme concluded with the suggestion that the experience of black pupils in mainstream (white) schools would be considerably enhanced by better trained and more aware teachers and through the development of meaningful links between school and community. Entirely absent from the programme was any commentary on the conspicuous lack of black teachers in mainstream educational sites, especially compared with their incidence on teacher training courses, and/or how this absence might affect black pupils' expectations, performance and behaviour.

At no point in any of the programmes in the series was there a historical, political, social or economic context in which to locate different black experiences, nor were other contributing factors such as class position or the specific cultural environment explored. While black communities clearly experience British society in ways which are distinctive and different from those of the white majority, the stories of educational under-achievement, lone parenting and inappropriate diagnosis and care in psychiatric services would probably be the same if the series had focused on the white underclass, albeit that black communities suffer the additional pressure of discrimination and prejudice. The point is that the 'black' problems identified in this series are as much about class as they are about race, but the quest for a good story (and thereby good ratings) results in programmes which concentrate on outcomes rather than process, sacrificing insight for exposé.

The colour of sex

Channel 4's late-night sex show *Doing It with You . . . Is Taboo* was a three-part series broadcast in 1993 with a trailer which was quite explicit about its content, whetting the viewers' appetites with the report that the series 'boils up the melting pot of colour and sex'. It was clear, then, from the beginning that the series intended to provide more anecdote than analysis and its broadcast slot of 11 pm indicated that its content would be 'adult' in nature. However, it wasn't until the programmes were actually screened that the production team's preoccupation with sex between cultures became so apparent, such emphasis almost entirely obscuring the socio-political dimension of cross-cultural relationships. The three programmes looked at black–white relations from the viewpoint of the black partner in such relationships. Over the three-week viewing period, black women, black men and black lesbians and gay men were asked about their reasons for getting involved with white partners but were mostly interrogated about their sex lives.

The producer, Stella Orakwue, was keen to explore 'why black women have chosen to break what I call the final taboo' (cited in *The Voice*, 5.10.93) and the first programme looked at the

experiences of five women, all of whom currently had white partners or had had them in the past. The presenter, Donu Kogbara, was
clearly fascinated with the reasons why black women get involved
with white men and, by way of careful questioning, her guests
finally agreed that perhaps they chose white men as second best.
Despite her insistence that the desire of white men for black women
should be seen in terms of colonial conquest, or at the very least,
that black women were being objectified by white men, her invited
guests argued against her. One participant, Thelma, stated quite
unambiguously that the reasons why white men found black
women attractive were that black women were better lovers,
washed more often, and were more sensual, spiritual and physical,
than their white sisters. Where the other guests were clearly embar-
rassed and uncomfortable with these bold, personal statements,
Kogbara encouraged and supported Thelma, nodding her concur-
rence with Thelma's remarks. Throughout the programme,
Kogbara clumsily brought the discussion back to sex whenever it
threatened to take off into more interesting territory and only
towards the end did she probe the wider questions relating to
society's views on cross-cultural relationships and her guests' own
personal experiences of being seen as part of a 'mixed' couple. She
asked if any of them ever felt guilty about dating white men,
suggesting that they were betraying the wider black community,
and although this was initially denied, careful rephrasing once
again encouraged the response that perhaps women did feel guilty,
sometimes, especially when they were berated for their choice of
partner by other black men and women. However, all the participants insisted that they chose and were chosen, on the basis of
attraction not ethnicity and that it was the person that mattered not
the skin. But Kogbara refused to let this pass and asked if people
from different cultures could ever fully understand each other.
When her guests said no, she instantly followed up by asking why
then did they date white men? And the circle/circus began again.

The second and third programmes largely followed the same
format, with Kogbara sticking to her own specifically sexual agenda
and constantly bringing the discussion back to these themes irrespective of what her guests wanted to debate. In the second programme, focusing on black men, the same kinds of strategies were
again employed, with Kogbara encouraging the guys to admit
white women's fascination with black male (super)sexuality. At one
point, she asked if white women expect 'jungle sex'. Although the
men were more than happy to collude with the notion that black
men are better lovers than white guys, they denied that they were

objectified by white women as empty-headed studs. Where the
black women on the previous programme had been frank and explicit in talking about sex, the men were altogether more coy, gig-
gling and gesticulating rather than actually using the language of
sex. The format for this programme was also slightly different, with
the discussion taking place around a table, and included one (well-
known) participant who was vehemently opposed to 'mixing it'.
When he – Ray – spoke, Kogbara attended carefully, but when his
equally articulate South African colleague argued against all
Kogbara's prejudices, she looked bored and distant, smoking lazily
and drinking wine. Commenting on the series, Smith argues that,

> focusing on sexual techniques and racial physical characteristics, to
> the exclusion of historical and political analysis, the programmes
> served to confirm rather than question persistent stereotypes and
> myths about black women being 'exotic' and 'sexy' and black men as
> well-endowed studs. Furthermore the choice of interviewees, the
> limited views expressed, and the shallow level of debate all helped to
> reinforce stereotypical images of black people as lacking in any intel-
> lectual depth. (Smith, 1994: 58)

The last programme, which discussed trans-cultural gay relationships, was by far the most interesting in that Kogbara simply wasn't
allowed to dominate the debate with her sex-talk. Instead, her
guests swung the discussion round to what they wanted to talk
about, which was the dimension of race in sexual/gay politics and
the social context of being in a cross-cultural and gay relationship.
Whilst this group again made the point that partners are chosen for
who they are rather than what they are, they nonetheless argued
that because of the additional oppression of homophobia, they were
more likely to choose a black partner. Most had had white partners
and some were still involved in such partnerships, but in general
there was much more acknowledgement made of the socio-political
context of cross-cultural relationships than was expressed by the
two previous groups. Each time Kogbara tried to refocus the
group's attention on the 'abnormal' sexual expectations that white
partners might have of them, participants deflected the question or
ignored it entirely. That they were able to do this was due in large
part to the fact that members of this group were much more politically aware than members of the other two, and seemed to want to
use the opportunity they had been given to their own ends, rather
than be bound by someone else's agenda. Ironically, throughout the
series, the real taboo of describing a loving and fulfilling black-on-
black partnership remained elusive and hidden. Even the gay black

relationships were construed as the result of convenience and pressure rather than choice.

Black futures

But what do series such as *Taboo* and *All Black* indicate about the direction of black broadcasting in the 1990s? As with many series which ultimately disappoint, *All Black* was widely anticipated, fuelled both by pre-publicity hype and by the expectations of a black viewing public eager to see authentic portraits of itself for a change, keen for images of black communities constructed from the inside rather than from without. It was presumably with some considerable regret that black viewers felt compelled to denounce the series in the pages of the black press, their feelings of betrayal palpable through their prose. The series has been attacked for being sensationalist, for demonstrating tabloid journalism at its worst, for perpetuating existing negative stereotypes and castigated for washing the black community's dirty linen in public, providing more ammunition, if any were needed, to the racists. Speaking in defence of the series during the BBC's consumer rights programme *Biteback* in September 1993, the Managing Editor of the Multicultural Programmes Department, Narendhra Morar, lamely argued that the series was a topical current affairs programme and was only one part of the total output from the Multicultural Programmes Department. *Taboo* also evoked unfavourable viewer responses when it was featured on Channel 4's *Right to Reply* programme. When confronted by hostile audiences, the producers of both these series simply denied that what they had done could possibly have caused offence. When Stella Orakwue was asked during the November 1993 edition of *Right to Reply* how participants had been chosen for *Taboo*, she reported that her research team had conducted a rigorous study to identify suitable guests. However, several participants were well-known (at least within the black community) commentators on race with equally well-known viewpoints.

Narendhra Morar glibly suggested that all current affairs programmes are, by their very nature, problem-oriented and that he was therefore simply obeying the conventions of the genre in highlighting black problems in the *All Black* series. But this is to imply that factual programmes, as opposed to fiction, are entirely value-free and neutral, that in some mysterious way current affairs programme-makers are able to suspend their own beliefs and produce programmes which are impeccably impartial. Documentary programme-makers seem to believe what fiction filmmakers only pretend to: that film and programme making is an objective process where the text provides a representation of the way things *really* are. Very few practitioners working within factual programming strands seem prepared to admit that all filmmaking is a form of discourse which fabricates its effects, impressions and perspective (Nichol, 1985). The documentary programme's illusion of objectivity is further enhanced when the production company making a 'black' programme is itself comprised of black professionals, according the subsequent narrative an additional authenticity.

But the crucial point at issue is the requirement to represent African Caribbean and other black diaspora communities in Britain in all their diverse realities in the face of a white-dominated media industry which regularly constructs images of the black 'other' out of nothing more rooted than its own collective imagination. Much of the criticism against *All Black* has been for its concentration on negativity, but the call to provide only positive images of black communities is also misplaced. The positive vs. negative debate has in any case been going on for a very long time. During the 1920s and 1930s, the African American filmmaker, Oscar Micheaux, had precisely these same positive-only arguments levelled against his films which were berated for their lurid presentations of the more salacious and controversial aspects of African American life. More recently, African American filmmakers such as John Singleton and Mario Van Peebles have been denounced for their preoccupation with the gun culture of young African American men and their perpetuation of associated negative stereotypes. Gurinder Chadha and Meera Syal have been amply criticized for their exploration, in *Bhaji on the Beach*, of the cultural mores of some Asian families and the authoritarian patriarchy exercised by husbands and fathers in the household. However, what the positive-only lobby fail to grasp is that the real issues are about showing authentic and diverse experiences rather than concentrating on the positive ones. It is the lack of access to media production by black practitioners which ultimately circumscribes and limits the nature and form of black representation. Individual film- and programme-makers should be allowed to tell their own story in their own way and should not have their creative impulses gagged for the sake of trying to create a new 'positive' black mythology in the mould of *The Cosby Show*. But equally, the political context in which black programmes are made must also be acknowledged and consideration given to who and what these programmes are for. There is no homogeneous black community, there is no one black perspective, there is no one black story, nor one black story-teller. The relative absence of media opportunities through which black creativity is given expression means that those few programmes which do get made have to shoulder the unbearable burden of representing *all* black communities, despite their distinctions and stand accused of not being all those black programmes and films which have never been made. It thus seems a doubly cruel blow when an entire series dedicated to exploring African Caribbean communities in Britain and, moreover, a series produced by black programme-makers, cannot manage to include a single programme which focuses on the positive contribution that black people have made to British culture or which maps the progress that black communities are making in their own lives in their own way.

Evidence of otherwise hidden problems and issues facing black individuals and communities should of course be disclosed and brought to public attention, but whether it is appropriate to spend an entire series peddling negativity, racism and black victim consciousness or to reduce discussions of cross-cultural relationships to straightforward considerations of sexual appetite and performance, is arguable. That these topics are inappropriate foci for TV programmes has been clearly demonstrated by attending to viewing figures. For *All Black*, one million people tuned in to watch the first programme in the series, but a clear dislike for the orientation of the programme resulted in a swift downturn in the audience to 500,000 for programme two and then a continuing downward trend through programmes three to seven. Both *All Black* and *Taboo* came out under the banner of multicultural programmes and it is not enough simply to argue, as Narendhra Morar does, that *All Black* was only one part of his department's total output. It was after all the *only* output of that department to be broadcast over two months and comprised the major strand of its summer schedule. It is not enough to argue that the series was simply good journalism and that in any case, television does not have a responsibility to tell only positive stories about black people. Departments which have a specific remit for multicultural programmes have different and unique responsibilities from those of other departments, not least because of the perception of (white) viewers that programmes from this source are especially authoritative. If a multicultural programmes department chooses the race-relations issue as the primary focus for any given series then, ipso facto, that issue becomes *the* agenda. The mechanisms through which such vital decisions as agenda-setting are made must be carefully considered in any department, but even more so in departments whose output constitutes their channel's

primary forum for debating black issues. If this burden of representation seems unfair, so it is, but it is undoubtedly true that black
media professionals who do have access to audiences through their
programmes are accorded a special legitimacy. It is all the more
damaging then, when those few precious 'black' spaces are occupied by programmes which rehearse the same old tired stereotypes. When Darcus Howe, ex-Black Panther and now host of
Channel 4's *Devil's Advocate* series expounds on what being West
Indian means to him, his voice is not heard as if it is just another
black voice but is perceived as being especially 'real' by a public
whose experiences of black communities are mostly vicarious and
third-hand. He states that being West Indian means,

> I make children all the time. Why? Because I climb up on top of them
> and make sex. They didn't mind and I didn't mind and when I see the
> results I am pleased I didn't mind. It's wonderful. It is not odd. My
> brothers and I have different mothers – and my father was an Angli-
> can priest. (Howe in interview with Andrew Billen, *Sunday Times*,
> 21.11.1993)

Watching me watching you

What both *All Black* and *Taboo* exemplify is that there are no longer
aspects of black community life which can or should remain private:
everything is now available for scrutiny, exposure and exploitation
but for what and to whom? Who is the imagined audience for these
tales of failure and sexual preoccupation and how does the fact that
these programmes are made by black production teams, with black
producers and presenters, fit with their provocative content and
hostile black audience reaction? Are programmes more authentic
because the programme-makers and the subjects share the same
ethnicity? Perhaps these programmes are being cynically targeted
at a prurient white audience, eager to see evidence of the failures of
black British life and the crucial role that white people continue to
play in the lives and loves of black communities. It is in any case
interesting that both these series use the term 'black' to describe
African and African Caribbean people and concentrate exclusively
on this black community as the subject for their series. There are no
spaces in which to tell other black stories, to sing other black songs.

If the struggles to achieve more genuine representations of black
communities were won in the 1970s and 1980s with innovative
series such as *Black on Black*, *East*, *Ebony* and *Empire Road*, the
politics of representation have now been subordinated to a new

harder-edged politics of sensationalism, where high ratings at any cost appears to be the ruling principle. Viewer response to series such as *All Black* and *Taboo* has sent clear messages to programme-makers in terms of what is desired both from departments which have a specific remit for responding to the needs of Britain's 'multicultural' society, and more generally, from programmes which focus on the particularity of Britain's black minority communities. Whose voices are privileged to be heard and which stories allowed to be told will continue to constitute the contested terrain of 'appropriate' and acceptable representation. It should be acknowledged, though, that one year later, the 1994 series of *All Black* appeared to have taken seriously the criticisms made of the previous series and presented stories which were more innovative and imaginative than had been managed before. Subjects included black networking strategies, black fathers and their children and the influence of black churches on social relations. Here, at last, were stories about black communities which did not require a white racist backdrop to contextualize black experiences. Rather, here were black men and women getting on with their lives, refusing to be bowed by others' expectations and showing precisely the entrepreneurial spirit which is supposed to be lacking within black community settings. This kind of programming is both energizing for black audiences and also subversive and challenging for white viewers, but it was one lone series in the wilderness. That it was scheduled against Britain's most popular soap meant that despite its original and fresh perspective on African Caribbean communities, the series was destined to be seen by only a dedicated and already converted minority.

The power that commissioning editors wield is considerable. Such individuals operate effectively to deny or enable work to be produced and screened and it is hard to see evidence of any serious strategies which aim to bridge the producer–consumer divide. While Narendhra Morar defends his corner at the BBC, Farrukh Dhondy at Channel 4 seems to believe he can respond effectively to the concerns of all Britain's black communities. Answering the question, 'How do you as part of the Asian community address the needs of the Afro-Caribbean community?', he replied,

> Just through familiarity with what the Afro-Caribbean community wants, needs, and does. I do not conduct any surveys. I do not attend any committees to advise me on it because my brains are better than any group of advisors I could gather. (1993: 38)

If black programmes are, ostensibly, geared towards satisfying a black audience, there is nonetheless scant evidence to affirm that such programmes are actually watched by black viewers. What still remains unknown and possibly unknowable, is the audience profile for black programming. Without a better understanding of the way in which the audience (both black and white) interprets television's messages, programme-makers will continue to give the public what they think they want and viewers will continue to complain about it. In a so-called multicultural society, the existence of a specific black programming strand could in any case be seen as something of an anachronism. The arguments for a discrete black strand are numerous, including the provision of a dedicated space in which black issues and voices can be articulated, a training ground whereby media workers can learn their craft and make the transition, if they want, into the mainstream, and an easy access point for black production companies wanting to sell their products. Black broadcasting could, in principle, encourage the development of a viable bank of knowledge and expertise and provide regular opportunities to explore issues and topics of interest to black communities. To overcome the one-only problem, regular programmes could focus on different types of issues or topics, perhaps one strand dealing with the arts and another with current affairs, and such programmes should be a permanent part of the television landscape, recording, monitoring and reflecting changing black experiences for anyone who wants to watch. Samir Shah, responsible for BBC TV's current affairs output and previously the producer on *Eastern Eye*, argues that as long as terms such as 'Asian' continue to have meaning, then there will continue to be a need for programmes which address the context of that meaning. 'It seems to me that there will always be a need for programmes aimed separately at Asian and Afro-Caribbean viewers – until the difference between Afro-Caribbeans and Asians becomes the same as the difference between the Angles and the Saxons' (Shah, 1992: 159). Similarly,

> If we abandon black programme-making and pretend that we don't want to have separate black programmes, then we're also saying that we think our experience is second-rate, not worth preserving, not worth having in its clear and separate form. And that's really why I think we need to battle for television slots that are about black programme-makers speaking to black audiences. (T. Phillips, 1992: 155)

On the opposite side, is the argument which says that the low level of resource accorded such strands leads to programmes falling into the ghetto trap. The writer Trix Worrell, for example, argues that the existence of multicultural programme departments simply lets everyone else off the hook of having to deal with black Britons and perpetuates the thinking that as long as there is one of something – one black sitcom, one black comedy show – then sufficient progress has been made (Worrell, 1992). Similarly, Hanson argues that as long as *Desmonds* is being produced, it would be difficult to commission another black sitcom at the same time 'because commissioning editors would argue that their budget is going into *Desmonds*' (1992: 191). But this is not the basis on which other programmes in other departments are commissioned. The light entertainment department or the drama department simply agree to commission another programme or series for their particular schedules, irrespective of whether or not there is already a sitcom about an elderly married couple or a drama about the police force. As the novelist Mike Phillips argues:

> We are all multicultural in our homes and on the streets so we have a private multiculturalism which isn't reflected in the media. When I watch *Inspector Morse* I don't think of it as not belonging to me and there is no reason why a white person shouldn't feel the same about our programmes except that they are never given the chance to because those kind of programmes are very rarely made. (1992a: 27)

Phillips goes on to state that when he wanted to adapt his novel, *Blood Rights*, for television, it would have been ghettoized as a multicultural programme, of minority interest and therefore given a poor scheduling spot if he had taken it to Channel 4. 'I didn't want to be forced into an eleven o'clock slot with a production team which saw it as an experimental multicultural sort of thing' (1992a: 27). As it was, the BBC accepted the adaptation and it was subsequently made as a mainstream drama by the drama department. As well as the problem of sidelining, black programme units can also hinder the entry of black media practitioners into mainstream production because anything they want to do is necessarily seen as a 'black' thing and therefore the province of the multicultural department (Jivani, 1992). It is tempting to regard black broadcasting as an inevitable ghetto, where output is only watched by black audiences and which has little impact either on the wider society or on the commissioning decisions of other departments. However, there is no evidence that black programming does collapse in on itself in this way, or that media workers who start their careers in such departments can never enter mainstream production. What does seem to be happening, though, is an interest by the mainstream in taking up 'black' issues. In the mid-1990s, for example, programmes about black interests and concerns began to appear regularly in mainstream documentary strands such as *Arena* (BBC), *Without Walls* (Channel 4) and *Panorama* (BBC). It certainly seems to be the case that a more diverse range of documentary programmes which explore black community life is being made by mainstream production teams than is being commissioned by the 'race' units. For example, *Arena* made *Trouble Man: the Last Years of Marvin Gaye*, screened in March 1994; the following month, *Dispatches* (Channel 4) broadcast a programme looking at the changing political fortunes of Winnie Mandela; *Timewatch* (BBC2) screened *Racism or Realism? A History of Immigration*; and a new magazine series called *Africa Express* began on Channel 4 which aimed to provide an antidote to the ubiquitous themes of famine, Aids and civil war which usually attend programmes on Africa. With good quality mainstream programmes being made about black experiences and functioning outside the otherwise irresistible race-relations discourse which characterizes so much of what is supposed to be 'black' broadcasting, the arguments for retaining specific multicultural programme units look to be increasingly redundant. But how many black workers are employed on these programmes about their lives? On balance, no matter how much black broadcasting strands are criticized, they do perform at least one crucial function which is to provide a dedicated home to black-oriented work and thus provide the means by which emerging black professionals have the opportunity to hone the skills of their trade. Even as we creep towards the end of the millennium, it is still extraordinarily difficult for black media workers to break into the industry and any hard-fought entry routes must be protected.

What is clear from the new broadcasting legislation and the increasing deregulation of the media industry, is that the potential for innovative, challenging and 'political' work by black production companies will become more rather than less restricted, as channels bring their schedules down to the lowest common denominator in order to win market share. The principles of public service broadcasting have never really been applied to minority audiences, despite the easy rhetoric to the contrary. A deregulated media context could provide a genuine opportunity for community-based services but it is hard to see how small-scale black-oriented organizations could win in a straight fight for licences against larger and more established consortia.

Positive actions

That the portrayal of black people in film and television continues to be seen as problematic is evidenced by the number of research studies, conferences, seminars, and media-generated initiatives which have aimed to both identify the nature of the 'problem' but also offer some partial ameliorative strategies. The 1990s, in particular, have seen black representation on and in television taken up as an issue not just for individual nation-states but across Europe and beyond. Public broadcasting organizations have begun, slowly, to consider what they can do to halt the perpetuation of stereotypical portraits of black people. In 1992, for example, a conference was held in The Netherlands which looked specifically at public broadcasting for a multicultural Europe (PBME) with the express objective of developing a programme of action. Twelve countries sent delegates and as a result of the conference, a number of pan-European collaborative projects were set up and a resolution put to the European Commission to take a number of actions, including funding a European Coordination Point to facilitate positive actions against racism and xenophobia in radio and television. One very visible outcome of the conference has been the publication of *Spectrum* magazine by PBME, intended to 'present a voice of reason and a campaigning voice in a continent increasingly afflicted by racial violence and intolerance of cultural difference' (*Spectrum* editorial, 1993, issue 1). The magazine is distributed by BBC TV Equal Opportunities Department and by the summer of 1994 was already collecting material on European broadcast initiatives for inclusion in the third issue. *Spectrum* is produced with the help of a grant to PBME from the European Commission's EUROFORM Programme and the EC also funded, through its Horizon Programme, the Black European Media Project, which aimed to create employment and training opportunities for young black people in the European media industry. This one-year project (1992–3) was jointly supported by the Scottish Office. In 1995, PBME held a second conference to assess what the initiative had achieved over the previous two years and what still needed to be done in the future.

Also in 1992, the BFI made two documentaries for the BBC on the contribution of black people to British television as part of the BBC's *Black and White in Colour* season. In November 1992, a conference on the same topic – Black and White in Colour Conference: Prospects for Black Intervention in Television – took place and explored specific issues such as multicultural programming, black international production and the disjunction between black comedy's success and the neglect of black drama. The following year, the International Broadcasting Trust and the Centre for Multicultural Education (Institute of Education) organized a conference, Can We Get It Right?, which explored representation issues in programmes and reports made about the developing world. As Hall points out, what the media 'produce' are representations and images of the social world and frameworks within which to understand that world and amongst the definitions offered by the media is one about 'race' (Hall, 1981). No matter how well-meaning and empathic a production team is towards the developing world or other issues which highlight blackness, it seems almost inevitable that it is 'race' which is seen as the problem rather than racism.

Parts of the television industry itself have developed a number of initiatives aimed at enabling black media practitioners and/or aspirants to place their feet on the bottom rungs of the professional ladder. The BBC, for example, set up the Television Training Trust in 1990 (under Section 37 of the Race Relations Act) as a means by which people from black and 'ethnic minority' communities could be offered 'a chance to gain television production skills and pursue a career in programme-making' (BBC publicity material). This scheme has since been renamed the Television Production Trainee Scheme and is a general scheme for all-comers but with half the places (five) reserved for black candidates. This change has been prompted by the fact that within the BBC and by trainees themselves, the TTT scheme was seen as being of a lower standard/value than the mainstream training programme. The BBC also offer the Technical Operations Bursary Scheme to enable black entrants to gain technical skills and there are twelve bursaries available each year.

In addition to television network strategies, the Arts Council initiated the Black Arts Video Project Scheme in the late 1980s to support new directors in the production of imaginative arts documentaries on black cultural issues. There were ten winners in the 1992–3 competition, including five newcomers and five more established practitioners. Building on the success of this initiative, in 1992 the independent Carlton Television and the Arts Council ran a competition to offer commissions for the production of original, 5-minute films on any aspect of black arts, music and culture. The budget ceiling for each film was £10,000. In the literature accompanying the competition, the Arts Council reported that one of the objectives of the competition – subsequently marketed as Synchro – was to stimulate the production of videos about black arts and

cultural subjects by new video-makers and that as a result, pro-
fessionalism would be encouraged and a contribution made towards greater professional opportunities in the future. In the end,
eight films were commissioned and were subsequently screened as
two 30-minute compilations on Carlton TV in early 1994. Alongside
this initiative, the Arts Council and Carlton TV are also aiming to
establish a training programme to help encourage an understanding of the commissioning process and television production skills.
In 1993, the BBC ran a script-writing competition – *Black Screen* – to
develop new black writing talent and twelve writers subsequently
began working with BBC script-editors, although ultimately only
six scripts actually resulted in broadcast dramas. The competition
was repeated in 1994, with similar outcomes.

The British Film Institute recently established an African Caribbean Film Unit within the Institute which launched a new quarterly
journal in 1993 – *Black Film Bulletin*. The BFB aims to keep readers
up to date with the latest developments, projects and people involved in black film production and features both notice-board
items as well as more reflective pieces. During the summer of the
launch year, the *Bulletin* organized a summer screen celebration
which highlighted the range of new work produced by black British
filmmakers, including film school and independent productions,
TV previews and trailers for new British and American commercial
films. With more than four hundred people attending the screening,
it is clear that there is interest in black-originated work but, as
Adepegba argues, the appetite (and more importantly the funding
interest) is for commercial films which are popular and profitable.
'I'm not talking here about your avant-garde experimentalist Black
film co-op types. Just mention their names and the investors are
gone and the audience know enough not to show up' (Adepegba,
1993: 18).

The Commission for Racial Equality has also added its weight to
the debate and in 1992 launched its Race in the Media Awards to
'encourage more informed coverage of race relations issues' (RIMA
publicity literature). In its second year, the keynote speaker at the
Awards presentation in 1994 was Peter Brooke, the Heritage Secretary, who emphasized that responsible reporting and fair presentation of the issues was of crucial social importance. He added that
the Race in the Media Awards, by recognizing good practice in the
treatment of race and ethnic issues, made an important contribution
towards 'better journalism and . . . helped create a climate in which
sensitive reporting of race issues becomes a matter of course' (CRE
Press Release, 12.4.1994). It is worth noting that, of the seven cat-

egory winners in the competition, only two were black. One was Isabel Appio, editor of *The Weekly Journal*, winning in the specialist journal/magazine category, and the other was Celina Smith of Reel Life Television in the current affairs/documentary category, for her excellent *Crossing the Tracks* (for the BBC's *Birthrights* series). The predominance of whites at the winners table (and among the guests enjoying an expensive lunch) bears eloquent testimony to the distance yet to be travelled down the road of equal access to mainstream media: both *The Weekly Journal* and Reel Life operate as independents.

PART III

Film and Television

6

Reading Black Media

Maintaining an ironic distance from dominant, imposed and/or pre-existent discourses is recognised by many as a key characteristic of cultural manifestations in the black diaspora, and as a sign of resistance to colonial domination.

      Coco Fusco, 'The Other Is In: Black British Film in the US'

Given the wide variation of film forms and company structures which can be loosely described as 'black' and 'independent', can there be a movement or tradition which is essentially black and independent and which could be united under the inclusive description of 'black' film? Mercer argues that if the 'oppositional' aspect is identified and highlighted, then black independent filmmaking can be seen as constituting a counter-practice, one which opposes and critiques the traditional representation of black communities.

A consistent motivation for black filmmakers has been to challenge the predominantly stereotypical forms in which blacks become visible either as problems or victims, always as some intractable and unassimilable Other on the margins of . . . society and its collective consciousness. (1988: 8)

Hall argues that the history of marginalization, both cultural and socio-economic, has led to significant movements of resistance in late twentieth-century society, movements whose members contest the orthodox images of 'the other' and unite under a politically and self-constructed 'black' identity to represent themselves in their own images and develop their own black aesthetic and discursive code (1988). Ways have needed to be found whereby the voices of the silenced could be heard and the stereotypes residing in the white imagination could be confounded and displaced. Hall argues that such a cultural project had two main objects:

> first the question of access to the rights to representation by black artists and black cultural workers themselves. Secondly the contestation of the marginality, the stereotypical quality and the fetishised nature of images of blacks by the counter-position of a 'positive' black imagery. (1988: 27)

For Hall, the main issue in these early struggles centred on trying to change what he describes as the 'relations of representation', but the debate has moved on from there to a contemporary concern with the politics of representation itself which, among other things, heralds the end of the essential 'black' subject. Ceasing to idealize a fixed black subject enables a celebration of the diversity of black experiences, cultures and histories but also means that cultural artefacts produced by black artists are no longer guaranteed a positive or sympathetic reception simply because they are expressions of a special black artistic effort. 'Films are not necessarily good because black people make them. They are not necessarily "right-on" by virtue of the fact that they deal with the black experience' (Hall, 1988: 28). One consequence of admitting the end of the essential black subject is that black film is then placed in an open arena and subjected to mainstream critical scrutiny. This positioning of black film in the same frame as mainstream art works then prompts a return to the question of whether black film is a specific and different practice to that of other (mainstream or conventional) cinemas and if so, whether the critical criteria with which to read such films should be different.

Different types of black film are generated by attending to different types of filmmaking imperative. Mercer is keen to distinguish between two types of black filmmaking which he describes as the *monologic* and the *dialogic* (1990a). The former refers to productions which are identical in form, structure and convention to those offered by mainstream cinema and differ only in their content. Such artefacts are summarily dismissed by Mercer as examples of cultural mimicry and neo-colonial surrender. The dialogic film, on the other hand, not only contests racist stereotypes through its narrative, but also interrogates the dominant language and codes which inscribe mainstream products. An engagement with the politics of racism and representation thus produces a critical *dialogue* and what Mercer is arguing for, then, is not black film as art, but as politics. This requirement to privilege the educative and informational aspects of the medium rather than focus on pleasure and entertainment goes some way towards explaining the framing of the majority of contemporary films produced by black filmmakers, particularly in Britain, within the realist, sometimes experimental, paradigm, many in documentary format. Thus the key determinant which distinguishes black filmmaking as a specific practice which is qualitatively different from films simply made by black filmmakers, is the imperative to engage in a critical dialogue which explores the political, cultural, social and economic specificity of black experiences. The propensity for such a realist perspective to become so influential is rooted in a desire to produce counter-discourses to the traditional portraits and a refusal to engage with the race-relations master narrative. The hitherto unchallenged authority of traditional (racist) perceptions of the black subject is thus interrupted and opposed by black counter-narratives which give a voice to the silenced. The oral history accounts of black community life provided in a quartet of films produced by Britain's Institute of Race Relations, *Struggles for Black Community* (Colin Prescod, 1983) for example, provide authentic descriptions of community life which correct the largely ahistorical logic with which the conventional race relations discourse is inflected.

Although documentary realism is a useful technique with which to juxtapose the white imaginary with the black experience as lived, such a device is nonetheless part of mainstream cinema's structural repertoire. Black filmmakers thus find themselves attempting to provide a counter-narrative to the conventional assumptions about race but doing so within a framework which is irrevocably structured by dominance. 'It has been difficult for black practitioners to evolve a cinematic approach which is unaffected by the determinants of 'race-relations' discourse or which works outside documentary realism' (Pines, 1988: 29). If Pines's argument largely holds true for much of the work produced in the early years of black filmmaking, the 1980s witnessed a serious effort by a number of filmmakers to rupture the seduction of the realist style. The work of black workshops during the 1980s further strengthened the possibility of different styles, techniques and narrative interests being incorporated under the general rubric of 'black' film. In terms of developing a cinematic tradition which is essentially black, acknowledgement needs to be made of what cinema is and how it functions in the social world, that is, that it operates as an ideological signifier in much the same way as television, throwing back to the viewer particular perceptions of society. A black film practice must therefore begin by demystifying and demythifying traditional cinematic conventions and instead of mimicking them, must establish its own base, its own modes of production and symbolic images

(Yearwood, 1982b). Black film here, then, constitutes a particular practice of signification which is rooted in the specific experiences of black people in society and through history.

It should be clear that the very notion of what is 'black' is ambiguous and confused and Snead questions the meaning of black when considering the concept of black independent film, arguing that the indiscriminate way in which the word is used obscures the underlying tensions around political power and ideological control which are constantly and irresistibly present (1988). Although it is certainly important to unite in a positive and inclusive identity in order to counter the ubiquitous assumption of white as 'norm', it is equally important to preserve and explore the diversity of historical and cultural experiences. Yearwood is also keen to unpack what precisely 'black' film denotes and what kinds of film can properly be described as operating within an essentially 'black' film tradition (1982b). He identifies a number of criteria which are used to distinguish a black film from any other, for example, if the characters are black or the content is concerned with a 'race' issue, or if the filmmaker is black. These kinds of definitions are clearly inadequate and even inappropriate signifiers of black film, being iconic and superficial. 'The art work cannot be judged on the basis of who the artist is, or the artist himself, the artist's life, the artist's intentionality, nor his audience' (1982b: 70). The crucial distinguishing feature of black film for Yearwood is that it is created out of a shared historical and socio-cultural experience and that it displays a mode of production which retains control over the means of that production. Thus a black film is one which not only challenges the orthodoxies of image and representation of black communities derived from white perspectives but also contests the power relations which exist within conventional or 'institutionalized' cinema practice. Caution thus needs to be applied about the apparently unproblematic use of 'black' when describing films by black filmmakers and an appreciation of the full diversity of such art works needs to be exercised since the term subsumes a wide range of practitioners and areas of operation and interest within its embrace.

Notions of Third Cinema

If the early 1980s saw black independent film production become more coherent as a specific 'movement', nascent as it was, the mid- and late 1980s saw serious questions being asked about exactly where such filmic products might and ought to be located. The term which was often (and is still) used to describe the particular set of film practices which constitute black and Third World films is 'Third Cinema', derived from that set of counter or oppositional film practices which were characteristic of radical filmmakers in Latin America in the 1960s and 1970s and more recently typified by filmmakers working elsewhere in the developing world. The term incorporates not just a set of practical and critical criteria which are unique to Third Cinema but also implies a range of possibilities about the emergence of a militant cinema through which cultural change and national liberation might be wrought (Akomfrah, 1988a). But what has become clear is that nothing can be taken for granted any more, not least the future of (black) independent film. Akomfrah therefore suggests that it is now timely to re-examine the possibilities of meaning that Third Cinema now has and, in revisiting the term, perhaps enable it to move on once more as a consequence of mature reflection and as part of the onward march of evolutionary progress. There is a certain caution about using the term to describe oppositional practices which are generated from outside developing world cultures, even when such practitioners are part of the black diaspora. Auguiste suggests that the casual use of the term eventually reduces its potency as an accurate descriptor but also argues that there may be a link between the 'Third Cinema of the Third World' and that which is in the process of evolving out of diaspora communities in the West (1989).

The notion of a Third Cinema was (probably) first developed in the 1960s in Latin America, rooted in the Cuban Revolution of 1959 and incorporated as part of a movement of revolutionary consciousness (Pines and Willemen, 1989). The concept was formulated as a way of producing a new cinema aesthetic which would be more relevant to the revolutionary and radical period of the 1960s and which would engage with and inform a new set of cultural and political practices within the cinematic enterprise. While this new film focus was opposed to the pre-existing Eurocentric traditions, certain film techniques and genres, most notably Grierson's pioneering documentary work, were appropriated for their technical qualities. What was particularly appealing about documentary film practice was its association with low budgets and its tendency to focus on parochial rather than global concerns. Gabriel traces the development of Third World film over three phases, suggesting that the genealogy of Third World film culture,

> moves from the First Phase in which foreign images are impressed in an alienating fashion on the audience, to the Second and Third

Phases in which recognition of 'consciousness of oneself' serves as the essential antecedent for national and, more significantly, international consciousness. (1989: 31)

By this account, then, Third World cinema began by mimicking Hollywood in its form and emphasis on entertainment values. There is a thinly veiled contempt for the perceived decadence of Western artistic (film) traditions when Gabriel argues that 'Aping Hollywood stylistically, more often than not, runs counter to Third World needs for a serious social art' (1989: 32). The second phase down the path of enlightenment is described as 'remembrance' and is the place where he locates most contemporary Third World film practitioners. This phase is essentially about film looking back, often to a mythic past and is typified by narratives which revolve around old and probably lost values and the celebration of customs and folklore, particularly where old ideas come into conflict with the more ruthless mores of the modern world. The danger of sentimentality to which Gabriel alludes is precisely discussed in *The Passion of Remembrance* which engages with the problematic of misremembering, sharply contrasting fond but erroneous recollections of yesterday with the critical discourse of today.

There is nothing very radical about exalting traditional culture and practice if, at the same time, the more restrictive and repressive features of that culture are not challenged and questioned. The third phase in Gabriel's journey towards a Third Cinema nirvana is the 'combative' phase, which disavows the conventions of dominant cinematic practice and becomes a cinema of and by the people, owned by the nation, managed and operated by and for them. It is characterized by deliberately naive techniques because 'technical and artistic perfection in the production of a film cannot be aims in themselves' (1989: 33), presumably because such objectives are overtly commercial. The style of phase three is cinema as ideology and the filmmaker who operates at this level must be one who is perceptive of and knowledgeable about the pulse of developing world peoples.

The filmmaker Haile Gerima also juxtaposes the ethos and rationale of the 'good' Third Cinema practice with the craven and decadent 'bad' of the conventional cinematic tradition (1989). Commenting specifically on the development of African American cinema, but with perceptions which are essentially about Third Cinema and Hollywood, Gerima argues that the dependence of African American filmmakers on the dominant power structures has meant that authentic artistic impulses to produce cinema out-

side the orthodox cinematic formats are persistently thwarted. This
argument could also be made about the position of black
filmmakers in Britain. But whilst it is a commonplace to promote
theory X by pointing to the shortcomings of theory Y, in this case
identifying Third Cinema as an antidote to the intellectually barren
posturing of mainstream cinema, there is a danger of not seeing the
wood for the trees. In critiquing mainstream film, Gerima describes
the practitioner working in that medium as 'by and large egotistical,
psychologically deformed and individualistic, incapable of intro-
ducing the necessary historic vision that can activate the progressive cultural energy of the masses of people' (1989: 67). This does
seem a rather sweeping and unproveable generalization, although
Gerima's points were originally made at the 1986 Edinburgh Film
Festival and should therefore be read as being intentionally in-
flammatory, controversial and polemic. As with Gabriel, Gerima
appears to be arguing for a black cultural and moral superiority
which has emerged through a history of exploitation, suggesting
that the conventional (white) filmmaker is incapable of producing
authentic work since s/he is unavoidably disabled by her/his imperial past. It is tempting to cite all those white (and black)
filmmakers working within conventional narratives who have
nonetheless made powerful and political films, but that is to enter a
debate which is endlessly circular. What is more pertinent is to
query the evidence upon which Gerima bases his assumption that
the 'masses' are impatient to be saved. They are apparently waiting
to be released from the bondage of Hollywood where unrelenting
exposure to mainstream film has left the audience,

> castrated of their own potential to be human beings . . . full of self-
> hatred; constantly wishing for some kind of miraculous alteration of
> their nose, their lips, their hair, hoping to turn overnight into models
> of what they see in commercial cinema. (1989: 68)

The audience, like the hapless filmmaker, has been brought to this
state by what Gerima describes as the 'brainwashing' which has
attended long years of colonization and a diet replete with distorted
expectations of what cinema (and society) is or should be. It becomes clear that when Gerima argues for the development of new
relationships between filmmaker, audience and critic whereby all
three, working in harmony, can effect social change, his address is
to a wholly black constituency. For Gabriel, too, Third Cinema
products, or what he prefers to describe as Third World cinema, are
not only located specifically in the developing world context but

also intended for an exclusively Third World audience (1989). He
argues that screening these cultural products to viewers in the West
is problematic because such an audience has difficuties dealing with
a filmic technique which confounds the conventions of dominant
mainstream cinema. The white viewer is unable to maintain her
position as ultimate arbiter of codification and interpretation, since
the subject matter of Third Cinema is outside her realm of experience. However, while black and white viewers of the same film
will undoubtedly derive different pleasures and different themes
will cue a diverse range of resonances, these interpretations do not
necessarily have to be perceived in a hierarchical relationship, as
better or worse than each other, but viewed merely as different.
Commenting on the impact of his films on a Western audience,
Satyajit Ray suggests that though his works are about human beings, human relationships and social problems, the specifically 'Indian' context and orientation of his art means that some of the more
symbolic aspects are missed by the Western viewer (1992). Ray
states quite frankly that his films are intended for an Indian audience and contain cultural codes and iconography which can only be
understood and appreciated by a knowing and informed audience.
While his more general themes – boy meets girl, family relationships or socially contentious issues – could easily be grasped by an
international audience, Ray argues that in order to read and appreciate the film properly, the audience or critic needs an open mind
and a profound knowledge of India and her culture.

But the audience for any particular film, certainly while it is in
production, must necessarily be an imaginary one and thereafter
self-selecting at the point of actually choosing to watch it. For films
such as *Handsworth Songs*, the imagined audience had been one
made up of a diaspora constituency (Auguiste, 1988b) but it is no
longer commercially sensible to be quite so rigid. The filmmaker
John Akomfrah, answering a question relating to the intended audience for his films, suggests that during the early 1980s it would have
been possible to say that black film was made for black people and
that the productions were framed with that audience in mind
(1988a). However, in the harsher reality of the late 1980s (and certainly in the 1990s) it is no longer feasible to consider an exclusively
black constituency and 'the more one continues to want to get the
films shown in centres which are largely dominated by art cinema,
other audiences must be taken into consideration. That seems to me
to be obvious' (Akomfrah, 1988b: 9).

Although the debate around defining a specifically black film
praxis has been going on since the first efforts of black filmmakers in

the early years of this century, the greater visibility of films by black filmmakers at mainstream cinemas and on television during the 1980s and 1990s has given the debate a renewed impetus. For example, in 1988 a conference was held at the Institute of Contemporary Art to discuss the state of black filmmaking in Britain which used as its focus, three films produced by contemporary black production companies in 1986: *The Passion of Remembrance, Playing Away* and *Handsworth Songs* (see chapter 2). These three films were emblematic of what black film could be, with one of the films – *Playing Away* – adopting a traditional narrative structure to tell its story and the other two using more experimental and innovative techniques. In the context of the reception of black film productions, however, the less conventional the format, the more likely a negative reading. *Songs*, for example, won widespread critical acclaim, including the Grierson Award from the British Film Institute, but was dismissed by critics such as Salman Rushdie and the black newspaper *The Voice* for being just another riot movie. As Gates points out, to the extent that black film is perceived as a political act, it then becomes vulnerable to a political reproach which sees such work as both elitist and uninterested in a mainstream black audience (Gates Jr, 1992). Rushdie, in particular, attacks the film for speaking with only one voice, that of riot, while ignoring Handsworth's other songs which speak of a changing culture and community (1987). His central criticism relates to the need to find a language through which the voiceless can speak, suggesting that the language developed by *Songs*, whereby it 'attempts to excavate hidden ruptures/agonies of "race" [and] looks at the riots as a political field coloured by the trajectories of industrial decline and structural crisis' (*Songs* publicity literature), is not one which can be communicated easily to a mainstream audience. There does appear to be a persuasive logic in his argument that language, whether written or visual, must communicate to be effective. But at base, the argument is less to do with the film's ability to communicate or not than with the general paucity of black films which gives those which do exist a totemic significance and a burden of unrealistic expectations.

Mercer suggests that the contradictory responses of different audiences to works by new black filmmakers such as *Songs* and *Passion of Remembrance* need to be understood in the context of an emergent film tradition which, as yet, does not have the framework of an appropriate critical language with which to discuss it (1990a). He argues that white audiences and critics look to Euro-American avant-garde film practice as their framework through which to categorize something which appears to confound their expectations of

what black films should be like. Black audiences, he argues, are
equally mystified and are 'bemused by the originality of a practice
that explicitly draws on a dual inheritance from both Third World
and First World cultures' (1990a: 26). The absence of an ongoing
discourse of radical black film criticism is largely due to the
marginalization of black filmmakers and the consequent desire to
celebrate any film which has emerged simply because it has been
made at all. As black filmmaking begins to function as a viable,
vibrant and more visible tradition in its own right, it is appropriate
to begin to develop a rigorous and relevant critical framework. 'My
concern is to explore whether a more adequate model of criticism
might not be derived from the critical practice performed in the
films themselves' (1990a: 27). What Mercer wants to put forward as
a critical tool is the concept of 'interruption', whereby the critic
engages directly with the text rather than attempting to interpret
it within the existing grammar of mainstream film theory and
criticism.

Who can throw stones?

One of the problems with attacking or at least opposing mainstream
cinema criticism is that mainstream cinema itself, that is, the *practice*, is often conflated with the *theory*, so that both films and criticism are elided and treated as if they were the same thing.
Williamson wants to make a clear distinction between these two
activities, since she is generally hostile to the assumptions that
inflect mainstream criticism (and critics) but rather less rigid in her
views on mainstream films and their audiences (1988). For
Williamson, part of the problem of criticism is that black filmmakers
appear to be more interested in receiving feedback from their peer
professionals than with a critique emanating from the viewing public. If artists cannot make or take criticism openly then it goes
underground, becoming more malevolent and fuelling artistic para-
noia. Williamson pointedly states that 'I don't want to spend too
much time picking out particular films, but for example I have yet to
read or participate in a free-ranging critical discussion of *Passion of
Remembrance*' (1988: 33).

Williamson is describing precisely the danger that Hall and
others have cautioned against, of fêting a film because it is black and
then abstaining from providing the kind of critical response which
would be routinely given to other types of film effort and which
would in turn push black film practice forward. The reasons for this
refusal to criticize are complex, including the general desire to

support any film whose makers have heroically struggled to get it made in the face of extreme adversity. But Williamson touches on a much more prosaic reason which, as a white critic and a woman, she feels is more pertinent. This is that as a woman she has tirelessly fought against the tendency of male critics to intervene in and engage with feminist film discourse and now recognizes that as a white critic, she (and others like her) may well be seen as committing the same act of appropriation: 'There is a reluctance by white critics to make criticisms of films by black filmmakers because they feel (sometimes quite rightly) not qualified to do so, or to put it more bluntly, they are afraid of appearing racist' (1988: 33). It is important to identify exactly who is doing the criticizing since there are obvious problems in black films simply providing the artistic food for white intellectual consumption so that 'white institutions provide structures of control in which white intellectuals theorise about racism while ethnic film and video producers supply "experimental" materials in the form of testimony and documentary' (Fusco, 1988b: 82). But it is equally important to guard against dismissing the critical gaze simply because the object and the subject do not share the same ethnicity. The recent imperatives towards political correctness militate to some extent against taking a determinedly critical view of black film, since political support becomes confused with aesthetic and critical judgement. Black film works then become in danger of being valued for the blackness of their directors rather than the strength of their narratives, carefully insured against criticism by the white audience. It is right to be cautious about commenting on films which can only ever have second-hand resonances for an individual, but that is not to say it should not and cannot be done. Such responses will undoubtedly be different from those made from a more personally informed position, but they are not automatically of lesser or no value. Otherwise all that is left is a separatist critique where only black-on-black or women-on-women criticism is deemed acceptable and valid. The white critic's anxiety about appearing racist in critiquing black film is further exacerbated when black commentators dismiss those white critiques which do emerge on the grounds that white critics/audiences cannot understand black film because they are impeded by their Eurocentric history and lack of shared experiences (cf. Mercer, 1990a).

Towards a critical framework for black film: ins and outs

The need to develop an appropriate framework through which to critique black media has preoccupied a number of commentators, particularly now that black film and other cultural and artistic activities are more visible. As Henriques points out, when the publication of a black novel or book of poetry or the production of a play or film constituted a significant event, the enormous struggle that the black artist had gone through in order to actually produce something which the public would be able to see or hear was worthy of praise in its own right, sometimes regardless of the content. 'One of the reasons for this, perhaps as a hang-over from earlier days, has been the tendency to rely on a kind of siege mentality which says that anything we do must be good' (1988: 18). Now that black arts and culture have established themselves as a particular set of practices, it is necessary to be rather more rigorous in making critical responses. Yearwood argues that instead of considering black film outside the framework of conventional film criticism, historians and commentators have used the Hollywood tradition and its system of ideological support as the bases for understanding black cinema (1982b). This has meant that differences in style, tone and content of black films, when judged against mainstream white films, have tended to be misunderstood as indicative of poor production values, inexperienced filmmakers and/or symptomatic of technical and artistic limitations. Thus innovation and experimentation have been regarded not as an exciting subversion of otherwise stale formulae but rather the consequence of over-ambitious amateurs trying, and conspicuously failing, to play in the big league. Crusz puts the dilemma succinctly when he argues that the technology of filmmaking has developed within a specific historic and cultural space – Euro-American – which has traditionally marginalized 'other' voices.

> The Euro-American history and world view has misrepresented and marginalised black people. Therefore, when black people choose film as a means of earning a living, as a channel for political action, for our particular and specific aesthetic creations, for entertainment and for pleasure, we constantly have to work with and against a technology which is not neutral. (1985: 154)

Arts institutions firstly ignored black arts, then regarded them as exotic and marginal activities and finally acknowledged their worth, but ultimately damned with faint praise. Fusco suggests that one of the problems in developing a critical framework for interrogating black film is the tendency to construct theories retrospectively and, as a result, to then have problems relating to the texts. 'Conceptual difficulties arise when one attempts to create movements retroactively ... there are frequent attempts to define in theory what was never made clear in practice' (1989: 9). For Fusco, then, speaking specifically on filmmaking practices in Latin America, films are the individual efforts of a range of diverse filmmakers on an equally varied number of themes which cannot now bear scrutiny as if they were all of a piece, all part of the same movement. For example, all the individuals who are given the credit for constituting the first wave of Third Cinema filmmakers, such as Fernando Solanas, Octavio Getino or Julio García Espinos, are men. Such filmmakers, producing films and 'film acts' and working in guerrilla film units, produced films which reflected their preoccupation with global and political oppression rather than the more mundane social and sexual oppression routinely experienced by women. While race and class almost always inflected the narrative themes of oppositional Latin American films of the 1960s and 1970s, questions of gender were strangely absent. If these 'radical' films were, undoubtedly, *one* expression of an authentic Latin American experience, they were not the definitive statement of what it was like to live in those countries for everyone. Of equal significance was the disjunction between the articulated rhetoric of the makers of such films, that their efforts were 'for the masses' as part of a mass act of consciousness-raising, and their subsequent screening through art house film venues to highly selected audiences (Fusco, 1989). The point here is that Latin American film, Third Cinema or 'black' film do not constitute a homogenous and inclusive set of practices and concerns, except in so far as they are determinedly *oppositional* to the mainstream, including mainstream film practice, emerging as they do from a specifically minority experience and perspective.

Part of the problem involved in the construction of an appropriate critical framework for black film is its relative newness as a popular form and the difficulty for audiences to adapt existing terms of reference to a new type of work. The fact that different members of the same audience can read a film in many different ways is not, in itself, unusual. But what is perhaps new is the way in which image-making and representation have become sites of contestation, where notions of what it means to be British or American, for example, have begun to be debated, as well as speculating on what British or American cinema is or might become.

The innovative project with which black arts is now engaged is not simply to challenge that obsolete conception of Western homogeneity but to contest the very notion of what culture is or could be, what identities are possible, asserting that culture must be celebrated for its diversity rather than constrained by its sameness. (MacCabe, 1988)

Williamson argues that not only has the development of a black/good–white/bad orthodoxy within black cultural practices hampered the construction of an appropriate critical framework, but that such a tension is accompanied by two further dichotomous sets which encourage non-critical readings of black film works. First is one that says: realist, narrative, mainstream cinema = bad: non-narrative, difficult, oppositional cinema = good; and the other which polarizes Hollywood and/or mainstream cinema with the avant-garde and/or difficult cinema (Williamson, 1988). What this tendency encourages is that if a film is black, oppositional and avant-garde, then it is intrinsically 'good' and needs no further critical consideration. Similarly, films displaying the opposite characteristics are 'bad' and are thus undeserving of serious scrutiny. It cannot be accidental that the majority of black British films (and filmmakers) which have received the most attention – both critical and theoretical – and the most exposure in terms of distribution and screenings, have been those films which would sit comfortably in the avant-garde category, regardless of any other description they might carry, such as Third Cinema. In addition, Fusco makes the point that part of the 'success' in America of black British independent film is that it is infinitely easier to deal with an imported 'other' and the other's problems than to face up to the internal problems of one's own (1988b). Despite the self-identification of such films as essentially 'black' or from a Third Cinema perspective, their technical closeness with a Euro-American avant-garde film tradition makes such products especially inviting to an informed avant-garde audience eager for new material.

But Fusco also argues that the conformity of such films to the Euro-American avant-garde tradition is only 'apparent', and that the white cognoscenti's insistence on defining them as part of that practice is the result of a determinedly innocent view of modernist aesthetics which is seen as colour-blind. In other words, a white audience sees what it wants to see because it does not have the experience or understanding to fully comprehend the meaning of the message. Whilst Fusco acknowledges the very real influence that the modernist tradition has had on independent black film, she maintains that a critical framework with which to evaluate black artistic products should not be over-determined by modernist cri-

teria at the expense of a discourse which is actively (and construc-
tively) critical.

But of course, until a new language and critical framework is
established, not to mention a new and different cinematic form
which is sufficiently distinct from both mainstream and avant-
garde film practice to require a new vocabulary, filmmakers, critics
and audiences will necessarily be forced to adopt one or other of the
postures and attitudes which are already pre-existing, or else be
unable to communicate at all. Hall is also keen to construct a critical
framework within which to evaluate black film and argues that
bringing into play mainstream conventional criteria for judging
films is inadequate and inappropriate. Such criteria do not recognize the very particular circumstances in which most black films are
made, nor acknowledge their political underpinning, nor appreciate
their innovation. 'I no longer believe we can resolve the questions of
aesthetic value by the use of these transcendental, canonical cultural
categories' (1988: 30). Perhaps not, but while the rejection of the
existing framework of film criticism because of its Eurocentric assumptions is an entirely legitimate position to take, moving the
debate on to discuss the actual substance of an alternative one is still
stubbornly elusive. Gilroy, however, has one suggestion to make.
'The most productive way to proceed is to think about how certain
antagonisms might be sharpened, with a view to giving this "community" a way of having disagreements publicly and productively,
rather than simply rationalising the domination which exists'
(Gilroy, 1988a: 44). As another concrete step towards developing a
critical theory, Mercer suggests that any such critical framework
needs to take account of the multiple ethnicities which can be contained within the 'black' enterprise. Instead of developing a pre-
scriptive framework which seeks to judge black art, Mercer argues
for a gentler, more reflexive strategy, of criticism as conversation or
dialogue (1990b). In fact, Mercer's idea of such a strategy is that it
isn't a strategy at all, that there is no need to develop a general
theory or framework for interpretation but that dialogues about
film and between authors and readers should be played out in the
public domain, with acknowledgement that there is no one reading
or definitive statement. However, Mercer also acknowledges the
need for a more general theoretical framework for black art and
cultural criticism which enables something more grounded to develop than simply stating individual satisfactions and criticisms. He
argues that far from inventing something new, principles can be
derived from engaging in a critical dialogue with the aesthetic prin-

ciples with which art works are already inscribed. There is little point in reinventing the wheel when critical and theoretical texts, analyses and discourses are already available to be appropriated and recycled with a 1990s orientation. The 'philosophy of language' thesis elaborated by Bakhtin (1981) provides an appropriate 'analytic vocabulary which can be re-used for "making" sense of the struggle-in-language inscribed in the artistic text of the black diaspora' (Mercer, 1990b: 76). The appropriation of language for political and other ends has always been a subversive activity and as Gates points out, the deconstruction of language has been an ongoing project of oppressed populations since the colonial adventure first began,

> let me state clearly here that only a black person alienated from black language-use could fail to understand that we have been deconstructing white people's languages and discourse since that dreadful day in 1619 when we were marched off the boat in Virginia. Derrida did not invent deconstruction, *we* did! (1987: 38)

Black filmmakers working in Britain and America are put in the ambiguous position of being both part of society and altering its culture forever, while at the same time being excluded and marginalized by and from that society. Crusz suggests that as long as black filmmakers and theorists explore and debate issues within traditional structures of domination, they are simply colluding with and adding to that domination even while recognizing what is happening, resulting in a classic double bind. 'If we choose to work uncritically within the dominant traditions of practice and theory we face participating in our own subordination, mis-representation and marginalisation. Working completely outside the system is naive and impossible (Crusz, 1985: 156). But part of the project of challenging dominant discourse is to identify it and acknowledge its power. That, at least, is taking place.

7

Twenty-first Century Blues

No one today is purely *one* thing. Labels like Indian, or woman, or Muslim, or American are no more than starting points, which if followed into actual experience for only a moment are quickly left behind. Imperialism consolidated the mixture of cultures and identities on a global scale. But its worst and most paradoxical gift was to allow people to believe that they were only, mainly, exclusively, white, or black, or Western, or Oriental. Yet just as human beings make their own history, they also make their cultures and ethnic identities.

Edward Said, *Culture and Imperialism*

The original idea which prompted this book was to ask how, in developed societies fractured by ethnic hostility and nationalist fervour, television programmes and films portray black diaspora communities living in those societies, focusing specifically on the British and North American experience. What the preceding chapters have shown is that in mainstream (white) examples of those media, black people continue to be routinely portrayed within a restricted repertoire of types and genres which, though 'better' than in previous years, are still limited by an imaginative stasis among many media workers. There are, of course, some notable exceptions to this rather dreary conclusion, not least the influence that black media professionals are exerting on the media landscape by exploding many of the myths around ethnicity, identity and nation. It is becoming a little less unusual to see black people in ordinary roles, as shoppers, lawyers and office workers, appearing in narratives which are not explicitly about 'race'. Such characters are mostly allowed to act outside their skin where their ethnicity is not constantly highlighted as emblem, symbol, blackness. But more generally, the picture is still one of strict colour-coding. While it is certainly the case that mainstream American narratives tend to be much less self-conscious in their use of black actors than their British counterparts, integrated casting across all genres is still some way off. On the other hand, the cinema scene has been partially transformed by the emergence of black filmmakers producing mainstream and popular films to an enthusiastic mixed audience and subverting, however fleetingly, the orthodox race motifs which inflect many Hollywood texts.

A key feature of Western media industries is their dominance by white people and many of the problems of black (mis)-representation are a consequence of this fundamental fact. Many media professionals operate within an implicit, albeit unconscious, ethnocentric framework which routinely inscribes all broadcast output and through which cosy lens the world is viewed. This is not to suggest a kind of simplistic conspiracy theory, where racist white folks do their best to sensationalize the unacceptable practices of the black 'other' or to racialize events which are more correctly about class, but rather to point to an altogether more dangerous liberal trap – that the best intentions do not guarantee successful outcomes. We are all products of our history, culture and socialization and we all function within a specific cultural framework of dominant norms and values. Thus it matters little what the avowed intention of a film or programme-maker actually is, the resulting product can too easily be framed within an imperialist (and inherently exploitative) code, of 'us' looking in on 'them' – yet more exotic spectacle on which to gaze.

It is the poverty of black images rather than their frequency that constitutes the real problem, images constrained and constructed within a narrow band of character types in comedy and drama, or fetishized within a racialized demonology in factual programming. It is the lack of diversity when encountering black images as well as the pejorative or negative connotations which such images provoke which lie at the centre of the representation debate in the media mainstream. There is absolutely nothing in it for white folks to give black communities a voice, to disrupt their cosy white world to make room for uppity black non-traditionals. The perpetuation of negative imagery and the reinforcement of cherished race preju- dices serve a valuable function both in deflecting comment away from the equally crucial and pertinent issues of class and gender and also in shoring up a disintegrating white hegemony through the celebratory invocation of a national (white) pride.

This book has concentrated on looking at the final product. It has focused almost exclusively on the screened image, but implicated in that cut is the decision-making process and editing strategies which have taken place along the way. Whatever research is conducted into how black communities are represented by the media and the effect that such representations subsequently have on the viewing public, it must be acknowledged that what appears on the large and the small screen is the result of a complex of decisions taken by the gate-keepers of the media industry. If the production of films is largely contingent on the potential marketability of the product as perceived by men (as they invariably are) in suits and the spin doctors, television programmes are made with one eye on the ratings while the other speculates on the limits of acceptability. Although the world of television prides itself on its accountability mechanisms, with various watchdog quangos sitting in judgement over programme content, the proliferation of satellite and cable across the globe is already making a mockery of 'regulation' and in any case, the media monitors have always been much more interested in sex and violence than in equality of image. The global reach of television networks such as CNN and BBC World Service has significant consequences for the circulation of particular images, particular stories, particular perspectives and the transfer of media power into fewer hands encourages the view that, as McLuhan and Fiore predicted, we already live in a global village (1968). In order to make sense of black images now and their importance for individual nations and communities, it is necessary to consider, albeit briefly, the development of a global media future.

Global futures, local lives

The increasing sophistication of electronic media and telecommunications systems, together with improvements in transport systems, have resulted in a diminishing world in time and space and the task is to identify the importance of global media for nation-states and their black diaspora communities, to get behind the rhetoric and explore the potential of globalization. The 'global' idea has concerned cultural commentators, political economists and various other theorists for many years although the 1990s have seen a significant growth in rhetorical enquiry around the notion (see for example Featherstone (ed), 1990; King (ed), 1991; McGrew, Lewis et al., 1992). But Robertson cautions against the notion of globalization being regarded as a 'play zone' and a site 'for the expression of residual social-theoretical interests, interpretive indulgence, or the display of world-ideological preferences' (1990: 16). He points out that although a body of analysis and research has been conducted around globalization, work has tended to focus on the general idea rather than concentrate on the concept itself and the notion remains largely fixed in the domain of the theoretical as a fiercely contested topic. For every theorist who rehearses the push towards globalization there is another who demonstrates the durability of defining categories such as First World/Third World, over-developed/developing, North/South.

At least one of the anxieties surrounding the notion of a global culture is its tendency to smooth away local, regional and national distinctions in favour of a bland and homogenized global soup. As the distribution of an entertainment channel like MTV across the world demonstrates, media products which are destined to travel the globe are likely to be culturally 'neutral', with a 'downgrading of cultural specificity in themes and settings and a preference for formats and genres which are thought to be more universal' (McQuail, 1994: 112). The potential for negative media stereotypes to circulate internationally, 'maintaining unequal relations of race and gender, and fuelling cross-national misunderstanding, mis-trust, and conflict' (Sreberny-Mohammadi, 1990: 306) is clearly sig-nificant. And as Appadurai points out, fears about homogenization can be exploited by nation-states in relation to their own minority groups, by suggesting that this external enemy is more real than its own hegemonic imperatives (1990). For Appadurai, models of global culture which posit a simple centre-periphery tension are analytically inadequate and he advocates instead a more sophisti-cated framework which can analyse the complex of overlapping disjunctures. His model is based around an exploration of the inter-actions between five dimensions of global cultural flow which he terms ethnoscapes, mediascapes, technoscapes, financescapes and ideoscapes. These 'scapes' form the building blocks of the 'im-agined worlds', that is, 'the multiple worlds which are constituted by the historically situated imaginations of persons and groups spread around the globe' (1990: 296–7). Crucially, global cultural flow occurs because ideas and images, people, money and machin-ery move at different speeds within and between different commu-nities. Notions of nationality and national identity thus become complicated as people move between continents and develop mul-tiple identifications and attachments. Images and ideas circulate internationally, becoming absorbed or remaining alien but either way, irrevocably changing indigenous cultures with their constant flux. Contradictions and disjunctures continually occur as nations embrace some aspects of cultural flow such as entertainment tele-vision, new technology and cash even while they reject others, such as democracy.

But concrete evidence to support the existence of a global culture is still difficult to find. Smith questions totalizing theories of cultural globalization, asking whether such systems really are fusing national cultures or at any rate overlaying them with a new 'cosmopolitan' culture (Smith, 1991). Though he acknowledges the undoubted sophistication and reach of global media and technology, he theorizes global culture as constituting a pastiche of borrowed styles and concerns which masquerade as something new and decidedly postmodern, as standing in for a pseudo-classical postmodernist mass culture. This culture is not fixed in time or space but is floating and forever fluid, truly global and spectacularly false. If the vast variety of different cultures which have been rehabilitated and reshaped for global packaging are, at base, simple human products – culture as artistic construction – then a global culture is surely the most ambitious project of human imagination. 'It is not enough to imagine the global community; new and wider forms of political association and different types of cultural community will first have to emerge. It is likely to be a piecemeal movement, disjointed and largely unplanned' (Smith, 1991: 160). But new models of globalization stress the interconnectivity between nations and describe the breakdown of the time–space dialectic where nowhere is any longer remote, everywhere is connected. Diaspora communities are able to inhabit two different worlds simultaneously and, as McNeill notes, 'human communities . . . are becoming partially detached from geography' (McNeill, 1994: 304). Contrary to the more pessimistic view of globalization, cultural flows are not just one-way, not just American imports invading the rest of the world. Although the world-wide consumption of Western cultural products remains significant there is increasing interest by the West in the importation of media products from the developing world. This impulse can be partially explained by the flows of communities across the globe – the changing 'ethnoscape', to use Appadurai's term – encouraging a sense of deterritorialization not just in terms of 'images and texts, but also of peoples, creating a highly mobile, nomadic, restless global environment' (Sreberny-Mohammadi and Mohammadi, 1994: 6). As cultural artefacts journey across the world, they are received, transformed and hybridized in an ongoing process of cultural (re)production.

But despite the cosy inclusivity implied by 'global' labelling, culture still has to be conceptualized along a range of dimensions – spatially, politically, economically, historically and socially – the global is also the local, the international is also the national (King, 1991). Talking global-speak conceals the myriad differences between all the locals, all the regions, all the nationals and in any case, global media messages are still capable of multiple interpretations contingent on local circumstances and dominant ideas. As Wallerstein points out, despite the fashionable suggestion that we are all global now, world history demonstrates conclusively the opposite (1991). Culture is associated with the nation and the state and distinguishes us from them, almost always with a degree of xenophobia so that culture operates as a specific source of identity. Recent internecine struggles across the world attest to the power of ethnic absolutism and its insistence on purity, and the various 'returns' to traditional culture which have taken place in former colonized regions have generated a variety of religious and nationalist fundamentalisms (Said, 1994). But a growth in global culture would not necessarily mean that local, regional and national identifications would have to be sacrificed and indeed a retreat into localism would be a perfectly logical counter-response to the homogenizing tendencies of a voracious globalism.

If it is not yet possible to talk of a global culture, in the sense of a unitary and homogenized world perspective which is actually in existence, it *is* relevant to talk about the global reach of popular media and to contemplate what this means for the production and circulation of black images. The trend towards the internationalization of mass communication is now assumed to be underway but little is known about the cultural consequences of these global media flows. As already noted, the major problem with globalization is its imperialist tendencies and its potential to displace indigenous cultures in favour of poor imitations of the West. For the celebrants, global culture offers the promise of an expansion of 'good' ideas such as democracy to a wider public as well as offering an escape from the restrictive and repressive regimes of some nation-states. But even taking this more optimistic view of a global media culture, the implication remains a homogenizing one. Despite its postmodern nod to inclusivity, global media remains firmly centred in the West, responding to the interests, assumptions and images demanded by Western audiences. While a global culture may acknowledge difference and celebrate diversity at a superficial level, its primary task lies in the absorption of distinctiveness to produce a kind of stratified homogeneity – the same but different (Hall, 1991a). The resolution of contradiction provides the motor for change since globalization cannot continue without learning how to live with and work through difference. The global space is not uncontested, but the site of constant struggle: the struggles over identity occur on the same plane. While global media may open up and add to the cultural options of some, it may at the same time and in the same place function to usurp the cultural space of minority others. In a deregulated media environment which is keen to distribute media products around the globe as well as domestically, less popular and more challenging oppositional work is likely to receive less exposure. The subversive potential of black media texts is unlikely to be realized in a media environment where the national lottery (in Britain) or the O. J. Simpson trial (in America) is the most popular show in town.

An alternative media future

One clear mode of resistance to globalizing tendencies and white-dominated Western media has been through the development of minority media (film and television) and the rejection, in some brave countries, of US programming. It is hard to fight against global forces which are intent on making the media world a blander place to be, and so a more fruitful enterprise perhaps lies in constructing an oppositional media practice at the local level. This return to a smaller space, a smaller place is now being appropriated by those who have traditionally occupied the margins. It is there at the periphery that meaningful change, tangible change, graspable change is taking place. The push towards authentic representations of those dispossessed others, the peoples of the various diasporas, has resulted in a journey of redemption where marginalized communities are exploring their own histories and communities, singing their own songs. This process of recovery is a painful, joyous, grassroots movement, a way of refiguring and re-presenting history as a bottom-up project of recuperation rather than a top-down doctrine of subordination.

The developments in cable technology and its widespread availability, at least in America (less so in Britain, but it is a growing market), has opened up new possibilities for black viewers and black media professionals working in broadcasting. That there is a vibrant and enthusiastic audience for popular black-originated work can be seen by the success of the US cable network, Black Entertainment Television, which was launched in 1980 with $15,000 of Robert Johnson's personal cash and $500,000 of Telecommunications Inc. investment. In 1992, BET was valued at between $220 million and $250 million. When he conceived the project in 1979, Johnson's objective was for the company to become the primary producer-distributor of black-oriented cable programming as well as the most significant vehicle through which to reach black consumers (Salmas, 1992). By the mid-1990s BET was the only cable channel of its kind, reaching 31.9 million households with a schedule of entertainment, music, news, current affairs and sport. In 1990, the British-born *Desmonds* was the first British show to be broadcast on BET. As well as BET which is geared towards an African American audience, America's other significant ethnic minority, the Hispanic-speaking communities, are also being catered for through cable stations such as the New York-based Spanish International Network (SIN) and other Spanish language channels such as Telemundo and Univision. These channels specialize in soaps, variety shows and football, and their development can be seen as a response to the poverty and paucity of black and other minority images which are available across mainstream programming. They represent a serious critique of the failure of television to adequately represent its viewing community to itself and suggests that the future for mass media may lie in specialization and niche marketing rather than the bland and numbing globalization promised by universal MTV.

The success of BET in exploiting the potential of an eager black audience has now made the transatlantic crossing to Britain and Identity Television (IDTV), marketed as Britain's first black entertainment channel, was launched in June 1993. IDTV is backed by BET and began transmitting on the London Interconnect system to approximately 150,000 homes. As with BET, IDTV's objectives are clear: to provide a quality black entertainment channel on the UK cable television networks, 18 hours a day, 7 days a week. The publicity material for the channel boldly says: 'it's your identity – get to know it!' The schedule is a mix of programmes from America, the Caribbean, Africa and the UK and includes soaps, music, comedy and current affairs programmes. Although it is currently only available to London-based households, IDTV intends to raise awareness amongst all those who currently receive cable – about 600,000 nationally – but the total market is thought to be in the region of 2.9 million homes. In September 1993, IDTV secured a major deal with the American channel NBC, to show the new comedy series *Here and Now*, starring Malcolm-Jamal Warner of *The Cosby Show* fame. Like BET, IDTV aims to set up a production arm so that it can produce and commission programmes as well as broadcast imported material. IDTV is only the latest player in the alternative black media network which is establishing itself in Britain: the satellite channel TV Asia has been operating in Britain for some time and black radio stations are already an integral part of the local radio landscape.

In addition to the challenging work being produced by black film- and programme-makers, former Wall Street banker Stephen Byrd formed American Cinema Group in 1993 to develop films for, by and about African Americans. Byrd reports that he is eschewing the urban violence genre which has been so popular in recent years, and claims to have uncovered a significant amount of interest in Japan and Europe for alternative types of black film product. 'I think the market is clamouring for fascinating characters [and] I am keen to emphasise the stories that African Americans have to tell, but I would also like to see integrated casts' (Byrd quoted in Screen International, 30.4.1993). Current projects include a remake of *A Streetcar Named Desire* to include an all-black cast. Polygram, the financier to Van Peebles's *Posse*, is also planning to establish a Motown-style film company devoted to black artists and the black cable channel, BET, is partnering Blockbuster Entertainment Corporation to form BET Pictures, a joint venture which will fund, produce and distribute low-cost, black-themed, family-oriented films. BET is already identifying film projects and overseas finance, and productions are expected to be budgeted at between $1.5 and $3 million.

The involvement of more black people in the media, both in front of and behind the camera is, as has already been indicated, a necessary first step in securing more authentic representations of black communities in television and film. Although this is not to say that always and everywhere it is absolutely necessary to be black in order to write convincingly about that reality, it is to suggest that the experiences of black people are most authentically enunciated and explored by themselves. But there needs to be an acknowledgement that there is no one black voice, no one black perspective. Those (few) black-originated works which do manage to achieve a public airing, on television or at the cinema, do not represent the entirety of black experiences and cannot be expected to do so. Nor should such works be criticized when they refuse to play the 'positive' images game or reject the imperatives of what Malik describes as the cinema of duty (1994). 'I can't take seriously the notion that one is doing a disservice to black people by writing about all the different sorts of black people in our community . . . I think that if you're any kind of artist, you have to deal with the whole spectrum of human experience' (M. Phillips, 1992b: 177). It is precisely the paucity of black images in the media, outside of race-relations narratives which are clearly about some aspect of the black 'condition', which causes those few which are screened to bear the unacceptable burden of representing all. If the organizational culture of the media

industry itself does not change fundamentally, it is hard to be optimistic about significant shifts in representation and improved access for black media practitioners into the industry more generally.
Although the institutional structure of many public (and private)
media organizations is beginning to change with the setting up of
monitoring committees and the development of codes of conduct
the pace of change is painfully slow. Without the gift of clairvoy-
ance, it is fruitless to predict what a deregulated media environment
might look like in the future, although it is not outside the realms of
possibility to think that more will probably mean less. Where that
leaves imaginative and oppositional texts which challenge the cosy
hegemony of white Western societies is unclear, but it will be a sad
day if the precarious foothold that black media professionals have
managed to obtain in the industry is blithely kicked away in the
rush to embrace global EmpTV.

Bibliography

Adepegba, Ade 1993: Blackchat. *Artrage*, April, 18–19

Adorno, T., Frankel-Brunswick, E., Levinson, D. J. and Nevitt, Sanford 1950: *The Authoritarian Personality*. New York: Harper and Row

Akomfrah, John 1988a: Introductory Address to Third Scenario: Theory and Politics of Location Conference, 6 October 1988, Midlands Art Centre, Birmingham, UK. *Framework*, 36, 5–6

—— 1988b: Interview with Paul Gilroy and Jim Pines. *Framework*, 35, 9–17

—— 1992: Interview with Pervaiz Khan. *Sight & Sound*, 2:3, 30–1

Alexander, Karen 1989: Mothers, Lovers and Others. *Monthly Film Bulletin*, 56:669, 314–16

—— 1993a: Film Review: Malcolm X. *Sight & Sound*, 3:3, 46–7

—— 1993b: Film Review: Daughters of the Dust. *Sight & Sound*, 3:9, 20–2

Ali, Yasmin 1993: Address to the Ninth Birmingham Film and Television Festival, 15 October

Alvarado, Manuel and Thompson, John O. 1990: *The Media Reader*. London: British Film Institute

Andersen, Erica Surat 1993: Film Review: Mississippi Masala. *Film Quarterly*, 46:4, 23–6

Anderson, Beverley 1988: How Television Depicts Blacks. *New Society*, 11.3.1988, 20–1

Annan, Lord 1977: *Report of the Committee on the Future of Broadcasting*. London: HMSO Cmnd 6753

Ansorge, Peter 1989: Interview with Author

Anwar, Mohammed 1978: *Who Tunes in to What?* London: Commission for Racial Equality

Anwar, Mohammed and Shang, Anthony 1982: *Television in a Multi-Racial Society*. London: Commission for Racial Equality

Appadurai, Arjun 1990: Disjuncture and Difference in the Global Cultural Economy. In Mike Featherstone (ed.), *Global Culture: Nationalism, Globalization and Modernity*, London and New Delhi: Sage, 295–310

Armstrong, Paul B. 1991: Play and Cultural Differences. *Kenyon Review*, NS 13. Cited in Mick Gidley (ed.) (1992), *Representing Others: White Views of Indigenous Peoples*, Exeter: University of Exeter Press

Atkin, David 1992: An Analysis of Television Series with Minority-lead Characters. *Critical Studies in Mass Communication*, 9, 337–49

Attile, Martine 1988: The Passion of Remembrance: Background. In Kobena Mercer (ed.), *Black Film: British Cinema*, ICA document no. 7, London: British Film Institute/ICA, 53–4

Attile, Martine and Blackwood, Maureen 1986: Black Women and Representation. In Charlotte Brunsdon (ed.), *Films for Women*, London: British Film Institute, 202–8

Auguiste, Reece 1988a: Handsworth Songs: Some Background Notes. *Framework*, 35, 4–8

——1988b: Interview with Paul Gilroy and Jim Pines on Handsworth Songs. *Framework*, 35, 9–17

——1989: Black Independents and Third Cinema: the British Context. In Jim Pines and Paul Willemen (eds), *Questions of Third Cinema*, London: British Film Institute, 212–17

Baker, Houston A. Jr 1993: Spike Lee and the Commerce of Culture. In Manthia Diawara (ed.), *Black American Cinema*, New York and London: Routledge, 154–76

Bakhtin, Mikhail 1981: *The Dialogic Imagination* (edited by Michael Holquist). Austin and London: University of Texas Press

Baldwin, James 1955: Life Straight in de Eye. *Commentary*, 19:1, 74–9. Cited in Lindsay Patterson (1975), *Black Films and Film-makers*, New York: Dodd Mead & Company

Baraka, Amiri 1993: Spike Lee at the Movies. In Manthia Diawara (ed.), *Black American Cinema*, New York and London: Routledge, 145–53

Barry, Angela 1988: Black Mythologies: Representations of Blacks on British Television. In John Twitchin (ed.), *The Black and White Media Book*, Stoke-on-Trent: Trentham Books, 83–102

Bergan, Ronald 1995: Black and Proud in the West. *Guardian*, 14.1.95

Bhabha, Homi 1983: The Other Question: the Stereotype and Colonial Discourse. *Screen*, 24:4, 18–36

——1989: The Commitment to Theory. In Jim Pines and Paul Willemen (eds), *Questions of Third Cinema*. London: British Film Institute, 111–32

Bhuchar, Suman 1989: I'm British But . . . Interview with Gurinder Chadha. *Bazaar*, 8, 9

Biddis, M. 1970: *Gobineau: Selected Political Writings*. London: Jonathan Cape

Birt, John 1980: Press Release Launching London Weekend Television's London Minorities Unit. *Broadcast*, 1040, 14.1.1980, 6

Bobo, Jacqueline 1991: Black Women in Fiction and Nonfiction: Images of Power and Powerlessness. *Wide Angle*, 13:3, 72–81

——1992: The Politics of Interpretation: Black Critics, Filmmakers and Audiences. In Michele Wallace with Gina Dent (ed.), *Black Popular Culture*, Seattle: Bay Press, 65–74

Bogle, Donald 1985a: A Separate Cinema. *Film Comment*, 21:5, 29–30

——1985b: 'B' . . . is for Black: No Business like Micheaux Business. *Film Comment*, 21:5, 31–8

——1989: *Blacks in American Film and Television*. New York: Simon & Schuster (Fireside)

——1994: *Toms, Coons, Mulattoes, Mammies and Bucks: an Interpretive History of Blacks in American Films* (3rd revised edn). Oxford: Roundhouse Publishing

Bourne, St Clair 1982: The Development of the Contemporary Black Film Movement. In Gladstone Yearwood (ed.), *Black Cinema Aesthetics: Issues in Black Filmmaking*, Ohio: Ohio University Papers on Afro-American, African and Caribbean Studies, Ohio University Centre for Afro-American Studies, 92–105

Bourne, Stephen 1983: Star Equality. *Films and Filming*, 351, 31–4

——1984: Star Equality. *Films and Filming*, 352, 24–5

——1993: Funny Ladies. *Artrage*, May: 11, 17

Bowser, Pearl 1982: Sexual Imagery and the Black Woman in Cinema. In Gladstone Yearwood (ed.), *Black Cinema Aesthetics: Issues in Black Filmmaking*, Ohio: Ohio University Papers on Afro-American, African and Caribbean Studies, Ohio University Centre for Afro-American Studies, 42–52

Brown, Colin 1991: Lost in the Pack. *Screen International*, 15.11.1991, 10–11

Browne, Lincoln 1979: Babylon Bridges the Black Gap. *TV Times*, 97:48, 22.11.1979, 34

Buckingham, David 1987: *Public Secrets: EastEnders and Its Audience*. London: British Film Institute

Caesar, Imruh, Martin, Henry, Prescod, Colin and Shabazz, Menelik 1981: Review of Wolcott. *Roots*, March. Reprinted in Thérèse Daniels and Jane Gerson (eds) (1989), *The Colour Black: Black Images in British Television*. London: British Film Institute, 79–84

Cantor, Muriel G. and Cantor, Joel M. 1992: *Prime-time Television: Content and Control* (2nd edn). London and New Delhi: Sage

Carby, Hazel 1987: *Reconstructing Womanhood: the Emergence of the Afro-American Novelist*. New York: Oxford University Press

Carey, J. 1975: A Cultural Approach to Communication. *Communication*, 2, 1–22

Cashmore, Ellis 1994: . . . *and There Was Television*. London and New York: Routledge

Cham, M. and Andrade-Watkins, C. (eds) 1988: *Blackframes: Critical Perspectives on Black Independent Cinema*. Cambridge, Mass: MIT Press

Clark, Steve (ed.) 1993: *Nelson Mandela Speaks*. New York: Pathfinder

Cohen, Phil and Gardner, Carl 1982: *It Ain't Half Racist, Mum*. London: Comedia

Cottle, Simon 1992: 'Race', Racialization and the Media: a Review and Update of Research. *Sage Race Relations Abstracts*, 17:2, 3–57

Cripps, Thomas 1967: The Death of Rastus: Negroes in American Films since 1945. *Phylon*, 28:3, 267–75

——1977: *Slow Fade to Black: the Negro in American Film 1900–1942*. Oxford: Oxford University Press.

——1978: *Black Film as Genre.* Bloomington and London: Indiana University Press

——1980: The Dark Spot in the Kaleidoscope: Black Images in American Film. In Randall M. Miller (ed.), *The Kaleidoscopic Lens: How Hollywood Views Ethnic Groups*, Englewood, NJ: Jerome Ozer, 15–35

——1982: New Black Cinema and Uses of the Past. In Gladstone Yearwood (ed.), *Black Cinema Aesthetics: Issues in Black Filmmaking*, Ohio: Ohio University Papers on Afro-American, African and Caribbean Studies, Ohio University Centre for Afro-American Studies, 19–26

——1993: *Making Movies Black: the Hollywood Message Movies from World War Two to the Civil Rights Era.* New York, Oxford: Oxford University Press

Crusz, Robert 1985: Black Cinemas, Film Theory and Dependent Knowledge. *Screen*, 26:3/4, 152–6

Curran, James, Ecclestone, Jake, Oakley, Giles and Richardson, Alan (eds) 1986: *Bending Reality: the State of the Media.* London: Pluto Press

Dabydeen, David 1980: Eighteenth Century English Literature on Commerce and Slavery. In David Dabydeen (ed.), *The Black Presence in English Literature*, Manchester: Manchester University Press

Daniels, Thérèse 1990: Beyond Negative or Positive Images. In Janet Willis and Tana Wollen (eds), *The Neglected Audience*, London: British Film Institute

——1992: *Black and White in Colour (Programme Notes)*, London: British Film Institute

——1993: Address to the Ninth Birmingham Film and Television Festival, 15 October

——1994: Programmes for Black Audiences. In Stuart Hood (ed.), *Behind the Scenes: the Structure of British Television in the Nineties*, London: Lawrence & Wishart

Daniels, Thérèse and Gerson, Jane (eds) 1989: *The Colour Black: Black Images in British Television.* London: British Film Institute

Dash, Julie 1986: Interview. *Independent*, 9:10, 16–20

Dates, Jannette and Barlow, William (eds) 1990: *Split Image: African Americans in the Mass Media.* Washington: Howard University Press

DelGaudio, Sybil 1983: The Mammy in Hollywood Film: I'd Walk a Million Miles for One of Her Smiles. *Jump Cut*, 28, 23–5

Dhillon-Kashyap, Perminder 1988: Locating the Asian Experience. *Screen*, 29:4, 120–7

Dhondy, Farrukh 1984: Black Is a Point of View. *Broadcast*, 10.8.84, 20

——1988: Interview. *The Listener*, 8.7.1988

——1992: Interview. In Jim Pines (ed.), *Black and White in Colour: Black People in British Television since 1936*, London: British Film Institute

——1993: Interview with Julia Knight. *Spectrum*, 1, 36–9

Diakité, Madubuko 1980: *Film, Culture and the Black Filmmaker: a Study of Functional Relationships and Parallel Developments.* New York: Arno Press

Diawara, Manthia 1988: Black Spectatorship: Problems of Identification and Resistance. *Screen*, 29:4, 66–79

—— 1993: Black American Cinema: the New Realism. In Manthia Diawara (ed.), *Black American Cinema*, New York and London: Routledge, American Film Institute Readers Series, 3–25

Dovey, Jon 1993: Old Dogs and New Tricks: Access Television in the UK. In Tony Dowmunt (ed.), *Channels of Resistance: Global Television and Local Empowerment*, London: British Film Institute in association with Channel 4 Television, 163–75

Downing, John 1988: The Cosby Show and American Racial Discourse. In G. Smitherman-Donaldson and Teun van Dijk (eds), *Disclosure and Discrimination*, Detroit: Wayne State University Press

Downing, John, Mohammadi, Ali and Sreberny-Mohammadi, Annabelle 1990: *Questioning the Media: a Critical Introduction*. Newbury Park: Sage

Dyer, Richard 1988: White. *Screen*, 29:4, 44–65

—— 1993: *The Matter of Images: Essays on Representation*. London and New York: Routledge

Dyson, Michael 1992: Out of the Ghetto. *Sight & Sound*, 2:6, 18–21

—— 1993: *Reflecting Black: African-American Cultural Criticism*. Minneapolis: University of Minnesota Press

Eliot, M. 1981: *American Television: the Official Art of the Artificial*. New York: Anchor

Eriksen, Thomas Hylland 1993: *Ethnicity and Nationalism: Anthropological Perspectives*. London and Boulder, Colorado: Pluto Press

Fanon, Frantz 1970: *Black Skin, White Masks*. London: Paladin (first published in 1952)

Fareed, Anjum 1992: The Wild Frontiers of Southall. *Bazaar*, 20, 5

Featherstone, Mike (ed.) 1990: *Global Culture: Nationalism, Globalization and Modernity*. London and New Delhi: Sage

Fife, Marilyn 1987: Promoting Racial Diversity in US Broadcasting: Federal Policies versus Social Realities. *Media, Culture and Society*, 9, 481–504

Forna, Memuna 1993: What's Race Got to Do with It? *Guardian*, 13.9.93

Fountain, Alan 1988: Channel 4 and Black Independents. In Kobena Mercer (ed.), *Black Film: British Cinema*, ICA document no. 7, London: British Film Institute/ICA, 42–4

—— 1989: *Workshop Policy in the 1990s*. London: Channel 4

Fraser, Nicholas 1993: Right to Be Wrong. *Guardian*, 29.11.1993

Fryer, Peter 1984: *Staying Power: the History of Black People in Britain*. London: Pluto Press

Fusco, Coco 1988a: The Other Is In: Black British Film in the US. In Kobena Mercer (ed.), *Black Film: British Cinema*, ICA document no. 7, London: British Film Institute/ICA, 37–9

—— 1988b: Fantasies of Oppositionality: Reflections on Recent Conferences in Boston and New York. *Screen*, 29:4, 80–93

—— 1989: About Locating Ourselves and Our Representation. *Framework*, 36, 7–14

Gabriel, Teshome H. 1989: Towards a Critical Theory of Third World Films. In Jim Pines and Paul Willemen (eds), *Questions of Third Cinema*, London: British Film Institute, 30–52

Gardner, Carl and Merck, Mandy 1980: Minority Reports. *Time Out*, 512, 8–14

Gates, Henry Louis 1989: TV's Black World Turns – but Stays Unreal. *New York Times*, 12.11.1989. Cited in Justin Lewis (1991) *The Ideological Octopus: an Exploration of Television and Its Audience*. New York and London: Routledge

Gates, H. Jr 1987: Authority (White) Power and the (Black) Critic: It's All Greek to Me. *Cultural Critique*, 7, 19–46

——1992: The Black Man's Burden. In Michele Wallace with Gina Dent (ed.), *Black Popular Culture*, Seattle: Bay Press

Gerima, Haile 1982: On Independent Black Cinema. In Gladstone Yearwood (ed.), *Black Cinema Aesthetics: Issues in Black Filmmaking*, Ohio: Ohio University Papers on Afro-American, African and Caribbean Studies, Ohio University Centre for Afro-American Studies, 104–13

——1989: Triangular Cinema, Breaking Toys and Dinknesh vs. Lucy. In Jim Pines and Paul Willemen (eds), *Questions of Third Cinema*, London: British Film Institute, 65–89

Ghani, Atif 1994: Projecting the Diaspora. *Black Film Bulletin*, 2:3, 3–4

Gidley, Mick 1992: Representing Others: an Introduction. In Mick Gidley (ed.), *Representing Others: White Views of Indigenous People*, Exeter: University of Exeter Press, 1–13

Gilbert, W. Stephen 1981: Off Air. *Broadcast*, 117, 10–11

Gilroy, Paul 1983: Channel 4: Bridgehead or Bantustan? *Screen*, 24, 130–6

——1987: *There Ain't No Black in the Union Jack*. London: Unwin Hyman

——1988a: Nothing but Sweat Inside My Hand: Diaspora Aesthetics and Black Arts in Britain. In Kobena Mercer (ed.), *Black Film: British Cinema*, ICA document no. 7, London: British Film Institute/ICA, 44–6

——1988b: Cruciality and the Frog's Perspective: an Agenda of Difficulties for the Black Arts Movement in Britain. *Third Text*, 5, 33–44

——1990a: It Ain't Where You're From, It's Where You're At. *Third Text*, 13, 3–16

——1990b: Art of Darkness: Black Art and the Problem of Belonging to England. *Third Text*, 10, 45–52

——1991a: Flipper Purify and Furious Styles. *Sight & Sound*, 1:4, 8–12

——1991b: Spiking the Argument. *Sight & Sound*, 1:7, 29–30

——1993: *The Black Atlantic: Modernity and Double Consciousness*. London and New York: Verso

Gitlin, Todd 1983: *Inside Prime-time*. New York: Pantheon

Gitlin, Todd (ed.) 1986: *Watching Television*. New York: Pantheon

Gittens, Tony 1982: Cultural Restitution and Independent Black Cinema. In Gladstone Yearwood (ed.), *Black Cinema Aesthetics: Issues in Black Filmmaking*, Ohio: Ohio University Papers on Afro-American, African and Caribbean Studies, Ohio University Centre for Afro-American Studies, 115–18

Givanni, June 1988: In Circulation: Black Films in Britain. In Kobena Mercer (ed.), *Black Film: British Cinema*, ICA document no. 7, London: British Film Institute/ICA, 39–41

—— 1993: Screen Scenes. *Black Film Bulletin*, 1:3, 4

Gledhill, Christine 1992: Pleasurable Negotiations. In Frances Bonner, Lizbeth Goodman, Richard Allen, Linda Janes and Catherine King (eds), *Imagining Women: Cultural Representations and Gender*, Cambridge: Polity Press in association with the Open University, 193–209

Gray, Herman 1993a: The Endless Slide of Difference: Critical Television Studies, Television and the Question of Race. *Critical Studies in Mass Communication*, 10:2, 190–7

—— 1993b: African-American Political Desire and the Seductions of Contemporary Cultural Politics. *Cultural Studies*, 7:3, 264–373

Greenberg, Bradley S. and Atkin, Charles K. 1982: Learning about Minorities from Television: a Research Agenda. In Gordon L. Berry and Claudia Mitchell-Kernan (eds), *Television and the Socialization of the Minority Child*. New York and London: Academic Press, 215–43

Guerrero, Ed 1993: Spike Lee and the Fever in the Racial Jungle. In Jim Collins, Hilary Radner and Ava Preacher Collins (eds), *Film Theory Goes to the Movies* (AFI Film Readers), New York and London: Routledge

Hacket, T. 1566: A Summary of the Antiquities and Wonders of the World. Cited in P. Fryer (1984), *Staying Power: the History of Black People in Britain*. London: Pluto Press

Hall, Stuart 1980: Coding and Encoding in the Television Discourse. In Stuart Hall/Centre for Contemporary Cultural Studies (eds), *Culture, Media, Language*. London: Hutchinson in association with CCCS, Birmingham, 197–208

—— 1981: The Whites of Their Eyes: Racist Ideologies and the Media. In George Bridges and Rosalind Brunt (eds), *Silver Linings: Some Strategies for the Eighties*. London: Lawrence & Wishart, 28–52

—— 1987: The Real Me: Postmodernism and the Question of Identity. London: ICA. Reproduced in Ann Gray and Jim McGuigan (eds), *Studying Culture*, London, New York, Melbourne and Auckland: Edward Arnold, 134–8

—— 1988: New Ethnicities. In Kobena Mercer (ed.), *Black Film: British Cinema*, ICA document no. 7, London: British Film Institute/ICA, 27–31

—— 1989: Cultural Identity and Cinematic Representation. *Framework*, 36, 68–81

—— 1991a: The Local and the Global: Globalization and Ethnicity. In Anthony D. King (ed.), *Culture, Globalization and the World-System*, Basingstoke: Macmillan in association with Department of Art and Art History, State University of New York, 19–40

—— 1991b: Old and New Identities, Old and New Ethnicities. In Anthony D. King (ed.), *Culture, Globalization and the World-System*, Basingstoke: Macmillan in association with Department of Art and Art History, State University of New York, 41–68

—— 1992: What Is This 'Black' in Black Popular Culture? In Michele Wallace with Gina Dent (ed.), *Black Popular Culture*, Seattle: Bay Press, 21–36

—— 1993: Culture, Community, Nation. *Cultural Studies*, 7:3, 349–63

Halstead, B. 1989: Is Science Racist? *The Salisbury Review*, 8:2, 10–15

Handelman, David 1992: The Last Time We Saw Richard. *Premiere*, 5:5, 78–90

Hanson, Charlie 1992: Interview. In Jim Pines (ed.), *Black and White in Colour: Black People in British Television since 1936*. London: British Film Institute

Hartmann, Paul and Husband, Charles 1974: *Racism and the Mass Media: a Study of the Role of the Mass Media in the Formation of White Beliefs and Attitudes in Britain*. London: Davis-Poynter

Hartsbough, D. 1989: *The Cosby Show* in Historical Context: Explaining Its Appeal to Middle-class Black Women. Paper presented to the Ohio State University Film Conference. Cited in Justin Lewis (1991), *The Ideological Octopus*, New York and London: Routledge

Head, Angela 1991: A History and Evaluation of the Workshop Declaration and the Future of Workshops. MA diss. University of Leeds

Hebdige, Dick 1987: Digging for Britain: an Excavation in Seven Parts. Cited in Kobena Mercer (ed.) (1988), *Black Film/British Cinema*. ICA document no. 7, London: British Film Institute/ICA

Henriques, Julian 1988: Realism and the New Language. In Kobena Mercer (ed.), *Black Film British Cinema*. ICA document no. 7. London: British Film Institute/ICA, 18–20

Hill, George and Hill, Sylvia Salverson 1985: *Blacks on Television*. London: Scarecrow Press

Hoberman, James 1976: A Black Pioneer: the Case of Oscar Micheaux. *No Rose*, 1:2, 23–31

Hood, Stuart 1980: *On Television*. London: Pluto Press

hooks, bell 1991: *Yearning: Race, Gender and Cultural Politics*. Boston: Turnaround

——1992: *Black Looks: Race and Representation*. London: Turnaround

——1993: The Oppositional Gaze: Black Female Spectators. In Manthia Diawara (ed.), *Black American Cinema*. New York and London: Routledge, 288–302

Hussain, Humayun 1992: Film Review: Bhaji on the Beach. *Artrage*, December, 24

Jackson, Lynne and Rasenberger, Jean 1988: Young British and Black. *Cineaste*, 16:4, 24–6

Jacobs, Lewis 1939: *The Rise of the American Film*. New York: Harcourt

Jamal, Mahmoud 1987: Dirty Linen. *Artrage*, 17:40

James, Nick, 1993: Film Review: Posse. *Sight & Sound*, 3:12, 49–50

Jhally, Sut and Lewis, Justin 1992: *Enlightened Racism: The Cosby Show, Audiences and the Myth of the American Dream*. Boulder and Oxford: Westview

Jivani, Alkarim 1991: Black Box. *Time Out*, 8.5.91

——1992: Multiculture Clash. *Impact*, 2, 26–7

Johnson, Albert 1959: Beige, Brown or Black. *Film Quarterly*, 13:1, 38–43

——1990: Moods Indigo: a Long View (Part 1). *Film Quarterly*, 44:2, 13–27

—— 1991: Moods Indigo: A Long View (Part 2). *Film Quarterly*, 44:3, 15–29

Jones, Jacquie 1990: In Sal's Country. *Cineaste*, 17:4, 34–5

—— 1991: The New Ghetto Aesthetic. *Wide Angle*, 13:3/4, 32–43

Jules, Jason 1994: Best Actress in a Submissive Role. *Sunday Times*, 13.3.94

Julien, Isaac 1985: Interview with Jim Pines on Territories. *Framework*, 26/27, 2–9

—— 1990: Interview with Andrea Stuart. *Producer*, 13, 18–19

—— 1992: Black Is, Black Ain't. In Michele Wallace with Gina Dent (ed.), *Black Popular Culture*, Seattle: Bay Press: 255–83

Julien, Isaac and Mercer, Kobena 1988: De Margin and de Centre. *Screen*, 29:4, 2–10

Kael, Pauline 1972: Notes on Black Movies. *New Yorker Magazine*. Reprinted in Lindsay Patterson (ed.), 1975, *Black Film and Film-makers*. New York: Dodd Mead & Company

Kagan, Norman 1970: Black American Cinema. *Cinema*, 6:2, 2–7

Kelemen, Paul 1992: Spike Lee's Jungle Fever. *Sage Race Relations Abstracts*, 17:4, 23–6

Kennedy, Lisa 1990: Women on the Edge of Male Violence. *Cineaste*, 17:4, 39

Kiernan, V. G. 1969: *The Lords of Humankind: European Attitudes towards the Outside World in the Imperial Age*. London: Weidenfeld & Nicolson

King, Anthony D. 1991: Spaces of Culture, Spaces of Knowledge. In Anthony D. King (ed.), *Culture, Globalization and the World-System*, Basingstoke: Macmillan in association with Department of Art and Art History, State University of New York, 1–18

King, Anthony D. (ed.) 1991: *Culture, Globalization and the World-System*. Basingstoke: Macmillan in association with Department of Art and Art History, State University of New York

King, Catherine 1992: The Politics of Representation: a Democracy of the Gaze. In Frances Bonner, Lizbeth Goodman, Richard Allen, Linda Janes and Catherine King (eds), *Imagining Women: Cultural Representations and Gender*, Cambridge: Polity Press in association with the Open University, 131–9

Kureishi, Hanif 1988: England, Bloody England. *Guardian*, 22.1.1988

Leab, Daniel J. 1975: *From Sambo to Superspade: the Black Experience in Motion Pictures*. London: Secker & Warburg

Lee, Spike 1986: Interview with Marlaine Glicksman. *Film Comment*, 22:5, 46–9

—— 1991: *Five for Five: the Films of Spike Lee*. New York: Stewart, Tabori and Chang

Lewis, Justin 1991: *The Ideological Octopus*. New York and London: Routledge

Lorimer, D. 1978: *Colour, Class and the Victorians*. London: Holmes and Meier

MacCabe, Colin 1988: Black Film in 80s Britain. In Kobena Mercer (ed.), *Black Film: British Cinema*, ICA document no. 7, London: British Film Institute/ICA, 31–2

McClelland, D. 1987: *Blackface to Blacklist: Al Jolson, Larry Parks and the Jolson Story*. New Jersey: Scarecrow Press

McDonald, J. Fred 1992: *Blacks and White TV: African Americans in Television since 1948* (2nd edn). Chicago: Nelson-Hall

McGrew, Anthony G., Lewis, Paul G. et al. 1992: *Global Politics: Globalization and the Nation-State*. Cambridge: Polity Press

McLuhan, Marshall and Fiore, Q. 1968: *War and Peace in the Global Village*. New York: McGraw-Hill

McNeill, William 1994: Reasserting the Polyethnic Norm. In John Hutchinson and Anthony D. Smith (eds), *Nationalism*, Oxford and New York: Oxford University Press, 300–5

McQuail, Denis (ed.) 1972: *Sociology of Mass Communication*. Harmondsworth: Penguin

McQuail, Denis 1994: *Mass Communication Theory: an Introduction* (3rd edn). London and New Delhi: Sage

McQuail, Denis, Blumler, Jay G. and Brown, J. R. 1972: The Television Audience: a Revised Perspective. In Denis McQuail (ed.), *Sociology of Mass Communication*. Harmondsworth: Penguin, 135–65

Malik, Sarita 1994: Beyond Identity: British Asian Film. *Black Film Bulletin*, 2:3, 12–13

Mapp, Edward 1972: *Blacks in American Films: Today and Yesterday*. City Metuchen: Scarecrow Press. Reprinted in Lindsay Patterson (1975), *Black Films and Film-makers: a Comprehensive Anthology from Stereotype to Superhero*. New York: Dodd Mead & Co.

Marshall, Tim 1988: Whiteness Test. *The Listener*, 14.4.1988, 4–6

Medhurst, Andy 1989: Introduction to Laughing Matters: Situation Comedies. In Thérèse Daniels and Jane Gerson (eds), *The Colour Black: Black Images in British Television*, London: BFI, 15–21

Melly, George 1988: Dark Divas. *The Listener*, 25.8.1988, 4–5

Mercer, Kobena 1988: Recoding Narratives of Race and Nation. In Kobena Mercer (ed.), *Black Film: British Cinema*, ICA document no. 7, London: British Film Institute/ICA, 4–14

——1989: Introduction. In Thérèse Daniels and Jane Gerson (eds), *The Colour Black: Black Images in British Television*, London: BFI, 1–111

——1990a: Diaspora Culture and the Dialogic Imagination: the Aesthetics of Black Independent Film in Britain. In Manuel Alvarado and John O. Thompson (eds), *The Media Reader*. London: British Film Institute, 24–35

——1990b: Black Art and the Burden of Representation. *Third Text*, 10, 61–79

——1990c: Black People in British Television. *Artrage*, 27, 5–8

Michener, Charles 1972: Black Movies. *Newsweek*. Reprinted in Lindsay Patterson (1975), *Black Films and Film-makers*. New York: Dodd Mead & Co.

Miles, Robert 1989: *Racism*. London: Routledge

Miller, James 1993: The Case of Early Black Cinema. *Critical Studies in Mass Communication*, 10:2, 181–4

Miller, Randall M. (ed.) 1980: *The Kaleidoscopic Lens: How Hollywood Views Ethnic Groups*. Englewood, NJ: Jerome Ozer

Millwood Hargreave, Andrea 1992: *The Portrayal of Ethnic Minorities on Television*. Broadcasting Standards Council working paper no. 7, London: BSC

Minh-ha, Trinh T. 1989: Outside In Inside Out. In Jim Pines and Paul Willemen (eds), *Questions of Third Cinema*. London: British Film Institute, 133–49

Mitchell, W. J. T. 1990: Representation. In Frank Lentricchia and Thomas McLaughlin (eds), *Critical Terms for Literary Study*. Chicago and London: University of Chicago Press, 11–22

Moir, Jim 1989: Interview with Author

Morar, Narendhra 1989: Interview with Author

Morris, Jeff 1991: Study of Deregulation in UK Public Service Broadcasting. MA thesis. University of Bristol

Morrison, Toni 1993: Black Matters. *Independent*, 5.10.93

Muwakkil, Salim 1990: Spike Lee and the Image Police. *Cineaste*, 17:4, 35–6

Neale, Steve 1993: The Same Old Story: Stereotypes and Difference. In Manuel Alvarado, Edward Buscombe and Richard Collins (eds), *The Screen Education Reader: Cinema, Television, Culture*, Basingstoke: Macmillan, 41–7 (first published in *Screen Education*, 32/3, 1979–80)

Nelson, Derek 1985: One Step Forward . . . One Step Black: interview with David Howsham. *Broadcast*, 19.4.1985, 61

Nichol, Bill 1985: The Voice of Documentary. In Bill Nichol (ed.), *Movies and Methods*, Vol. 2. Berkeley: University of California Press, 253–73

Null, Gary 1975: *Black Hollywood: the Black Performer in Motion Pictures*. New Jersey: Citadel Press

O'Hagan, Sean, 1992: Malcolm, *Observer*, 11.10.1992

Oguibe, Olu 1993: In the 'Heart of Darkness'. *Third Text*, 23, 1–8

Okri, Ben 1995: Time to Dream the Best Dream of All. *Guardian*, 7.1.95, 5

Patterson, Alex 1993: *Spike Lee: a Biography*. London: Abacus

Patterson, Lindsay 1975: *Black Films and Film-makers: a Comprehensive Anthology from Stereotype to Superhero*. New York: Dodd Mead & Co.

Perkins, Eric 1990: Renewing the African-American Cinema: the Films of Spike Lee. *Cineaste*, 17:4, 4–8

Petrie, Duncan (ed.) 1992: *Screening Europe: Image and Identity in Contemporary European Cinema*. London: British Film Institute Working Papers

Phillips, Mike 1992a: Interview. *Impact*, 2, 27

——1992b: Interview. In Jim Pines (ed.), *Black and White in Colour: Black People in British Television since 1936*. London: British Film Institute, 173–81

——1994: White Lies. *Sight & Sound*, 4:6, 69

Phillips, Trevor 1992: Interview. In Jim Pines (ed.), *Black and White in Colour: Black People in British Television since 1936*. London: British Film Institute, 145–55

Pieterse, Jan Nederveen 1992: *White on Black: Images of Africa and Blacks in Western Popular Culture*. New Haven and London: Yale University Press

Pines, Jim 1975: *Blacks in Film: a Survey of Racial Themes and Images in American Film*. London: Studio Vista

——1988: The Cultural Context of Black British Cinema. In M. Cham and C. Andrade-Watkins (eds), *Blackframes: Critical Perspectives on Black Independent Cinema*, Cambridge, Mass: MIT Press

——1989: Introduction to: I Fought the Law. In Thérèse Daniels and Jane Gerson (eds), *The Colour Black: Black Images in British Television*. London: British Film Institute, 63–70

——1991a: *Representation and Blacks in British Cinema*. London: BFI Education

——1991b: *Representation and Blacks in American Cinema*. London: BFI Education

Pines, Jim (ed.) 1992: *Black and White in Colour: Black People in British Television since 1936*. London: BFI

Pines, Jim and Willemen, Paul (eds) 1989: *Questions of Third Cinema*. London: British Film Institute

Rapping, Elayne 1987: *The Looking Glass World of Nonfiction TV*. Boston: South End Press

Ray, Satyajit 1992: Interview with Kerstin Andersson. *Cinema Papers*, 88, 44–50

Real, Michael 1989: *Super Media: a Cultural Studies Approach*. London and New Delhi: Sage

Reddick, Lawrence 1944: Of Motion Pictures, Radio, the Press and Libraries. *The Journal of Negro Education*. Reprinted in Lindsay Patterson (1975), *Black Films and Film-makers*. New York: Dodd Mead & Co., 3–24

Reid, Mark A. 1993: *Redefining Black Film*: Berkeley, Los Angeles and Oxford: University of California Press

Rense, Rip 1991: Color Blind. *Emmy*, 13:1, 33–7

Rhodes, Jane 1993: The Visibility of Race and Media History. *Critical Studies in Mass Communication*, 10:2, 184–9

Rich, B. Ruby 1992: In the Eyes of the Beholder. *The Voice*, 28.1.92, 60 and 65

Ridley, H. 1983: *Images of Imperial Rule*. London: Croom Helm

Riggs, Marlon 1991: *Color Adjustment* (a film produced, directed and written by Marlon Riggs), San Francisco: California Newsreel

Robertson, Roland 1990: Mapping the Global Condition: Globalization as the Central Concept. In Mike Featherstone (ed.), *Global Culture: Nationalism, Globalization and Modernity*. London, and New Delhi: Sage, 15–30

Robinson, Andrew 1985: Boys from the Currystuff: Interview with Farrukh Dhondy. *Sight & Sound*, 55:1, 14–18

Robinson, M. 1979: Prime-time Chic: between Newsbreaks and Commercials the Values are LA Liberal. *Public Opinion*, 2, 42–7

Ross, Karen 1992: *Television in Black and White: Ethnic Stereotypes and Popular Television*. Research paper no. 19, Warwick: Centre for Research in Ethnic Relations, University of Warwick

——1994: Review of *The Portrayal of Ethnic Minorities on Television* (A. Milwood Hargreave). *Media, Culture & Society*, 16:1, 160–3

Ross, Leone 1993: Home Boy Rides into Town. *The Voice*, 23.11.93

Roy, Somi 1993: Asian American Cinema. *Black Film Bulletin*, 3, 7

Rushdie, Salman 1984: Outside the Whale. *Granta*, 11, 123–38

——1987: Songs Doesn't Know the Score. *Guardian*, 12.1.87

Said, Edward 1978: *Orientalism*. New York: Pantheon Books

——1994: *Culture and Imperialism*. London: Vintage

Salaria, Fatima 1987: New Stereotypes. *Artrage*, 17:41

Salmas, Eileen Becker 1992: One Smart Bet. *Emmy*, 14:3, 58–62

Sampson, Henry T. 1977: *Blacks in Black and White: a Source Book on Black Films*. New Jersey: Scarecrow Press

Seaton, Jean 1991: How the Audience is Made. In James Curran and Jean Seaton (eds), *Power without Responsibility: the Press and Broadcasting in Britain* (4th edn), London: Routledge, 212–33

Shah, Samir 1992: Interview. In Jim Pines (ed.), *Black and White in Colour: Black People in British Television since 1936*. London: British Film Institute, 156–62

Small, Stephen 1993: *Racialised Barriers: the Black Experience in the United States and England in the 1980s*. London and New York: Routledge

Smith, Anthony 1991: *National Identity*. Harmondsworth: Penguin

Smith, Celina 1994: Whither Multiculturalism? *Spectrum*, 1, 58

Smitherman-Donaldson, G. and van Dijk, Teun (eds) 1988: *Disclosure and Discrimination*. Detroit: Wayne State University Press

Smurthwaite, Nick 1991: Talking about a Revolution. *Television Today*, 5750, 23

Snead, James 1988: Black Independent Film: Britain and America. In Kobena Mercer (ed.), *Black Film: British Cinema*, ICA document no. 7, London: British Film Institute/ICA, 47–50

Spencer, Neil 1993: Beating the Rap with a Send-Up: Interview with Nelson George. *Observer*, 21.11.93

Sreberny-Mohammadi, Annabelle 1990: US Media Covers the World. In John Downing, Ali Mohammadi and Annabelle Sreberny-Mohammadi (eds), *Questioning the Media*, London and New Delhi: Sage, 296–307

Sreberny-Mohammadi, Annabelle and Mohammadi, Ali 1994: *Small Media, Big Revolution: Communication, Culture and the Iranian Revolution*. Minneapolis and London: University of Minnesota Press

Stein, B. 1979: *The View from Sunset Strip: America as Brought by the People Who Make Television*. New York: Basic Books

Stone, Norman 1988: Through a Lens Darkly. *Sunday Times*, 10.1.1988

Stuart, Andrea 1994: Blackpool Illumination. *Sight & Sound*, 4:2, 26–7

Synmoie, Donovan 1993: Sneaking Ghosts through the Back Door . . . *Black Film Bulletin*, 1, 3

Taubin, Amy 1993: Girl N the Hood. *Sight & Sound*, 3:8, 16–17

——1994: The Odd Couple. *Sight & Sound*, 4:3, 24–5

Taylor, Clyde 1986: The Master Text and the Jeddi Doctrine. *Screen*, 29:4, 96–104

——1989: Black Cinema in the Post-aesthetic Era. In Jim Pines and Paul Willemen (eds), *Questions of Third Cinema*. London: British Film Institute, 90–110

——1991: The Re-birth of the Aesthetic in Cinema. *Wide Angle*, 13:3–4, 12–29

Thomas, Sari 1990: Myths in and about Television. In John Downing et al., *Questioning the Media: a Critical Introduction*. London and New Delhi: Sage, 330–44

Torode, Brian and Silverman, David 1978: *The Material Word: Some Theories of Language and its Limits*. London: Routledge

Tulloch, John 1990: Television and Black Britons. In Andrew Goodwin and Gary Whannel (eds), *Understanding Television*. London: Routledge, 141–52

Tunstall, Jeremy 1994: *The Media Are American: Anglo-American Media in the World* (2nd edn). London: Constable

Turan, Kenneth 1992: Daughters Recaptures Power of Gullah Past. *Los Angeles Times*, 6.3.1992

Twitchin, John (ed.) 1988: *The Black and White Media Book*. Stoke-on-Trent: Trentham Books

Van Peebles, Melvin 1972: *The Making of Sweet Sweetback's Baadasssss Song*. New York: Lancet Books

Vidmar, Neil and Rokeach, Milton 1974: Archie Bunker's Bigotry. *Journal of Communication*, 24, 36–47

Wadsworth, Marc 1986: Racism in Broadcasting. In James Curran et al. (eds), *Bending Reality: the State of the Media*. London: Pluto Press, 38–46

Wallace, Michele 1970: *Black Macho and the Myth of the Superwoman*. New York: Dial Press

——1989: The Politics of Location: Cinema/Theory/Literature/Ethnicity/Sexuality/Me. *Framework*, 36, 42–55

Wallerstein, Immanuel 1991: The National and the Universal: Can There Be Such a Thing as World Culture? In Anthony D. King (ed.), *Culture, Globalization and the World-System*, Basingstoke: Macmillan in association with Department of Art and Art History, State University of New York, 91–106

Walvin, James 1973: *Black and White: the Negro and English Society – 1555– 1945*. London: Allen Lane

Wambu, Onye 1989: Obstacle Race, *The Listener*, 1.6.1989, 15–16

Weaver, Harold 1982: The Politics of African Cinema. In Gladstone Yearwood (ed.), *Black Cinema Aesthetics: Issues in Black Filmmaking*, Ohio: Ohio University Papers on Afro-American, African and Caribbean Studies, Ohio University Centre for Afro-American Studies, 83–91

Wesley, Richard 1973: Which Way the Black Film? Cited in Lindsay Patterson (ed.) (1975), *Black Film and Film-makers*, New York: Dodd, Mead & Co.

Westley, B. and MacLean, M. 1957: A Conceptual Model for Mass Communication Research. *Journalism Quarterly*, 34, 31–8

White, Mimi 1991: What's the Difference? *Frank's Place* in Television. *Wide Angle*, 13:3/4, 82–93

Wilkins, Mike 1989: I'm Gonna Git You Sucka: a Glance at the Blaxploitation Era. *Black Face*, 1, 36–43

Willemen, Paul 1989: The Third Cinema Question: Notes and Reflections. In Jim Pines and Paul Willemen (eds), *Questions of Third Cinema*, London: British Film Institute, 1–29

Williamson, Judith 1988: Two Kinds of Otherness. In Kobena Mercer (ed.), *Black Film: British Cinema*, ICA document no. 7, London: British Film Institute/ICA, 33–7

Willis, Janet and Wollen, Tana 1990: *The Neglected Audience*. London: British Film Institute

Winokur, Mark 1991: Eating Children Is Wrong. *Sight & Sound*, 1:7, 10–13

Withall, Keith 1990: How Not to Tackle Racism on TV. *Race & Class*, 31:3, 49–60

Woffinden, Bob 1988: Blacking Up, Backing Down. *The Listener*, 30.6.1988

Woll, Allen and Miller, Randall 1987: *Ethnic and Racial Images in American Film and Television: Historical Essays and Bibliography*. New York and London: Garland

Woodford, Sue 1983: Has C4 Locked the Black Door? Interview with Roma Felstein. *Broadcast*, 1223, 30–1

Worrell, Trix 1992: Interview. In Jim Pines (ed.), *Black and White in Colour: Black People in British Television since 1936*. London: British Film Institute, 182–7

Yearwood, Gladstone 1982a: The Cult of the Hero in Traditional Cinema. *Wide Angle*, 5:2, 43–50

——1982b: Towards a Theory of a Black Cinema Aesthetic. In Gladstone Yearwood (ed.), *Black Cinema Aesthetics: Issues in Black Filmmaking*, Ohio: Ohio University Papers on Afro-American, African and Caribbean Studies, Ohio University Centre for Afro-American Studies, 9–18

General Index

Vidmar, Neil and Rokeach, Milton 93
Vithana, Kim 48
Voice, The 54

Wadsworth, Marc 95, 129
Walker, Alice 22, 50
Walker, Rudolph 94
Wallace, Michele 39
Wallerstein, Immanuel 174
Walvin, James 5, 6
Wambu, Onye 120
Wang, Wayne 76
Washington, Booker T. 59
Washington, Denzil 25, 28–9, 68, 69, 76
Washington, Fredi 13
Wayans, Keenan Ivory 105–7
Weekly Journal, The 149
Wesley, Richard 63
Whitaker, Forest 75, 77
white
audience(s) xx, xxii, 31, 82, 88, 110, 161, 163, 166
chauvinsm xix
essentialism xix
hegemony 170
imagination 3, 18, 154
media ix, xxi
perspectives 156
viewers 122, 140, 160
White, Mimi 100
whiteness xxiii, 4–5, 7, 27
Williams, Vanessa 75
Williamson, Judith 162–3, 166
Willis, Shauntisa 30
Winokur, Mark 71
Woffinden, Bob 96
Woll, Allen and Miller, Randall 93
Woodbine, Bokeem 75
Woodward, Alfre 30
Workshop Declaration, The 35, 37
Worrell, Trix 144

xenophobia 99, 146, 174

Yearwood, Gladstone 8, 63, 156, 164

Index of Films

Index of TV Programmes